MW01205285

# Preparing for the 2023 California MFT Law & Ethics Exam

# Preparing for the 2023 California MFT Law & Ethics Exam

Benjamin E. Caldwell, PsyD

Copyright © 2023 by Benjamin E. Caldwell. All rights reserved. Except as permitted under the United States Copyright Act of 1976, no portion of this publication may be reproduced or redistributed in any manner whatsoever without the prior written permission of the publisher.

ISBN: 979-8-9864668-1-1

Ben Caldwell Labs
346 Kanan Rd, Suite 103
Oak Park, CA 91377

www.bencaldwelllabs.com

Ordering Information:

U.S. trade bookstores and wholesalers: Please contact Ben Caldwell Labs via email at support@bencaldwelllabs.com.

*To you*
*You've got this*
*Pass*

# Contents

# Acknowledgements

Profound thanks to Marcia Castro-Rohrer, who makes all our systems here at Ben Caldwell Labs work. Thanks as well to Emma Ekum and Jeff Liebert, my friends and former teammates here at Ben Caldwell Labs, without whom this book would not exist.

Thanks to my wife Angela and our two amazing daughters, who I am humbled to call my family, for their unwavering support and encouragement. Not just with this book, but with all my advocacy efforts on behalf of therapists across career stages.

My gratitude as well to all those associates, students, instructors, and supervisors who used and provided feedback on earlier generations of this book. Your feedback has likely had some influence here.

And most importantly to you, using this book to prepare for your exam: Thank you for the good and important work you do. The path to becoming a therapist is not easy, nor should it be. That you have chosen this path says a great deal about who you are, and how much you have to give to your community. I'm proud to be part of your journey.

# About the author

Benjamin E. Caldwell, PsyD is a California Licensed Marriage and Family Therapist and Adjunct Faculty for California State University Northridge. His research papers have been published in the *Journal of Marital and Family Therapy, American Journal of Family Therapy, Journal of Divorce and Remarriage, Journal of Systemic Therapy*, and elsewhere. He regularly gives presentations around the country on legal and ethical issues impacting therapy work.

Other books by Benjamin Caldwell:

*Basics of California Law for LMFTs, LPCCs, and LCSWs*
*Preparing for the California Clinical Social Work Law & Ethics Exam*
*Saving Psychotherapy*
*User's Guide to the 2015 AAMFT Code of Ethics (editor)*

# Disclaimers

The information in this book is believed to be accurate at the time of printing. However, mistakes can happen, and legal and ethical standards can change quickly. It is the responsibility of each individual therapist to make sure they are remaining current with legal and ethical standards of practice.

Neither this book, nor *any* book or test preparation program, can guarantee success on the exam. While of course we do the best we can to assist, and we believe that our guidance here can be a critical element in a successful study plan, your success on the test depends on your ability to learn and recall key information and apply it in the test setting.

Finally, while this book discusses legal and ethical requirements for the practice of family therapy, it is intended to be used exclusively in the study process for the California MFT Law and Ethics Exam administered by the Board of Behavioral Sciences. It is not intended as case-specific legal or ethical advice. **No part of this book should be construed as legal advice or as a substitute for consultation with a qualified attorney.** If you need legal guidance, your professional liability insurer and your professional association may provide legal resources to you at no cost.

# Introduction

# First thing's first:
## *You've got this.*

The California MFT Law and Ethics Exam is 75 questions over 90 minutes, and it is *absolutely* a test that you can pass. You've taken a graduate-level course in Law and Ethics that was probably pretty good, and probably not all that long ago. But even if it was a while back or a bit lacking in quality, you can catch up with the current standards quickly.

As licensing exams go, this exam is narrowly focused. Later, when it comes time to take the California MFT Clinical Exam, you'll need to know the theory and interventions involved in many different models of treatment, you'll need to know assessment issues and techniques, and you'll need to know a wide variety of additional information on effective clinical care *in addition to* knowing the legal and ethical rules governing the profession. But **this first test is just about those legal and ethical rules.** In that way, it's a better test all around: It's shorter, it's more clearly geared to public safety, and on your side, it's easier to prepare for.

You've got this.

# About this book

This book is meant solely to help you prepare for the California MFT Law and Ethics Exam. It aims to be as efficient as possible in providing the critical, current information you need to know to be successful on the test.

There are four main sources for this book:

1) The *AAMFT Code of Ethics*, available at aamft.org
2) The *CAMFT Code of Ethics*, available at camft.org*
3) *Basics of California Law for LMFTs, LPCCs, and LCSWs,* available at bencaldwelllabs.com and at amazon.com
4) California statutes and regulations, a summary of which is available at bbs.ca.gov (complete California law is available at leginfo.legislature.ca.gov)

In addition to those sources, several other articles and books were used in the development of this book. This is like how the test itself is developed: Licensed MFTs use source material common in the field, and they develop questions assessing an examinee's knowledge of 121 "knowledge statements" outlined in the BBS Exam Plan for this test.

That Exam Plan is a public document available on the BBS web site and in the Appendix here, where it also serves as an Index. Because it so clearly specifies the knowledge needed for the test, the exam plan was also key to the development of this book: **Next to each header in the study guide, you will see small numbers that start with the letter K. These numbers indicate the knowledge statements, in the BBS Exam Plan, that are addressed in that section of the book.** As you'll see, this book covers all 121 knowledge statements used in the development of the exam.

---

\* You might rightly wonder – wait, two codes of ethics? Short answer: Yes. The BBS has said in public meetings that they use both codes as reference points when writing exam questions and investigating possible unprofessional conduct. Thankfully, the two largely overlap. It's unlikely that you'll see exam questions on areas where the correct answer would be different depending on which code you're looking at, though you may see questions on areas one code covers that the other does not, or where one code is stricter than the other (the correct answer would uphold the more strict standard and thus be compliant with both codes).

Of course, this book is not a substitute for a graduate-level Law and Ethics course, or for the textbooks used in such a course. For a deeper dive on California law for clinical practice, I would recommend my *Basics of California Law for LMFTs, LPCCs, and LCSWs*. For more detailed texts on ethical issues for MFTs, I would recommend the following:

- ***Issues and Ethics in the Helping Professions*** by G. Corey, M. S. Corey, & C. Corey (10th edition, Brooks/Cole, 2018; the 11th edition is scheduled to publish in March 2023)
- ***Ethics and Professional Issues in Couple and Family Therapy*** Edited by M. J. Murphy & L. Hecker (2nd edition, Routledge, 2016)

This book doesn't contain secret knowledge. All the *information* you need to know for the exam comes from common materials in the field, including the AAMFT and CAMFT codes of ethics (freely available online), state law and regulation (also freely available online), and the same Law and Ethics textbooks (like my *Basics of California Law* text) commonly used in MFT graduate courses in the state. What this book does is **organize and filter** that knowledge in ways that should be useful, and then give you practice **applying** that knowledge in vignettes that approximate the actual exam.

# About the Exam

## Test basics

The California MFT Law and Ethics Exam is a 75-item, 90-minute test. Of those 75 items, only 50 count toward your score; the other 25 items are non-scored items that are being tested for possible inclusion as scored items in future test cycles. Of course, you have no way of knowing which exam items are scored and which are these experimental items, so it is in your best interest to do the best you can on every item on the test. All questions are four-option, multiple choice questions, where you are tasked with choosing the *best* response from the available options.

The test is administered via computer at testing centers around the state, and it can be taken at some centers outside the state as well. You can see a complete list of test centers by going to home.pearsonvue.com/cabbs (Pearson VUE is an independent company the BBS contracts with for the administration of their exams) and selecting "Find a Test Center." No personal items are allowed into the test centers. They have strict rules about the clothing that examinees can wear, to ensure the security of testing. Some test centers have lockers where you can store personal items during your test, but some do not.

You will be seated at a workstation where your exam has been preloaded into the computer, and you may be offered a set of earplugs or noise-cancelling headphones to use during the test if you wish. (Some examinees find these very helpful for blocking out the sound of other computers in the room, while others simply find them uncomfortable.) The Pearson VUE testing centers administer a wide variety of tests for federal and state government agencies as well as private businesses, so it is likely that the other examinees in the testing room with you will be working on several different kinds of tests. Once you've had the opportunity to get settled in and familiarize yourself with the computer you will be using, you follow the on-screen instructions to begin your exam.

## Content

Considered as a whole (but without considering the 25 experimental items), the test will break down into the following proportions:

| Topic Area | % of scored items | # of scored items (out of 50) |
| --- | --- | --- |
| **Law** | **40%** | **20** |
| Confidentiality, privilege, and consent | 14% | 7 |
| Limits to confidentiality, including mandated reporting | 16% | 8 |
| Legal standards for professional practice | 10% | 5 |
| **Ethics** | **60%** | **30** |
| Professional competence and preventing harm | 18% | 9 |
| Therapeutic relationship | 27% | 13-14 |
| Business practices and policies | 15% | 7-8 |

The exam is not separated into these sections; you will get questions from various categories in random order. These are merely overall proportions. Still, they can be helpful to know. For example, knowing that ethical issues surrounding the therapeutic relationship make up more than a quarter of the test, you may place an emphasis in your studying on this area.

## Scoring

**Your score is based on the total number of non-experimental items that you answered correctly, out of 50 total.** Every item is worth one point – there is no weighting of items based on difficulty, complexity, topic (legal versus ethical), or any other factor. There is also no penalty for an incorrect response; it is counted as 0 points, just the same as if the item were left blank.

The minimum passing score on the test (sometimes referred to as the passing score cutoff) varies from one test cycle to the next, and sometimes among different versions of the test being given within the same test cycle. Some versions of the test are more challenging than others, so the BBS conducts careful statistical analysis of each test -- and of every *item* on each test -- to make sure they set the passing score appropriately. While the BBS no longer publicly announces the passing score, they used to. During that time, the minimum passing score was consistently *around* 35 out of 50 scored items (70%). It would be unusual for the minimum passing score to be above 38 or below 33 for any specific test cycle.

## Strategy

There are many different test-taking strategies that can help you perform well on the exam. Of course, no test-taking strategy will substitute for having detailed knowledge of the material you're being tested on. But strategies can help maximize your score by helping with items you don't know the answer to, and strategies can help with time and anxiety management.

In general, I defer here to your knowledge of your own strengths and challenges. You probably already know how good of a test-taker you are, and you probably already know what strategies will work best for you. (If you don't, it may be worth it to you to try the practice exam here in a couple of different ways, to see what strategies help you the most.) Just like for studying, the only bad strategy for test-taking is one that doesn't work for you.

If you're already clear on the strategies that help you the most on exams, you can safely ignore the rest of this section. If you're interested, here are some strategies specific to this exam that may help you. They aren't mutually exclusive, so you can use as many of these as you like.

**1, Take the easy ones first.** You can go forward and backward on the test as much as you like. Remember that you have a time limit and that items are not weighted, so a good way to start the exam (and possibly build some confidence) is to go through the whole test, marking the responses you are sure of. Then you can go back and spend more time on those items that need more time to consider. You may find that in a very short time period, you already have half or more of the test completed – and that almost all of those answers are likely correct.

**2, Use the process of elimination.** Even when you aren't certain of the *right* response on a particular question, there is a good chance you will be able to identify one or more of the response choices as obviously *wrong*. Eliminating wrong options greatly increases your chance of getting the question right, even if you're not ultimately sure what the best answer would be. One way of eliminating wrong answers is to notice when a question is asking specifically for a *legal* response or specifically for an *ethical* one – that will allow you to eliminate any response choices that would fall into the other category.

The line between legal concerns and ethical concerns isn't as clear in real practice as it is on the test. The fact is, the phrase "in accordance with applicable law" or its equivalent is all over our codes of ethics, and the (legal) unprofessional conduct category known as "general unprofessional conduct" can make ethical violations into legal ones as well. But for the purposes of the test, the two are distinguished – in ways that can help you succeed on the test, if you understand which issues fall into which category. The table on the next page addresses where several common concerns *generally* lie: Legal, ethical, or both. There may be exceptions within each.

**3, Don't get stuck in a rabbit hole.** You have 90 minutes to respond to 75 questions. That gives you a little more than 70 seconds per question. If you find yourself getting hung up on an especially difficult question, move on. Make a mental note (or, if you're using the blank paper provided at the test center, an actual note) of the question you're struggling with and any responses you have ruled out, and then go on to other questions you may be able to answer more quickly.

**4, Stay confident.** You'll encounter some weird questions on the test – either things that just don't make sense to you, or items that are strangely worded. You may even see bad grammar, spelling, and sentence structure. Don't panic. These kinds of items may be the non-scored, experimental items being tested for possible inclusion as scored items on future tests. This is precisely why they do that kind of experimentation: They need to weed out bad items. It's still worth it to answer them as best you can, but if you can't figure some items out, don't let that shake your confidence in your overall knowledge. If a question is confusing, consider it *a problem with the question,* not a problem with you.

# Legal, ethical, or both?

| Legal | Both | Ethical |
|---|---|---|
| Informed consent for telehealth | Minors' consent for therapy | Informed consent for therapy or research |
| Privilege | Confidentiality | |
| Scope of practice | | Scope of competence |
| Client access to records; retaining records 7 years | Maintaining records | Storage and destruction of records |
| Professional titles | Truth in advertising | Testimonials |
| Telehealth regulations | Telehealth competence | |
| | | Personal values, attitudes, and beliefs |
| | | Countertransference |
| Ownership of records | Client autonomy | |
| | Non-discrimination | Cultural competence |
| Fee disclosures | Fees for referrals | Bartering |
| Child, elder, & dependent adult abuse reporting | | |
| Involuntary hospitalization | Crisis management | |
| Insurance parity | | Advocacy with payors |
| | | Termination and non-abandonment |
| Providing *Therapy Never Includes Sexual Behavior* brochure | Sexual relationships | Multiple relationships |
| | Monitoring self for impairment | Assisting impaired colleagues |
| Licensure requirements | Supervision | |

See the important cautionary notes about this chart on the previous pages. In real life, the categories aren't as cleanly divided as they are here. Also, a quick reminder: Stuff like this takes a long time to put together. **Please don't share this or other content from this guide online.** Doing so violates our copyright (there's some irony in breaking the law while preparing for a law and ethics test), and ultimately drives up prices for everyone. Thanks for being awesome and not doing that. ☺ Like the rest of this book, this chart is © Copyright 2023 Ben Caldwell Labs Inc.

**5, Go ahead and guess.** Because there is no penalty for an incorrect response, if there are items you are truly unsure about, it is in your best interest to go ahead and mark your best guess. **Use the last few minutes of your test to mark your best guess on all remaining items you haven't already answered.** The worst thing you can do is leave an item blank, since that gives you a 0% chance of getting the point for it. Even if you're not able to eliminate *any* of the response choices from consideration, guessing at it gives you at least a 25% chance of getting it right.

## Accommodations

Accommodations are available for examinees with recognized disabilities. If you need accommodations, you will need to arrange for a letter to be sent from your health care provider documenting your disability. Common accommodations include a quiet room for testing, or additional time to complete the exam. It is Pearson VUE, and not the BBS, who determines accommodations for examinees with documented disabilities. More information about the process of applying for accommodations, as well as the forms that must be completed, are at home.pearsonvue.com/Test-takers/Accommodations.aspx

As a separate process, the BBS will also allow additional testing time for those who do not speak English as their native language. There are strict requirements to qualify for this additional time, however. The form to apply for this additional time is at www.bbs.ca.gov/pdf/forms/esl_specaccom.pdf

If you are considering applying for accommodations, it's important to plan ahead. All requests for accommodation should be received at least 90 days prior to scheduling your exam. Actual processing time varies based on time of year, application volume, staffing, and other variables.

While many examinees with disabilities report that it is beneficial to receive accommodations, I have also sometimes observed those who do not have recognized disabilities trying to receive accommodations to get extra time on the exam. You should note here that 1) test anxiety is not a recognized disability, and 2) unless you have a history of benefiting from disability accommodations, you probably don't need accommodations for this exam. Remember that the majority of those who attempt this exam pass on their first try, and among those who don't, rarely does inadequate time come up as an issue.

# Before the test

## Weeks and months before

The material on which you will be tested is largely consistent with what you would have learned in graduate school, particularly what you learned in your Law and Ethics class. So a lot of your preparation will simply be re-familiarizing yourself with that material, and making sure you're caught up on any recent changes that have taken place in the legal and ethical rules governing our profession.

There are, of course, lots of ways to **study the material for the exam.** Do what you know works for you. The law and ethics exam does not contain trick questions, and there is no "secret" way to study. The only wrong way to study is a way that doesn't work for you. If you work well with flash cards, make them. If you're someone who does better with reading and rereading, well, hopefully this book is helpful! The point is, trust your instincts and experience when deciding how to study, and how much. Some will find that an hour a night is all they can handle, while others will want to take several-hour-long blocks of time to study. Similarly, some find it more useful to study with friends or colleagues who are also about to test, while others prefer to study on their own.

The most important thing to do several weeks before the test is to **schedule your exam.** Review the list of test centers on the Pearson VUE website and choose the one that is most convenient to you. While all of the test centers are designed to have ample parking and similar testing conditions, you might want to consult with others who have recently taken exams at locations close to you. They can prepare you for things like the friendliness (or lack thereof) of test center staff, which can make a big difference in your testing experience. Note that the center you choose to schedule might not be the one that is geographically closest to you; you might find there's one farther away that is easier to schedule on your preferred day and time, or in a neighborhood that you like to visit.

One thing you may find helpful once you have your test scheduled is to **clear your test day of other obligations.** Arrange to take the day off from work, and don't put any other appointments on your schedule. You will want to focus squarely on the test. And once it's over, you will not want to go back to work right away. If you pass, you'll want (and deserve!) a bit of celebration, and if you don't pass, you'll want some time to shake it off.

Another thing to address once your test is scheduled: **tell employers, supervisors, and loved ones about your upcoming test.** Part of this is simply pragmatic: They will need to know that you will be entirely unreachable, even in the event of an emergency, during the time you are taking the test. (Cell phones are, of course, not allowed in the testing room.) But part of it is also to shore up social support: It's good to go into a test knowing that a lot of people are cheering for you, and will be ready to celebrate with you once you pass.

## The week before

Since you schedule your exam by phone or online, you may not be familiar with the specific location of the test center where you will take the exam. It can reduce anxiety on your test day if you actually **visit the test center** during the week before the test. Try to go to the center in advance around the same time of day that you'll be going for the actual test. This can help you get a feel for traffic, parking, and the like. Based on how long it takes you to get there, you can better plan your actual test day, making sure to give yourself ample time for unexpected delays.

The week before the test is also the time to **wrap up studying**. Hopefully by this time you're feeling confident and ready. If not, it's worth taking an honest look at *why* you're not feeling that way. Is it simple anxiety about the test, or is it a recognition that you don't know the material as well as you should? Anxiety can be managed through relaxation techniques, time with friends, and perhaps a visit to your own therapist. If there are parts of the material you are struggling with, you still have time to shore up your weak points before going in to the exam.

The wrap-up process does involve studying, of course, but **take care of yourself** during this time. There is indeed such thing as too much studying: if it is interfering with sleep, your ability to care for your clients, or your relationships with loved ones, you may find that simply adding on more study time this late in the process will do you more harm than good.

Part of taking care of yourself can be to **adopt a mantra**, or a brief statement you can use repetitively to center yourself and calm your nerves. (A mantra can be part of a larger spiritual or meditation practice, but doesn't have to be.) Here are a few you can choose from, or create one that is a good fit for you:

> *It's just a test. It doesn't define me as a person or as a therapist.*
> *I am ready.*
> *I've had good education, good supervision, and good preparation.*
> *I will be the same therapist after the test that I am before it.*
> *This is a milestone, just one checkpoint on a larger journey.*
> *I will pass.*
> *My friends and family will love me the same no matter what happens.*
> *I know the things I need to know.*

Occasionally, people find that they are really not ready for the test at this point, and may consider rescheduling it for a later date. That's fine, but before taking this step, consider whether it is truly about your readiness, or whether it simply is a reflection of anxiety creeping up on you. If it's anxiety, putting off the test may just mean you repeat the experience a few weeks later.

## The day before

The day before the test, spend time reviewing what you know and making sure you have everything ready for the next day. You may want to prepare a checklist of things to do and things to bring to the test with you, such as a photo ID, paperwork confirming the test time and location, and the like. (Remember that most test centers will not allow you to bring personal items into the exam room. Some test centers have lockers you can use to store personal items during the test, but not all do.) Make sure you eat well and get a good night's sleep the night before the exam.

## The day of the test

Different people have different ideas about whether it is helpful to do some last-minute studying on the actual day of the test. Again, do what works best for you. Some find that reviewing material one last time increases their confidence, as they recognize material, get practice questions right, and generally go into the test feeling good about how much they know. Others find that continuing to review at the last minute only increases their anxiety.

The most important thing you can do on the day of the test is to keep your anxiety in check. Have a normal, healthy breakfast. (Food and drinks are not allowed in the testing room, so don't go in on an empty stomach.) Get a pep talk from your partner or a close friend. If you've chosen a mantra, spend time repeating it to yourself.

Before you leave home or work for the test, make sure you have the documents you will need to get in: your photo ID and the confirmation from Pearson VUE that includes the date, time, and location of your test. Without these materials, you may not be allowed to take the exam.

# After the test

Unless you have a disability accommodation that requires paper-and-pencil testing, or there is some other unusual circumstance, you will find out immediately whether you passed the exam. As of late 2022, some examinees were receiving their score notifications by email within 24 hours of their exams, but the norm is to receive a printout with your results at the test center.

If you pass, congratulations! You will not need to go through another test until you complete your 3,000 hours of supervised experience for licensure and are sitting for the Clinical Exam. Spread the word about your success to friends, family, colleagues, supervisors, social media, or anyplace else you want to announce it so that people can join in celebrating your accomplishment. **Please also let us know:** An email to **support@bencaldwelllabs.com** to share your success story gives me the chance to provide a personal congratulations!

If you do *not* pass on your first try, don't worry. You can take the test again after a 90-day waiting period, and pass on that attempt. You need to *attempt* the exam at least once during each one-year associate registration period, until you pass it.

The BBS will not allow anyone to register with a second associate number, or to sit for the MFT Clinical Exam, until they have passed the MFT Law and Ethics Exam.

# 2023 key changes in California law

There have been several recent changes in state law that impact the work of MFTs and associates. In 2022, most of the relevant legal changes surrounded the supervision process. There were relatively few major changes in law for 2023, though many of these will likely impact you directly:

- Video-based supervision is now legal across all work settings. Supervisors providing supervision via video now must assess each supervisee's appropriateness for video-based supervision at the beginning of the supervision process.
- All Associate MFTs now must take a 3-hour CE course in law and ethics for each registration renewal, regardless of whether you have already passed your Law & Ethics Exam. I have this course available at **bencaldwelllabs.com/associates** and plan to update it annually.
- All applicants for licensure as of July 1, 2023 must have completed at least 3 hours of training in telehealth, including specific content. The training can be from a CE course or have been included in your graduate degree.
- There are other new rules surrounding continuing education, including expanding the activities that can result in CE credit. Serving on an ethics committee, serving as a subject matter expert in a BBS disciplinary process, or completing an occupational analysis survey all can now result in CE credit.

As is usual, there were also several additional technical changes in law, though these are largely not substantive changes. Where the changes above (and other changes from 2022) link to topics in the Exam Plan, they have been included in the study guide portion of this book.

# Here we go!

The next section is a summary of information likely to be included on the exam. The BBS uses 121 "knowledge statements" outlining what they believe you need to know in order to practice therapy within your legal and ethical boundaries. They've been organized here in such a way that should make them easier to study and retain. I've kept the descriptions as brief and simple as possible.

This study guide is divided into subsections that correspond with the knowledge categories on the exam plan:

- Law: Confidentiality, privilege, and consent
- Law: Limits to confidentiality, including mandated reporting
- Law: Legal standards for professional practice
- Ethics: Professional competence and preventing harm
- Ethics: Therapeutic relationship
- Ethics: Business practices and policies

At the beginning of each subsection, you'll see the number of questions from that section you are likely to encounter on your actual exam, out of 50 total scored items. This should help you determine how much emphasis to give each section.

If you have questions about any of the explanations here, or want to dive deeper on any of the subjects covered in this book, you best first stop is the primary source material used in the development of this book.

You've got this.

Good luck!

# Study Guide

# LAW

# Confidentiality, Privilege, and Consent

**Scored exam questions (approximate): 7**

## Understanding confidentiality K1-2

**Laws about confidentiality.** Unless a specific exception to confidentiality applies, MFTs are legally required to keep the content of therapy confidential. This means that they do not share any information about clients, including even the existence of a therapeutic relationship, with outsiders.

Maintaining confidentiality means more than simply not sharing a client's identity. All information gained in a confidential context is deemed confidential under state law, unless the client has given permission to share that information or a legal exception to confidentiality applies.

**Laws about disclosure.** While confidentiality is the default state, several legal exceptions to confidentiality exist. In fact, there are more than 20 instances in state law where confidentiality either *can* or *must* be broken, and information shared with outside persons or agencies.

The times when an MFT is legally *required* to break confidentiality can be generally broken down into five categories:

- Suspected child abuse
- Suspected elder or dependent adult abuse
- Danger to self or others
- Legal authorization, such as a court order or client release
- Other, less common instances where disclosure is required

The first four categories will be discussed in greater detail within this study guide. As an MFT, you need to be keenly aware of each of them.

The fifth category – those less-common instances where disclosure is required – includes an investigation by a board, commission, or administrative agency; a lawful request from an arbitrator or arbitration panel; a coroner's investigation of client's death; and a national security investigation. These instances rarely come up in therapy, but they may be the focus of exam questions. In the event of a national security investigation, MFTs not only are required to turn over client records, but they are legally prohibited from informing the client that they have done so.

Those instances where confidentiality *can* be broken present more opportunity for professional judgment. Therapists will typically err on the side of confidentiality in such instances. However, there may be instances where a therapist breaks confidentiality because they legally *can* do so, and they believe it is in the best interest of the client to do so.

For example, the law allows but does not require disclosure of confidential information to the person or entity paying for services, to the extent necessary to determine who is responsible for payment and payment to be made. As another example that has become especially relevant during the pandemic, confidential information can be disclosed to public health authorities for the purpose of public health surveillance and intervention (in other words, to control disease spread).

# Understanding privilege K3-6

Privilege refers to information that can be excluded from court proceedings. Normally, all communications between a therapist and their client are considered privileged communications, meaning that they cannot be used in court. Other examples of communication that is usually privileged include communication between spouses, and communication between an attorney and their client.

This is particularly important in therapy. Clients need to be able to trust that information they have shared with their therapist about mental health symptoms or other emotional problems will not be used against them in court. If that risk exists, clients will understandably be less open with their therapists about struggles in the clients' lives.

**Clients generally hold their own privilege.** In other words, only the client can waive their own right to privileged communication in most instances. Even when the client is a minor, the client is usually considered the holder of their own privilege, although the minor may not be allowed to waive privilege on their own. A judge may block a minor (or an adult, for that matter) from waiving privilege if the judge believes that waiving privilege is not in the person's best interest. In any case, it is never up to the therapist to determine whether privilege will be waived. That is up to the client, the client's guardian, another court appointee, or a judge.

**Release of privileged information.** By definition, privileged information cannot be used in a court proceeding. Privileged information may only be released in court if the client has waived privilege, or if a judge has determined that privilege does not apply, based on one or more of the exceptions spelled out in state law (more on that in the next section).

**Responding to a subpoena or court order.** If an MFT receives a subpoena (a legal document requesting that the therapist produce records, appear in court, or both), MFTs are commonly advised to take these steps:

1. **Contact an attorney as soon as possible.** The MFT will benefit from legal guidance throughout this process.
2. **Assess the subpoena for its source and validity.** A subpoena from a judge is a court order – the MFT must obey it. A subpoena from an attorney, on the other hand, may be fought if the client wishes. Occasionally, an attorney may advise you to object to the subpoena, though this is less common.
3. **Contact the client to determine their wishes.** Often, the client will freely authorize the MFT to release the records or appear in court. Sometimes, the client will prefer that the MFT assert privilege on the client's behalf, asking that the therapist's records or testimony not be made part of the court proceeding.
4. Unless the client has specifically waived privilege or a judge has determined that privilege does not apply, **assert privilege on behalf of the client.** This is generally considered the best default position for a therapist to take in the absence of other guidance from the client or the court.

If the client does waive privilege, or if a court determines that privilege does not apply, you must comply with the subpoena. And regardless of what path you and the client choose, you always must respond to the subpoena in some form, even if to assert privilege. Simply failing to respond to a subpoena can result in sanctions from the court.

# Treatment of minors K7

**Treatment of minors.** In most cases, parents provide consent for the treatment of their child. Anyone under age 18 is a minor under state law, and parents can consent for treatment on their child's behalf. If a minor has two legal parents (either because the parents are married, or because they never were married and both have retained parental rights), then typically either parent can provide consent on their own for therapy for the minor.

If the minor's parents are divorced, consent becomes more complicated. The MFT can request a copy of the custody order to determine which parent's consent is necessary for treatment of the minor. In joint custody, typically either parent can provide consent on their own. If one parent has sole custody, typically only that parent can provide consent for the minor's treatment. If that parent refuses or withdraws their consent, the MFT should not treat the minor.

Other caregivers may sometimes bring a minor in for therapy. Another relative who lives in the same home as the minor may provide consent for the minor's treatment if they sign a "Caregiver's Authorization Affidavit." The necessary language of this document is specified in state law.

Minors as young as 12 can consent to mental health care on their own if the minor is mature enough to participate intelligently in treatment. That determination is made by the therapist. In these cases, the therapist still must either try to contact the child's parents to involve them in treatment, or document why they believe doing so would be harmful. Parents do not have a right to access records of their child's treatment if the child consented independently, and parents cannot be forced to pay for services provided without the parents' consent.

# Documentation K8-11

**Documentation of services.** Documentation of therapy is both a legal and ethical requirement. Neither state law nor professional ethical codes define the specific *content* that needs to be in treatment records, and there are many formats for things like assessments and progress notes. However, all MFTs are legally required to keep records that are consistent with "sound clinical judgment, the standards of the profession, and the nature of the services being rendered" (CA BPC 4982(v)). As we will see, there are some specific things that legally must be documented when they occur, such as client releases of information and specific consent for telehealth services.

If a client wishes, they have the right to include a statement in their treatment record of up to 250 words. Clients sometimes ask to do so when they disagree with some element of their clinical record, and want their disagreement included in case their file is ever released to a court or to another provider.

**Maintenance and disposal of records.** Under state law, records must be maintained for at least 7 years following the last professional contact. If you are working with a minor, records must be maintained for at least 7 years after the minor turns 18.

During the time you are maintaining records, you must take reasonable steps to ensure they are secure and confidential. When the time comes to dispose of old client records, this disposal must also be done in a manner that protects security and confidentiality (and, if you're a HIPAA-covered entity, is HIPAA compliant). You should never just throw old files in the trash.

**Client access to records.** Clients generally have a legal right to access their records, though there are some limitations on this. Unless you believe that the release of records to the client would be harmful, you must comply with their request in a timely manner: Within 5 days if the client simply wants to inspect their records, and within 15 days if the client wants a copy of their record. You cannot refuse a client's request for records simply because they owe you money. You can, however, charge for reasonable costs associated with accessing and copying the client's file, and you can provide a summary of the file rather than the full record if you prefer (this typically must be within 10 days of the client's request). Any client who inspects their record and believes some part of it to be incomplete or incorrect can submit a brief statement to be included in the client file.

If you believe that releasing records to a client would be harmful to them, you may refuse to do so. If you refuse, you need to document the request and your reason for refusal. The client may then request that a third-party professional review the records to see whether that third party agrees with you that the record should not be released.

In the case of couple or family treatment, MFTs get consent from all members of the treatment unit prior to releasing records.

**Release of records to others.** Records of treatment can be released to third parties if the client requests it or if there is some other appropriate legal authorization. Most commonly, clients request that their records be forwarded to another therapist or health care provider for continuity of care, or they request that records be provided to their insurance company for the purpose of receiving reimbursement.

When a client requests that their records be released to a third party, this request typically must be in writing, and it must be signed and dated by the client or their legal representative.

There are some instances when a specific authorization to release information is *not* required by law, such as when the information is needed by another active health care provider or health care facility to for the purposes of diagnosis or treatment (in an emergency, for example, there may not be time to gather written authorization), or when the information is required as part of a billing process.

As discussed previously, records are also sometimes released by court order, which is its own form of legal authorization.

On occasion, clients may ask MFTs to provide letters on the client's behalf. For example, an MFT may write a letter to a client's employer in support of the client's request for time off to address mental health needs. Such letters are typically legal so long as they are accurate and are released with the client's written permission. In 2022, California enacted specific rules around therapists writing letters in support of a client's request for an Emotional Support Dog. For the therapist to write such a letter, they must have had at least a 30-day clinical relationship with the client, and in that time the therapist must have completed a clinical assessment. The therapist must include their licensure information in the letter. The therapist also must inform the client that falsely presenting an ESD as a service animal is a crime.

# Telehealth laws K12-13

**Telehealth consent.** Under California law, therapists who offer services via telemedicine are legally required to first obtain specific consent for telemedicine (the consent can be verbal or in writing) and document this in the client's file. Failure to do so is considered unprofessional conduct. While purely administrative contacts, such as contacting clients by phone or email to schedule in-person sessions, would likely not qualify as telehealth, actually providing therapy by phone, videoconference, or other technology certainly would.

**Telehealth delivery.** California and federal laws govern the delivery of services by telehealth. When delivering services by telehealth, all the laws regarding scope of practice, client confidentiality, and client rights to information and records continue to apply. MFTs must be particularly cautious when considering using telemedicine to treat clients located outside of California, as a California MFT license only authorizes the MFT to provide services to clients who are physically located within the state at the time of service.

By regulation, California MFTs wishing to conduct therapy via telehealth need to take several specific steps. *At the start* of engaging a client in telehealth, the MFT must:

- Get specific telehealth consent (as noted above)
- Inform clients of the risks and limitations of telehealth services
- Provide the client with the MFT's licensure/registration information
- Document reasonable efforts to locate crisis resources local to the client

Regarding that last point: A low-risk client wouldn't require the same effort to locate crisis resources local to them as a high-risk client would. So based on your assessment of client risk, you may locate crisis resources local to them just in case they're needed. Whatever you do in this area, it should be documented.

In addition to the steps above, the MFT must do the following *at each instance* of telehealth:

- Obtain and document the client's full name and current location (this should be a specific location such as an address, to confirm that you are qualified to provide services where they are and to allow you to send help to the client if needed in an emergency)
- Assess whether the client is appropriate for telehealth (this may be based on their symptoms as well as the technology and privacy available to the client at that time, among other factors)
- Use best practices for security and confidentiality

**HIPAA.** Under the Health Insurance Portability and Accountability Act (HIPAA), MFTs covered by the act have specific additional responsibilities to protect the privacy of client records. However, not all MFTs are considered "covered entities" and bound to HIPAA's requirements. HIPAA applies to those providers who digitally transmit a client's protected health information as part of a health care transaction. Put plainly, this means that HIPAA applies to therapists who submit billing documents electronically, to insurers or other payors. Among the requirements for covered entities:

- Designating a privacy official
- Informing clients and staff of privacy policy and procedures
- Disciplining staff members who violate privacy or security rules
- Repairing harmful effects of privacy violations
- Maintaining safeguards against the release of private information
- Having complaint procedures for violations of privacy
- Ensuring confidentiality of electronic health information
- Protecting against threats to information security
- Notifying the department of Health and Human Services of breaches of unsecured health information
- Getting client permission before using unsecured email

Rather than memorizing that list, it may work best to simply recall that under HIPAA, MFTs need to have and enforce specific policies to protect the security and confidentiality of health information, and that clients are to be informed of the relevant policies. Most MFTs covered under HIPAA provide clients with a Notice of Privacy Policies that outlines how private information is gathered and used.

There is a specific category of documentation that HIPAA calls "psychotherapy notes," which are a therapist's notes documenting or analyzing conversation with a client that happens in a private psychotherapy session. Within this definition, psychotherapy notes cannot include information like session start and stop times, diagnosis, progress, treatment plans, symptoms, interventions, or prognosis. Psychotherapy notes, as defined under HIPAA, must be kept separate from the rest of the client file and are not considered part of the client record. However, under state law, these records would still be subject to subpoena.

## Sample Questions
See the next page for answers and rationales

1. A 13-year-old girl presents for treatment at a nonprofit agency that provides no-cost therapy. The girl is assigned to an LMFT. The LMFT determines the girl is not in crisis. The girl says she is suffering from distress related to family conflict. Legally, the appropriate first step for the LMFT at this point is to:

    a.   Contact the girl's parents to seek consent for treatment
    b.   Assess the girl's emotional maturity
    c.   Proceed with therapy, and involve the girl's parents
    d.   Assess whether the girl is engaging in substance abuse

2. An investigator with a federal law enforcement agency shows up unexpectedly at an LMFT's office. The investigator says she is looking into suspicious behavior by an individual the investigator knows is seeing the LMFT. The investigator demands access to all information the LMFT has about the client and says that the investigation is related to national security. The LMFT should:

    a.   Provide access to the records, and not inform the client she has done so
    b.   Provide access to the records, and immediately inform the client she has done so
    c.   Deny access to the records until she can contact the client and determine the client's wishes
    d.   Deny access to the records and assert privilege on behalf of the client

# Sample Questions: Answers and Rationales

1. A 13-year-old girl presents for treatment at a nonprofit agency that provides no-cost therapy. The girl is assigned to an LMFT. The LMFT determines the girl is not in crisis. The girl says she is suffering from distress related to family conflict. Legally, the appropriate first step for the LMFT at this point is to:

    a.  **Incorrect.** Contact the girl's parents to seek consent for treatment
    b.  **CORRECT.** Assess the girl's emotional maturity
    c.  **Incorrect.** Proceed with therapy, and involve the girl's parents
    d.  **Incorrect.** Assess whether the girl is engaging in substance abuse

Minors as young as 12 can independently consent for mental health care so long as they are mature enough to participate intelligently in treatment. The LMFT must make that determination to know whether consent for treatment can be present. Contacting the girl's parents to seek consent (A) would be necessary if the minor is assessed and determined not to be able to independently consent. Proceeding with therapy (C), and assessing for substance abuse (D), is appropriate after consent has been obtained.

2. An investigator with a federal law enforcement agency shows up unexpectedly at an LMFT's office. The investigator says she is looking into suspicious behavior by an individual the investigator knows is seeing the LMFT. The investigator demands access to all information the LMFT has about the client and says that the investigation is related to national security. The LMFT should:

    a.   **CORRECT.** Provide access to the records, and not inform the client she has done so. *MFTs can be required to turn over records in a national security investigation and cannot tell the client they have done so*

    b.   **Incorrect.** Provide access to the records, and immediately inform the client she has done so. *Informing the client in this instance would be a violation of federal law*

    c.   **Incorrect.** Deny access to the records until she can contact the client and determine the client's wishes. *In a national security investigation, an MFT can be required to turn over records. Denying the investigator access to the records could be a violation of federal law*

    d.   **Incorrect.** Deny access to the records and assert privilege on behalf of the client. *In a national security investigation, an MFT can be required to turn over records. Denying the investigator access to the records could be a violation of federal law*

**LAW**

# Limits of Confidentiality

| Scored exam questions (approximate): | **8** |

## Exceptions to confidentiality: Child abuse K18-19

**Laws about reporting child abuse.** MFTs are **mandated reporters** of suspected child abuse or neglect when serving in their professional roles. In other words, you are required to report abuse or neglect you observe or suspect while in the office, but not what you observe or suspect at the grocery store, at home, or in other non-professional settings.

Your mandated reporting responsibilities are triggered when, in your professional role, you develop **reasonable suspicion** that a minor has been abused or neglected. ("A minor" is important here. The victim does not need to have been your client, it can be any minor whose abuse you learn about in your professional role.)

Reasonable suspicion is a specific term with a specific meaning. As the law is written, if another MFT with similar training and experience, when presented with the same information, would reasonably suspect that abuse had taken place, then so should you. You do not need to be certain that the abuse happened to reasonably suspect it – for example, you do not need to have personally observed injuries to suspect physical abuse.

There are five categories of abuse that *must* be reported:

- **Physical abuse.** Anyone who willfully causes an injury to a child or engages in cruel or unusual corporal punishment is committing physical abuse. Key terms there include "willfully" and "injury" – accidental contact is not abusive, and the child must have suffered an injury (such as a scratch, bruise, or other observable impact) for an event to qualify as physical abuse.

The law makes an exception to the reporting requirement for physical abuse when the injury occurred in the context of a "mutual affray among minors." This is meant to exclude common schoolyard fights from being mandated abuse reports. However, it is possible for a minor to physically abuse another minor if the events in question do not qualify as mutual.

- **Sexual abuse.** This category includes sexual assault, sexual exploitation, and what the law calls "lewd and lascivious acts." When minors engage in consensual, **heterosexual intercourse,** the therapist must consider their ages, using these two rules:

*The 14th birthday rule:*
If one partner is 14 years old or older, and the other is under 14, the therapist must report.

*The 21/16 rule:*
This rule can be thought of as the "drinking and driving" age rule: If one sexual partner is old enough to drink (at least 21), the other partner needs to be old enough to drive (at least 16). To put this another way, if one partner is *under* 16 and the other is 21 or older, the therapist must report.

For any other age combinations, the therapist should consider the age and maturational levels of the partners in assessing their capacity to consent and the nature of the relationship (i.e., is it exploitive or otherwise abusive) when deciding whether to report.

Notably, the law specifically states that the pregnancy of a minor, in and of itself, is *not* sufficient grounds to suspect abuse. This remains true regardless of the age of the minor.

When minors consensually engage in **oral sex, anal sex, or object penetration,** the 21/16 rule applies, but the 14th birthday rule does not. Of course, any non-consensual oral sex, anal, object penetration, or intercourse will always be reportable when a minor is involved.

**"Lewd and lascivious acts"** may include non-penetrative sexual behaviors like mutual masturbation. These acts are a mandated report if performed on a minor under age 14, regardless of the age of the partner. If the act is performed on a minor age 14 or 15, it is a mandated report if the partner is 10 or more years older than the minor. If the minor is 16 or older, these acts are not a mandated report.

The law specifically defines both the **distribution and the intentional downloading of child porn** as child abuse.

- **Willful harm or endangerment.** Any person causing a child "unjustifiable physical pain or mental suffering," or any caregiver who allows it to happen, is committing child abuse.

- **Neglect.** Even if it happens by accident, children are being neglected if their basic needs for adequate food, clothing, shelter, medical care, or supervision are not being met. A child does not need to have suffered actual harm for a report of neglect to be made.

  Note that a parent's "informed and appropriate" medical choices, including choices to refuse medical treatment for their child based on religious belief, are not neglect. However, this only applies if the parents have taken the child to a physician for assessment. Otherwise, the parent's medical choices may not be considered "informed and appropriate."

- **Abuse in out-of-home care.** This is given its own category for reporting purposes. It applies to kids who are physically injured or killed in child-care or school settings.

In addition to those types of abuse, **emotional abuse** operates on a *permissive* reporting standard, which means that you can report this if you choose to, but you are not required to. Emotional abuse is defined in law as "serious emotional damage or [...] substantial risk of suffering serious emotional damage." Children who witness domestic violence are sometimes reported as victims of emotional abuse.

Once you have developed reasonable suspicion, there are specific **timeframes for abuse reporting** that must be followed. You must make a report by phone to your local child protective agency immediately and follow up with a written report within 36 hours. This timeframe does not change for nights, weekends, or holidays.

**Indicators of child abuse.** Since the reasonable suspicion standard relies on MFTs having a shared understanding of the times when abuse should be reported, it is critical that MFTs are aware of common physical and behavioral indicators of abuse, neglect, and exploitation. The National Children's Advocacy Center has compiled the following lists of indicators. While none of these indicators by themselves would lead to a conclusion of abuse, they should lead an MFT to *consider* whether abuse or neglect may be taking place. Common physical indicators include:

- Unexplained bruises
- Unexplained burns
- Unexplained fractures or cuts
- Evidence of delayed or inappropriate treatment for injuries
- Multiple injuries in various stages of healing
- Injury or trauma to genital area
- Sexually transmitted disease
- Pain, swelling, itching, bruising, or bleeding in genital area
- Unattended medical needs
- Consistent hunger or poor hygiene
- Consistent lack of supervision

Common behavioral indicators of abuse and neglect include the following. As with all child and adolescent behaviors, a therapist must be especially cautious not to reach premature conclusions on the basis of behavioral indicators alone, as there are a number of potential causes for each of these that would *not* indicate abuse. However, these behaviors should get a therapist's attention:

- Sudden withdrawn behavior
- Self-destructive behavior
- Bizarre explanations for injuries
- Shying away from contact with familiar adults
- Sleep disturbances, including nightmares or flashbacks
- Substance use
- Anger and rage
- Aggressive, disruptive, or illegal behavior
- Frequent absence or tardiness from school or other activities
- Consistent fatigue or listlessness
- Stealing food
- Extreme need for affection
- Extreme loneliness

# Exceptions to confidentiality: Elder and dependent adult abuse K14-17

**Laws about reporting elder and dependent adult abuse.** Under California law, you must report any time you observe, suspect, or have knowledge of elder or dependent adult abuse. For mandated reporting purposes, **an elder is anyone age 65 or older who resides in California.** (A 2022 change in state law impacted the definition of an elder for other purposes related to Adult Protective Service agency functions, but it did not change how an elder is defined for mandated reporting purposes.) **A dependent adult is anyone age 18 to 64 who resides in California and has physical or mental limitations** that restrict their ability to carry out normal activities or protect their own rights. Anyone admitted as an inpatient in a hospital or other 24-hour health care facility is, by definition, a dependent adult. Reportable types of abuse include:

- **Physical abuse, which includes willful over- or under-medication.** Be careful with this, though – an elder reporting that they are in pain does not mean they are being abused. As long as they are being given the correct amount of medication prescribed by their doctor, it would simply call for a referral back to the client's physician to make any necessary adjustments in medication dosage or type. Various forms of sexual abuse are also included here as physical abuse.

- **Financial abuse.** This category is not a form of child abuse but does apply to elders and dependent adults.
- **Abduction.** Specifically, the law refers to an elder or dependent adult being taken *outside of California*, or prevented from returning, against their will.
- **Isolation.** Elders who are physically restrained from seeing visitors, or who are being prevented from receiving mail, phone calls, or visitors (when the elder wants to see the visitor), are being isolated. In rare instances, a health condition may make limitations on mail and phone calls clinically appropriate, but there should be good medical documentation for such a decision, and other normal contact should not be restricted.
- **Abandonment.** Caretakers accept responsibility for the adults in their care. Abandonment occurs when a caretaker deserts their patient or gives up on their caretaking responsibilities when a reasonable person would not have done so.
- **Neglect, including self-neglect.** This is reportable not so that the elder or dependent adult will be punished, but so that they can be moved to a higher level of care if it is appropriate to do so.

Unlike child abuse laws, elder and dependent adult abuse reporting laws allow for permissive reporting of any other form of abuse not otherwise defined in the law. This gives an MFT broad latitude to report behaviors that the MFT considers to be abusive or exploitive, even if those behaviors do not fit neatly into any of the categories listed.

Similar to child abuse reporting, you do not need to have heard a direct report of abuse from the victim in order to develop suspicion that abuse has taken place. However, unlike child abuse reporting laws, the laws on reporting elder and dependent adult abuse say that **if you do hear of abuse directly from the victim, you *must* report it.** There is only a very narrow exception, for when the person has been diagnosed with mental illness, there is no other evidence of the abuse, and the therapist does not reasonably believe the abuse occurred.

The **timeframes for reporting** elder or dependent adult abuse are complex. If the abuse did *not* take place in a long-term care facility, then a phone report of the abuse must be made immediately to Adult Protective Services or another local agency authorized to receive adult abuse reports. You then must follow up with a written report within two working days. Recent state law allows for elder and dependent adult abuse reports to be made via Internet, in which case the Internet report should be done immediately, and it replaces both the phone *and* written reports.

If the abuse happened within a long-term care facility, the rules are more complicated. For example, physical abuse in a long-term care facility that results in serious bodily injury to the victim must be reported to law enforcement immediately, with written reports sent to law enforcement, the local ombudsperson, and the facility's licensing agency all within two hours.

**Indicators of elder and dependent adult abuse.** Common indicators of elder abuse include the following. As is the case with child abuse, it may be inappropriate to conclude that abuse has occurred based solely on an indicator here, as each of these can be caused by incidents that would not qualify as abuse. However, they can raise a therapist's suspicion, and suspicion is the standard for reporting:

- Physical or sexual abuse
  - Unexplained bruises, welts, or scars
  - Broken bones, sprains, dislocations
  - Restraint injuries (marks on wrists)
  - Unexplained bleeding or injury to genitals
  - Sexually transmitted disease
  - Medication over- or under-dosing relative to prescribed amounts
- Abandonment or neglect
  - Unusual weight loss
  - Poor nutrition or dehydration
  - Poor hygiene
  - Unsanitary or unsafe living environment
  - Inappropriate clothing (inadequate for cold weather)
  - Lack of needed medical aids, such as glasses

- Financial abuse
  - Sudden changes in financial status
  - Valuable items or cash missing from residence
  - Unpaid bills when the person has money to pay them
  - Unusual financial activity, or activity the person could not have done (e.g., large withdrawals, ATM withdrawal by hospital inpatient)
  - Sudden appearance of unnecessary goods or services
  - Signatures on checks do not match the person's
- Unusual caregiver behavior (can indicate risk any type of abuse)
  - Threatening, belittling, or controlling behavior
  - Deserting
  - Burnout (can be evidenced by mental health symptoms, substance use, poor resilience, irritability, or resentment toward the person being cared for, as examples)

It is important for MFTs to be aware that stress and burnout are common among caregivers, and these indicate a risk of abuse, but may also simply mean that the caregiver needs some time away from their responsibilities. Caregiving is difficult, particularly if the person being cared for has severe illness or dementia, is socially isolated, is physically aggressive, or has a history of domestic violence. These factors place the person at greater risk of abuse.

# Exceptions to confidentiality: Danger to self or others K20-25

**Identifying need for hospitalization.** Under state law, an individual can be hospitalized against their will if they are a danger to others, are a danger to themselves, or are gravely disabled. In such instances, the person is taken to a hospital or other county-designated facility for assessment for up to 72 hours, which you may know as a "72-hour hold" or a "5150."

**Legal requirements for initiating involuntary hospitalization.** When an MFT believes hospitalization is necessary, having a client go voluntarily is usually preferable to the process of involuntary hospitalization. However, if the MFT believes the client has a mental disorder that is causing them to be a danger to themselves or others or is gravely disabled, and the client refuses voluntary treatment, the MFT can begin the process of involuntary hospitalization. For a client to be hospitalized against their will, a therapist must be able to cite specific facts (client words, appearance, or behaviors) supporting the dangerousness of the client, and the conclusions the therapist drew from those facts. The therapist must then find what the county considers an "eligible professional" to write the 5150 application. (Usually, a police officer or other person designated by the county serves this role. MFTs can be the eligible professional in some counties, but they may need to first go through additional training and certification.) Ultimately, it is up to a professional at the facility designated by the county to receive involuntary holds to determine whether the client is to be involuntarily hospitalized. If that professional agrees, the client can be initially held for up to 72 hours. If the client remains dangerous to themselves or others, or gravely disabled, at the end of the 72 hours, they can be certified for an additional hold of up to 14 days for intensive treatment.

**Laws about confidentiality in situations of client danger to self or others.** Danger to self or others is commonly understood as an exception to confidentiality under the law. The *Tarasoff v. California Board of Regents* case established that danger to a reasonably identifiable victim outweighs client confidentiality. An MFT dealing with a client who poses an imminent danger of serious bodily harm to reasonably identifiable victims must take reasonable steps to resolve the threat, which typically include breaking confidentiality (see "Duty to protect law" below). When a client is suicidal, the *Bellah v. Greenson* case established that therapists have a responsibility to act to protect the client's safety, and this can involve breaking confidentiality if needed. If a client poses a general danger to others because of a mental health condition, *Tarasoff* does not apply, but the therapist still can move to have the client involuntarily hospitalized if necessary.

In each of these instances, the MFT can break confidentiality. The MFT shares information about therapy with others who are involved in resolving the immediate danger. Even in these situations, though, the MFT should share *only* the information necessary to resolve the immediate threat. Sharing unrelated information about the client's therapy may still be seen as a violation of confidentiality rules.

Sometimes, law enforcement and therapists work together in mental health crisis response teams. These teams must be supervised by mental health professionals. The therapists and law enforcement officers responding to mental health crises on these teams are not doing therapy, but they may benefit from knowing some information about the potentially dangerous person. If you are providing information about your client to emergency responders, it is up to your judgment to determine what information is appropriate to share to resolve the threat, and not to share more than necessary.

If a *Tarasoff* situation arises where the therapist resolves the immediate danger *without* notifying law enforcement, the MFT still must inform law enforcement of the threat within 24 hours. This relatively recent law was enacted to help law enforcement put potentially dangerous individuals into a federal database to prevent them from buying guns.

**Methods and criteria to identify when a client poses danger to self or others.** There are good, brief ways of assessing clients who may pose a danger to themselves or someone else, including screening instruments and structured interviews. Assessments for suicide and violence to others tend to focus on the following factors:

- **Ideation (thoughts).** Is the person actively considering harming themselves or someone else? If suicidal, are they romanticizing what their death would be like, for them or others around them?
- **Planning.** Do they have a specific plan for how they would hurt themselves or someone else? Is it immediate?
- **Intent.** Does the person intend to commit violence? How sure are they? Some clients will fantasize about violence or death without any intent to ever act on these fantasies.
- **Access to means.** How easy would it be to carry out the plan? If they are considering suicide or homicide by gun, is there a gun in the house?
- **Past experience.** Have they attempted suicide or been violent with others before? How? Note that *previous suicide attempts* is the strongest risk factor for future attempts.

- **Protective factors.** What are the reasons the person has not hurt themselves or someone else so far? What would prevent them from suicide or violence in the future?

Demographic factors are also important to keep in mind, though these are not predictive of violence. While suicide is a leading cause of death among adolescents (because other causes of death are not common at this age), statistically, the highest risk for suicide is among the elderly (85+) and the middle-aged (45-64). Men are at higher risk than women. Whites and Native Americans have the highest suicide rates among ethnic groups.

**Duty to protect law.** You are probably familiar with *Tarasoff v. California Board of Regents*, the court case that established a therapist's responsibility to act when a client poses an imminent danger of serious bodily harm to a reasonably identifiable victim or victims. In such instances, MFTs have a legal obligation known as "duty to protect." While this is not technically a duty to warn (and in rare instances, it might be inappropriate to warn the intended victim, such as times when doing so might trigger the victim to commit a violent act), the most common methods of protecting potential victims are to notify the victims and law enforcement of the threat. You also have additional protection from liability when you make reasonable efforts to notify both the victim and law enforcement.

The law does *not* require you to report or otherwise act on threats to property, so such threats typically must remain confidential. Animals are considered property under state law, so threats against animals do not provoke any obligations or opportunities for the therapist to break confidentiality. However, threats to property are not considered privileged communication under the law (more on Privilege is below), so they could be disclosed in the context of a court proceeding.

**Indicators of intent to harm.** Obviously, the strongest indicator of a client's intent to harm someone is when they tell you directly that they intend to harm someone. However, this is not the only indicator a therapist should be aware of. Third-party reports of a client intending to harm another person may be treated similarly to direct reports, if the therapist believes that the third party is a trustworthy reporter. Threats made in writing or by other means may be considered evidence of intent to harm. Indirect statements such as "after today, she won't be around any more" may also be reasonable indicators, based on the MFT's knowledge of the client. Threatening behaviors may also qualify. Clients who are actively using drugs or alcohol may present heightened danger to potential victims.

# Exceptions to privilege K26-31

As noted earlier, privilege refers to information that can be excluded from court proceedings. Normally, all communications between a therapist and their client are considered *privileged communications*, meaning that they cannot be used in court. However, there are several exceptions to this rule defined in law. Normally privileged information may be used in court if:

1) The client makes their mental or emotional condition an issue in a lawsuit.
2) The client alleges breach of duty by the therapist.
3) Evaluation or therapy is taking place by court order.
4) A defendant in a criminal case requested the evaluation or therapy to determine their sanity.
5) The client is under age 16 and is the victim of a crime, and the therapist believes that disclosing that information is in the child's best interests.
6) The therapist was sought out for the purpose of committing a crime or avoiding detection after the fact.

This list is worth memorizing. Each one of these exceptions gets its own Knowledge Statement in the BBS Exam Plan, so there is a strong likelihood you will be specifically asked to apply your knowledge of one or more of these on your exam.

Recall here that while clients can waive privilege, only a judge can determine whether an exception to privilege applies to a specific situation. That's never your determination to make. Even in situations where you believe a judge is likely to ultimately determine that an exception applies, if your client is asserting privilege, you should also assert privilege on the client's behalf until the judge makes that determination.

## Sample Questions
See the next page for answers and rationales

1. A 43-year-old man has been charged with a number of crimes related to an incident six months ago in which he stood on a freeway, stopping traffic. He has requested a mental health evaluation to show that the incident was due to a mental condition, and an LMFT the man selected has been approved by the court to provide the evaluation. Over the course of three interviews, the LMFT determines that the client qualifies for a mental health diagnosis, but that the diagnosis does not explain the incident. The client objects and demands that the LMFT not share this analysis with the court. The client threatens to sue the LMFT if the analysis is shared. When the court orders the LMFT to provide the evaluation report, the LMFT should:

    a.   Assert privilege on behalf of the client

    b.   Refuse to turn over the report on the grounds that it is the subject of a potential lawsuit

    c.   Provide the report as requested

    d.   Encourage the client to file a motion with the court requesting an injunction

2. An LMFT is working with a Latina mother and her 7-year-old son in therapy, when the LMFT observes unusual bruises on the boy's face and arms. The bruises seem to be in several different stages of healing. When the LMFT asks how he got the bruises, both the boy and his mother refuse to answer. The LMFT should:

    a.   Report suspected child abuse

    b.   Consider whether physical discipline is common in Latin cultures

    c.   Remind the mother of the limits of confidentiality

    d.   Ask the child to remove his shirt to inspect his torso for additional injuries

# Sample Questions: Answers and Rationales

1. A 43-year-old man has been charged with a number of crimes related to an incident six months ago in which he stood on a freeway, stopping traffic. He has requested a mental health evaluation to show that the incident was due to a mental condition, and an LMFT the man selected has been approved by the court to provide the evaluation. Over the course of three interviews, the LMFT determines that the client qualifies for a mental health diagnosis, but that the diagnosis does not explain the incident. The client objects and demands that the LMFT not share this analysis with the court. The client threatens to sue the LMFT if the analysis is shared. When the court orders the LMFT to provide the evaluation report, the LMFT should:

   a. **Incorrect.** Assert privilege on behalf of the client
   b. **Incorrect.** Refuse to turn over the report on the grounds that it is the subject of a potential lawsuit
   c. **CORRECT.** Provide the report as requested
   d. **Incorrect.** Encourage the client to file a motion with the court requesting an injunction

When a defendant in a criminal case requests evaluation or therapy to establish their sanity, this is a specific exception to privilege in state law. The court is entitled to a copy of the LMFT's evaluation of the client, and "the court orders" in the question makes clear that this is a demand, not a request. Encouraging a client to file a motion with any court would be providing the client with legal advice, which is outside of the LMFT scope of practice.

2. An LMFT is working with a Latina mother and her 7-year-old son in therapy, when the LMFT observes unusual bruises on the boy's face and arms. The bruises seem to be in several different stages of healing. When the LMFT asks how he got the bruises, both the boy and his mother refuse to answer. The LMFT should:

    a.  **CORRECT.** Report suspected child abuse
    b.  **Incorrect.** Consider whether physical discipline is common in Latin cultures
    c.  **Incorrect.** Remind the mother of the limits of confidentiality
    d.  **Incorrect.** Ask the child to remove his shirt to inspect his torso for additional injuries

While the injuries, and both clients' response to the therapist's inquiries, are not a guarantee that abuse has taken place, remember that the therapist does not need to be certain. They just need to reasonably suspect abuse. The location of the injuries, the fact that they are in multiple stages of healing, and the refusal to explain them would amount to reasonable suspicion in almost any LMFT's mind. B would not be correct because the abuse reporting standards do not change on the basis of client culture. C is not correct because it would be an insufficient response to what appears to be abuse. D is not correct because this would place the LMFT in the role of an investigator, which is not the proper role of a therapist.

# LAW
# Standards for Professional Practice

**Scored exam questions (approximate): 5**

## Sexual relationships K32-33

**Sexual relationship between therapist and client.** Sexual behavior between therapist and client is specifically prohibited under California law. (Such contact is also specifically prohibited by both the CAMFT and AAMFT codes of ethics, which we will discuss in the Ethics section.) "Behavior" here is a broader term than intercourse, and it applies to a wide range of sexual activities.

**Intimacy between therapist and *former* client.** For former clients, state law prohibits sexual behavior for two years after the last professional contact. Sexual relationships with former clients after this time may still be problematic and are further discouraged in our ethics codes. But they are not legally prohibited so long as two years have gone by since the last professional contact.

**The *Therapy Never Includes Sexual Behavior* brochure.** If your client informs you that they have had a sexual relationship with another therapist, you are required by law to provide for them the state-authored brochure *Therapy Never Includes Sexual Behavior*. (This was previously called *Professional Therapy Never Includes Sex*, which may be how your supervisor refers to it.) Failure to provide the brochure is considered unprofessional conduct. Many therapists keep a copy or two of the brochure readily available in their offices; it also can be downloaded and printed when you need it.

# Scope of practice K34

Your scope of practice is set in state law. It specifies what someone with an MFT license can legally do. California's MFT scope of practice language was updated in 2022, but just to modernize the language; it didn't change anything about what MFTs can do in practice.

The MFT scope of practice allows MFTs to work with individuals, couples, families, and groups. (Throughout this book, when you see the word "client," it may refer to an individual, couple, or family.) The MFT scope of practice specifically allows MFTs to use psychotherapeutic techniques, making MFTs psychotherapists. And it allows MFTs to integrate required graduate training into practice – which is key to understanding that MFTs can independently diagnose mental illness.

MFTs can use psychological tests under two conditions: It has to be in the context of a therapy relationship, and the MFT must have adequate training in administering the test.

One of the most important pieces in understanding scope of practice is understanding its limits. MFTs *cannot* provide legal advice, medical advice, or other forms of guidance that are outside the MFT scope of practice. Referring a client to a doctor, lawyer, or other professional is fine, and it's good to recognize when clients have these needs. But recommending that a client take a certain medication, for example, or change their medication dosage, would be outside of the MFT scope of practice.

It also is helpful to understand the difference between scope of practice – which is set in state law and is the same for every MFT in the state – and scope of *competence*, which is based on your specific education, training, and experience. Scope of competence varies by individual MFT and is primarily an ethical issue. It is discussed later.

# Unprofessional conduct laws K35

When a therapist violates professional standards, they are said to have committed unprofessional conduct. The BBS exists to protect the public, not the professionals, and will investigate and (if appropriate) punish unprofessional conduct when it is reported.

State law defines 28 specific categories of unprofessional conduct. For our purposes, it's most important to know what unprofessional conduct *means*: It refers to **actions taken in a professional role that are below minimum professional standards**. Unlike criminal cases (where you could go to jail) or civil cases (where you might have to pay damages to someone you have wronged), unprofessional conduct rules apply to your professional role. Unprofessional conduct can result in action being taken against your license or registration.

The types of conduct defined in state law as unprofessional conduct include the following. The language here is lightly edited from state law, and grouped into categories:

**Sexual misconduct**
Sexual contact with a client or former client
Committing a sex crime with a minor
Committing a sex crime
Sexual misconduct
Failure to provide *Therapy Never Includes Sexual Behavior* brochure

**Scope of practice and competence**
Performing or offering services outside of scope

**Impairment**
Impairment due to mental or physical illness or drug dependence
Drug dependence or use with a client while providing services

**Confidentiality**
Failure to maintain confidentiality

**Crimes and bad acts**
Conviction of a crime
Committing a dishonest, corrupt, or fraudulent act
Discipline by another board or by another state

**Fraud**

    Getting or attempting to get a license by fraud

    Misrepresenting your license or qualifications

    Impersonating a licensee

    Aiding someone else's unlicensed activity

**Testing**

    Violating exam security or integrity

**Supervision**

    Improper supervision of a trainee or associate

    Violations during or involving required hours of experience

**Fees and advertising**

    Failure to disclose fees in advance

    False, misleading, deceptive, or improper advertising

    Paying, accepting, or soliciting a fee for referrals

**Record-keeping**

    Failure to keep records consistent with sound clinical judgment

    Failure to comply with client requests for access to records

**Telemedicine**

    Violating state telehealth standards

**General misconduct**

    General unprofessional conduct

    Gross negligence or incompetence

    Intentionally or recklessly causing physical or emotional harm

    The category simply called "general unprofessional conduct" allows the BBS to act against you if you violate other law, professional ethical standard, or the professional standard of care while in your professional role. In this way, behaviors that are unethical can also be considered illegal, even if they aren't specifically designated as such in the law.

    I don't typically recommend trying to memorize the entire list above. Most of it, again, is simply what you would expect (and what is covered in this book). Knowing all the categories will not be nearly as helpful to you as being able to determine whether a particular behavior qualifies as unprofessional conduct under the law.

When a therapist engages in unprofessional conduct, the client may submit a complaint to the BBS. The BBS then has an investigations unit that assesses the complaint, determines whether it is actionable, and investigates if appropriate. During this time, the MFT can defend themselves. If the MFT is found to have committed unprofessional conduct, the BBS can levy fines, place the MFT on suspension or probation, restrict their practice, and in severe cases, revoke the MFT's license (or registration, in cases involving MFT associates). They also may require other actions, such as regular drug testing, while the MFT is on probation or to resolve the disciplinary issue. The disciplinary process is meaningfully different from a criminal trial or a civil lawsuit; the BBS only needs to find *clear and convincing evidence* that a violation occurred to issue a penalty.

# Disclosing fees K36

**Required disclosures.** Under state law, you must inform clients before treatment begins of (1) the fee they will be charged and (2) the basis upon which that fee was computed. If you're confused about that second part, think about the sliding-fee scales used at many training clinics: *Client income* is the basis on which the fee is computed. As another example, some MFTs charge more for couple and family sessions than they do for individual sessions. That's fine, but clients need to know about this before treatment starts. Failure to disclose fees and their basis prior to starting treatment is considered unprofessional conduct.

Every new clients also must be informed of the process of filing a board complaint, should the client choose to file a complaint in the future.

Starting in 2022, federal law requires therapists and other health care professionals to provide a Good Faith Estimate of a new client's treatment costs, if the client is not planning to use their insurance to cover those costs. The GFE provides more information about the anticipated treatment, including estimated costs over the next 12 months. There are specific legal requirements for the content of a GFE and the time by which it must be provided to the client.

# Third-party reimbursement K37-38

**Third-party reimbursement rules.** Health insurance coverage has expanded significantly since the passage of the Affordable Care Act. Of course, insurance is not the only form of third-party payment; employers, courts, nonprofit organizations, family members, and others may be the ones who are actually paying for client care. MFTs need to be aware of the rules surrounding third-party payment, including the limits on information that can be shared with third-party payers.

Some of the key legal rules regarding third-party payment include:

- **Freedom of choice.** Insurance companies typically must reimburse MFTs alongside other mental health providers. Associates do not have to be reimbursed, though some plans will pay for services provided by associates.
- **Mental disorder only.** Most insurers will only reimburse when there is a diagnosed mental disorder. Some will cover services like couple therapy when there is no diagnosis, but plans are not legally required to do so.
- **Protests and complaints.** Providers can (and generally should) appeal denials of reimbursement. Consumers and providers both can complain to the state about insurance company practices. Depending on the plan, it may be governed by the state Department of Insurance or the Department of Managed Health Care.

One of the most important legal rules regarding third-party reimbursement is the prohibition against insurance fraud, which can draw criminal and civil penalties in addition to action against your license. Any falsification of diagnosis, procedure code, amount paid, or any other information for the purpose of receiving insurance payment is insurance fraud.

**Parity laws.** State and federal law require parity in insurance coverage for mental health. What this means is that insurers cannot use a different deductible or other forms of treatment limitations for mental health that they do not apply to other medical coverage. Co-payments, deductibles, and treatment limitations (like caps on visits or days of coverage) for mental health must be equal to or better than the limits placed on other medical coverage. Under a new law for 2021, any plan language aiming to give the insurer "discretionary authority" to refuse coverage for medically necessary mental health or substance abuse treatment is invalid.

# Advertising laws K39

**Advertising laws.** Essentially any public statement where you suggest that you offer therapy or counseling services to the public would be considered an advertisement – the law is purposefully broad on that. The only exception is church bulletins.

State law is highly specific on the **licensure status** disclosures that need to be included in *any* advertisement of an MFT's services. A licensed MFT needs to include their name, their license number, and their title ("licensed marriage and family therapist") or an acceptable abbreviation ("LMFT" or "MFT"). An associate needs to include their name, their registration number, their employer's name, an indication that they are under licensed supervision, and their title ("registered associate marriage and family therapist"). That title can be abbreviated "Registered Associate MFT," but the abbreviation "AMFT" can only be used as a title in an ad if the ad *also* contains the fully-spelled-out title "registered associate marriage and family therapist."

MFTs and associates can advertise themselves as **psychotherapists** and say that they perform psychotherapy, as long as they clearly list their licensure type, something the law already requires anyway.

Therapists can advertise using **fictitious business names**, so long as those names are not misleading and clients are informed of the business owners' names and licensure status before treatment begins.

Ads making any kind of **scientific claims** must be backed by published, peer-reviewed research literature.

Any **fees** included in an advertisement must be exact; you cannot advertise fees in ways like "$95 and up." For this reason, many therapists and clinics choose not to list their fees in their advertising.

It is unprofessional conduct for any MFT to advertise in a manner that is **false, misleading, or deceptive**. Any claims that would be likely to create unjustified expectations of treatment success are also prohibited by law.

# Payment for referrals K40

Therapists are legally prohibited from accepting any form of payment for referrals. (There is a parallel ethical prohibition.) This includes payment from clients as well as payments from the professional you referred the clients to (sometimes called "kickbacks"). The idea here is that referrals should be made *solely* on the basis of what is in the best interests of the client. If you are getting paid for referrals, there is at least the *appearance* of a conflict of interests, as you might make a referral based more on what will financially benefit you than on what will clinically benefit the client.

This issue has become more complex in recent years. In some communities, MFTs participate in "networking groups," which are organizations of professionals who sell a wide variety of goods and services. These professionals join the networking group for the specific purpose of referring potential customers to one another. However, because these groups often operate in a structure where members are rewarded for the referrals they generate (the reward might be the *absence* of a fee that they would otherwise have to pay to participate), MFTs in such groups risk being disciplined for violating the standards against receiving payment for referrals.

## Sample Questions
See the next page for answers and rationales

1. An LMFT in a cash-pay private practice notices that several clients have unpaid balances. Some of those with unpaid balances attend the same religious service as the LMFT. As the LMFT considers how to resolve the unpaid balances, how can the LMFT best address their legal responsibilities?

    a. Forgive the balances of those in the religious group, and consider it a donation to that group

    b. Reconsider whether therapy with these clients is within the LMFT's scope of practice

    c. Work with each client with an unpaid balance to develop a payment plan

    d. Charge fees for unpaid balances, to discourage clients from carrying balances in the future. Inform all clients of the new fee and how much, if any, they additionally owe

2. An LMFT with an MA degree in marriage and family therapy is also completing a PhD in world religions. They only need to complete their dissertation to complete the degree. From that education, the LMFT takes an approach to therapy that recognizes the importance of the client's spiritual and religious experience. The LMFT also is a Certified Level I Track Coach, which clients who are involved in sports sometimes say they appreciate. How can the LMFT most appropriately advertise themselves, considering their legal obligations?

    a. [Name], LMFT, PhD-c, Certified Coach

    b. [Name], LMFT, MA

    c. [Name], LMFT, PhD (ABD)

    d. [Name], LMFT, Level I Certification

# Sample Questions: Answers and Rationales

1. An LMFT in a cash-pay private practice notices that several clients have unpaid balances. Some of those with unpaid balances attend the same religious service as the LMFT. As the LMFT considers how to resolve the unpaid balances, how can the LMFT best address their legal responsibilities?

    a. **Incorrect.** Forgive the balances of those in the religious group, and consider it a donation to that group

    b. **Incorrect.** Reconsider whether therapy with these clients is within the LMFT's scope of practice

    c. **CORRECT.** Work with each client with an unpaid balance to develop a payment plan

    d. **Incorrect.** Charge fees for unpaid balances, to discourage clients from carrying balances in the future. Inform all clients of the new fee and how much, if any, they additionally owe

Forgiving the balances of those who share the LMFT's religious practice, while not forgiving the balances of others (A), would likely be considered discrimination based on religion. While scope of practice (B) is a legal issue, there is nothing in the vignette to suggest that the treatment the LMFT has been providing is outside of their scope. Simply sharing a religious affiliation with some clients does not make that treatment outside of the MFT's scope of practice. While it is legal to charge fees for unpaid balances (D), such fees need to be spelled out to clients *before* they are implemented -- typically in the initial informed consent agreement. Imposing them before informing clients of them would be a violation.

2. An LMFT with an MA degree in marriage and family therapy is also completing a PhD in world religions. They only need to complete their dissertation to complete the degree. From that education, the LMFT takes an approach to therapy that recognizes the importance of the client's spiritual and religious experience. The LMFT also is a Certified Level I Track Coach, which clients who are involved in sports sometimes say they appreciate. How can the LMFT most appropriately advertise themselves, considering their legal obligations?

    a.  **Incorrect.** [Name], LMFT, PhD-c, Certified Coach
    b.  **CORRECT.** [Name], LMFT, MA
    c.  **Incorrect.** [Name], LMFT, PhD (ABD)
    d.  **Incorrect.** [Name], LMFT, Level I Certification

LMFTs are only permitted to advertise degrees that are directly relevant to their clinical practices. While some elements of the doctoral degree may inform the LMFT's work, advertising it as part of the LMFT's marketing would mislead clients into thinking that the LMFT has a doctorate (or is working on a doctorate) in therapy or a closely related field. The public also does not tend to recognize such modifiers as PhD-c or ABD, making the use of "PhD" further misleading. The track coaching certification also is not directly related to clinical practice and should not be mentioned, especially in examples such as these where the fact that it is a certification in track coaching is not mentioned.

## ETHICS

# Competence and Preventing Harm

| Scored exam questions (approximate): | 9 |

## Scope of competence K41-45

**Understanding scope of competence.** Your scope of competence is defined by your education, training, and professional experience, and so your scope of competence is unique to you and can change over time. Scope of competence is primarily an *ethical* issue, though practicing outside of one's scope of competence is also considered unprofessional conduct in state law.

**Knowing your own limitations.** Just as it is important to be able to identify actions that would be out of the MFT scope of practice, it is also critical to understand when issues come before you that are outside your scope of competence. You can't possibly have training and experience for every possible situation you will encounter in your practice, so acknowledging limitations in your scope of competence is not a weakness. It is good professional behavior.

**Need for consultation.** When a situation comes up in therapy that is outside of an MFT's scope of competence, a responsible MFT will consult with a supervisor or others to determine what appropriate next steps would be. However, a need for consultation is not the same as a need to refer the client out. In many cases, the therapist will work to expand their competence while continuing to work with the client.

**Protecting client rights in consultation and collaboration.** Of course, MFTs are encouraged to regularly consult with other professionals and community resources to promote quality client care. It is common for MFTs to collaborate and consult with physicians, teachers, social service providers, and other important persons in a client's life, on issues that are outside the MFT's scope of competence.

When doing such consultations, MFTs respect the confidentiality of their clients. Each member of the treatment unit must give their permission for clinical information to be shared with any outsider unless an exception to confidentiality applies. Even when client permission or an exception to confidentiality is present, the MFT should only provide the information necessary for the consultation.

**Expanding competence.** If one's scope of competence is determined by education, training, and experience, then it makes sense that MFTs can expand into new areas of practice, or improve their competence in existing ones, by getting additional education, training, and experience. One's competence in working with a particular population can be improved through exposure to that population, including visiting or interacting with members of that population. In many cases it also is appropriate for an MFT to seek out new knowledge through books, videos, and other research about a topic or population that is new to the MFT.

**Responsibility to remain current.** The MFT field is constantly growing and changing, with new treatment models and new scientific developments occurring on a regular basis. The training and experience that make you competent to work with a certain problem or population today may be considered outdated and inaccurate 10 years from now. MFTs have an ethical responsibility to remain current with new developments in the profession, through additional education, training, and supervised experience. This is part of the reason why licensed MFTs are required to get continuing education hours in each license renewal cycle.

# Self-awareness K46-50

**Impairments.** Good therapists are keenly aware of their own limitations. If you are struggling with a serious emotional problem, mental or physical illness, or substance use, it can interfere with your ability to provide effective therapy. Potential impairment is not limited to these specific issues, however. Therapists may struggle with grief, family stressors, or a wide variety of other problems that can interfere with clinical work. If you have a strong emotional reaction to a particular client – perhaps because their struggle mirrors one you have gone through, or because there is something in the client's behavior that you strongly dislike – you may not be able to provide that client with effective services.

Impairment tends to show up as difficulty with clinical judgment. The therapist becomes more friendly, or harsher and more judgmental, toward clients than they typically would be. Sometimes impairment becomes visible through changes in a therapist's ability to complete routine tasks like documentation or follow-up contacts with clients and others. Sometimes impairment is most clear when reviewing client outcome data.

**Responding to impairments.** MFTs need to know the referrals and resources available if the therapist is struggling with an impairment and needs to step away from client care, either temporarily or on a longer-term basis. (Knowledge of appropriate referrals and resources comes up multiple times in the BBS Exam Plan, as it is important in many different sets of circumstances. Obviously, the test will not ask what the closest hospital is, since the test is being given across the state. But you may be asked about the *kinds* of client referrals and resources that would be most appropriate to a given situation. Referrals should always be appropriate to the level and type of client need.)

For the therapist, obviously seeking treatment is appropriate when the problem is a serious emotional problem, mental or physical illness, or substance use. If the issue is a strong reaction to the client, the MFT should seek supervision and consultation, and consider going to therapy. In whatever time it takes for the MFT to resolve their impairment, protecting the welfare of the client is the highest priority.

**Methods to facilitate transfer.** In some cases, the impairment of an MFT will lead to their needing to transfer clients to other therapists. If it is possible and appropriate, the MFT may have a termination session with the client, focused on transitioning them to a new provider. The MFT should provide appropriate referrals based on client need. The MFT and client should consider a Release of Information authorizing the transfer of client records to the new provider, and authorizing the old and new therapists to communicate to ensure continuity of care. The MFT should follow up with the new provider to transfer the records and coordinate care appropriately.

**Personal values, attitudes, and beliefs.** MFTs are ethically prohibited from influencing client decisions on preferred treatment or outcomes based on personal values, attitudes, and beliefs. (Going forward, I'll just say "attitudes" to refer collectively to "values, attitudes, and beliefs.") Obviously, it is important for MFTs to be aware of their own attitudes and how they might impact the therapy process. Therapists allowing for their attitudes to influence them might pathologize the behavior of clients the therapist doesn't like, leading to incorrect diagnoses and poor treatment decisions. They might show bias toward one or more family members, impacting the effectiveness of couple or family work. They might become overly friendly (or overly hostile) with a client. They might place their own belief about a particular problem above current scientific knowledge in the field. Ultimately, the therapist is likely to miss or misinterpret important clinical information, decreasing the likelihood of effective therapy.

**Managing the impact of therapist attitudes.** So what happens, then, when an MFT becomes aware that they have personal attitudes that are entering into the therapy room? It depends on the nature of what is arising. You are of course allowed to hold whatever attitudes you hold, and even to discuss them in therapy when it is clinically appropriate to do so. What you cannot do is *impose* those attitudes on the client or the therapeutic process.

If the therapist is experiencing judgment or bias toward the client based on personal attitudes, the therapist should carefully consider how those attitudes are impacting treatment. The therapist may seek out supervision or consultation to ensure quality of care, and may go to their own therapy to identify the source of the attitude, working to change it if appropriate. If the therapist attitude is likely to continue interfering in the therapeutic relationship, the therapist may consider referring the client to another therapist – but must be cautious to avoid client abandonment, and to ensure that the referral is not discriminatory in nature. If the therapist refers clients out based on personal attitudes about race, gender, or other protected characteristics, the therapist may be engaging in discrimination.

# Multiple Relationships K51-55

A multiple relationship (or "dual relationship" -- the terms are used here interchangeably) occurs any time an MFT has a relationship with a client that is separate from being their therapist. Not all multiple relationships are unethical or illegal, and some can't be avoided, especially in rural areas or in work with more tight-knit communities.

**Problematic multiple relationships.** Sexual or romantic relationships with a client are expressly prohibited, and discussed in greater detail below. There are some other kinds of multiple relationships that are also specifically noted in the CAMFT code of ethics as being potentially problematic. These include:

- Borrowing money from a client
- Hiring a client
- Joining with a client in a business venture
- Having a close personal relationship with a client

If in MFT engages in any of these same actions with a client's spouse, partner, or family member, this may also be unethical.

Not all multiple relationships can be avoided, especially if you are working in a rural area or with a highly specific population. It is also true that not all multiple relationships are problematic. If a colleague tells you that you can't see a client because "that would be a dual relationship," they haven't adequately made their case.

Multiple relationships must be carefully examined to see whether they would potentially **impair clinical judgment** or create **risk of client exploitation**. These two considerations are critical to determining whether a multiple relationship can be allowed. If you know and like someone in your community and they ask to see you in therapy, your liking of them would surely influence how you observe them clinically -- in other words, your pre-existing view of them would impair your clinical judgment. (Impairment can mean positive bias as well as negative.) Having a client who coaches your daughter's soccer team could create risk of exploitation, as you could use your knowledge of the client's personal secrets to push for more playing time for your daughter. The fact that you wouldn't actually do this does not eliminate the risk of it, nor does it take away your responsibility to protect clients from that risk.

Even when such risks exist, though, in some cases it may be appropriate to continue with the therapy. If you are the only provider in a rural area, for example, the best interests of the client might be better served by going ahead with therapy. You would then need to take specific actions to reduce the risk of impaired judgment or exploitation.

**Managing boundaries.** MFTs commonly take steps to ensure the integrity and boundaries of the therapy relationship. This can be especially important when it appears that a client is becoming confused about the nature of the relationship, or is wanting more of a personal or social relationship than what therapy allows.

Some examples of methods for managing boundaries include having a conversation with the client to remind them of the boundaries of therapy; maintaining a clear treatment plan with identified therapy goals; making sure all contact between client and therapist stays focused on therapeutic issues; starting and ending sessions on time; and, when clinically appropriate, limiting contact by phone or other means between scheduled session times.

**Potential conflicts of interest.** MFTs are ethically obligated to be aware of potential conflicts of interest as they arise. The CAMFT Code of Ethics specifically identifies providing multiple forms of treatment (individual, couple, family, or group) to the same person or family as a potential conflict. Another potential conflict emerges any time a therapist engages in a non-therapist role, such as consultation, coaching, or behavior analysis, with people who are or have been clients in therapy. In any instance of potential conflict of interests, MFTs have an obligation to clarify their roles, and to distinguish how any non-therapist role is different from therapy. To avoid any risk to clients, it may be preferable to refer out for additional services that are different from those for which the therapist was initially hired.

**Potentially damaging relationships.** Sexual relationships, which are discussed at greater length below, are the best example of a relationship that can be damaging to the client. However, they are not the only example. Other forms of multiple relationships can harm clients directly, through poor care or exploitation, or they may harm clients more indirectly, by reducing their overall confidence in therapy as an effective and worthwhile treatment. Social relationships between MFTs and clients can create confusion about the therapist's role, for example, and can hinder success in therapy by clouding the MFT's clinical judgment.

**When multiple relationships can't be avoided.** Some multiple relationships are unavoidable, and others don't need to be avoided. For example, some level of multiple relationship is created any time an MFT gets a new client through a referral from an existing client. Another example occurs in a rural area, where an MFT may have regular interaction with many clients at community gatherings. In these and similar situations, the CAMFT Code of Ethics requires MFTs to "take appropriate professional precautions [...] to avoid exploitation or harm" (standard 4.2). In some cases, the precautions may be as simple as having a conversation with the client to reassure them of confidentiality and clearly separate roles. In other cases, more stringent precautions may be appropriate, like the MFT regularly consulting on the case with a colleague, or documenting their analysis of risks and benefits. The AAMFT Code requires that MFTs document the precautions they take when choosing to engage in a multiple relationship.

# Sexual relationships K56-58

**Risk of exploitation.** The rules prohibiting sexual contact between therapists and their clients come from a fundamental understanding that because the therapist has power in the therapy relationship, because clients are often emotionally vulnerable, and because the therapy process happens behind closed doors, sexual relationships between therapists and clients are likely to be exploitive and ultimately harmful to clients.

This exploitation does not require sexual *intercourse*, and the legal and ethical standards around sexual relationships are worded in such a way as to include romantically intimate relationships and sexual behavior generally, even if there has not been intercourse. The CAMFT code even includes sexually explicit communication without a clear clinical purpose in its prohibited sexual behaviors. (If you're working with a couple on sexual issues, that work might require candid conversation about their sexual behavior; that's clinically appropriate.)

**Intimacy between therapist and client.** As noted in the legal section, sexual conduct -- again, a purposefully broader term than intercourse -- between therapist and client is specifically prohibited under California law. Such contact is also specifically prohibited by both the CAMFT and AAMFT codes of ethics.

**Intimacy between therapist and *former* client.** For former clients, the CAMFT Code of Ethics reinforces state law in prohibiting sexual relationships for two years after therapy has ended. Even after that time, the CAMFT Code continues to discourage sexual relationships with former clients, due to the risk that they will be exploitive and harmful to the former client. The current AAMFT Code of Ethics includes a *lifetime* ban on sexual relationships with former clients.

**Intimacy between therapist and client's spouse, partner, or family member.** State laws about sexual relationships with clients and former clients apply only to the clients themselves. Under ethical guidelines, the prohibition is broader: Therapists *also* may not engage in sexually intimate relationships with clients' spouses or partners. The AAMFT Code of Ethics also prohibits sexual relationships with other known family members of the client's family system. The CAMFT code limits this to "immediate" family members, without further defining the term.

**Therapy with former romantic partners.** Just as it would be unethical to start having sex with a former client (subject to the rules noted above), it would also be unethical to accept a client in therapy who was a former sexual partner. This type of multiple relationship is expressly prohibited by the CAMFT Code of Ethics. Entering a therapy relationship with the partner or immediate family member of someone with whom the therapist has had a prior sexual relationship is also prohibited.

While these situations are not directly addressed in the AAMFT code, it is likely that they would still be considered unethical under the existing rules on multiple relationships.

## Sample Questions
See the next page for answers and rationales

1. An LMFT working in a rural area begins taking on clients who have friendships or professional relationships with other clients. The LMFT does not always know of these connections between clients when treatment begins with a new client. While the LMFT is confident that the LMFT can maintain strong boundaries, they wonder what will happen if one client starts speaking about someone else in session, not knowing that the person they are speaking of is also a client. How should the LMFT address this issue?

    a. Seek consultation from other therapists who are working in rural areas

    b. Considering the nature of the community, ask new clients not to speak about others during therapy

    c. Move part or all of their practice to telehealth to broaden their geographic service area

    d. If existing clients give permission, provide new clients with a list of current clients, defining those current clients as off-limits topics for the new client's therapy

2. An LMFT develops a no-harm contract with an adolescent client who has been expressing moderate levels of suicidal ideation. While the client has not expressed any suicidal intent, the LMFT has been concerned that the client's situation could worsen. The LMFT consults with a Psychologist, who expresses concern over the use of a no-harm contract. The Psychologist tells the LMFT that such contracts are no longer considered a best practice in caring for potentially suicidal clients. Ethically, the LMFT should:

    a. Provide more information to the Psychologist to support the use of a no-harm contract

    b. Refer the case to the Psychologist, who can employ more current techniques

    c. Renew the no-harm contract on at least a weekly basis

    d. Seek out training on current best practices for suicide prevention and intervention

# Sample Questions: Answers and Rationales

1. An LMFT working in a rural area begins taking on clients who have friendships or professional relationships with other clients. The LMFT does not always know of these connections between clients when treatment begins with a new client. While the LMFT is confident that the LMFT can maintain strong boundaries, they wonder what will happen if one client starts speaking about someone else in session, not knowing that the person they are speaking of is also a client. How should the LMFT address this issue?

    a. **CORRECT.** Seek consultation from other therapists who are working in rural areas

    b. **Incorrect.** Considering the nature of the community, ask new clients not to speak about others during therapy

    c. **Incorrect.** Move part or all of their practice to telehealth to broaden their geographic service area

    d. **Incorrect.** If existing clients give permission, provide new clients with a list of current clients, defining those current clients as off-limits topics for the new client's therapy

LMFTs are expected to engage in consultation to address ethical questions or concerns. In this instance, the LMFT is not obligated to move to telehealth, and asking clients not to speak of other people (with or without existing clients' permission) would make it difficult to assess or intervene in client relationships. But the LMFT may need to take steps to manage the dual relationships that can arise in rural areas, and consultation will help the LMFT determine how to best do so.

2. An LMFT develops a no-harm contract with an adolescent client who has been expressing moderate levels of suicidal ideation. While the client has not expressed any suicidal intent, the LMFT has been concerned that the client's situation could worsen. The LMFT consults with a Psychologist, who expresses concern over the use of a no-harm contract. The Psychologist tells the LMFT that such contracts are no longer considered a best practice in caring for potentially suicidal clients. Ethically, the LMFT should:

a. **Incorrect.** Provide more information to the Psychologist to support the use of a no-harm contract
b. **Incorrect.** Refer the case to the Psychologist, who can employ more current techniques
c. **Incorrect.** Renew the no-harm contract on at least a weekly basis
d. **CORRECT.** Seek out training on current best practices for suicide prevention and intervention

LMFTs have an ethical responsibility to remain current in their practices, and in this instance, the Psychologist is correct. No-harm contracts are not a current best practice, having been replaced with more detailed safety plans. Rather than attempting to justify their decision (a), referring the client out (b), or continuing with an outdated process (c), the therapist should improve the currency of their knowledge.

## ETHICS
# Therapeutic Relationship

**Scored exam questions (approximate): 13-14**

## Informed Consent K59-64

**Informed consent.** For a client to offer consent that is truly *informed*, they need a reasonable amount of *information* about the treatment process. MFTs have an ethical responsibility to provide clients with appropriate information about the treatment process, so that the client can make an informed decision about whether they want to participate. Because treatment plans and methods can change during therapy, informed consent for treatment is best understood not as a single event but as an ongoing process in therapy. Consent does not need to be given in writing, but it should be documented in the client file.

**Facilitating client decisions about treatment.** Professional ethics codes require MFTs to provide enough information to clients that the clients can make meaningful choices about whether to start therapy. The nature of this information may vary by therapist and by treatment type. MFTs are specifically obligated to inform clients of the limits of confidentiality, the client's right to autonomy in decision-making (more on that below), and of potential risks and benefits of any new or experimental techniques. MFTs are also encouraged, but not required, to give clients information about the therapist's education, training, theoretical orientation, specialties, and any other information the MFT thinks will be helpful.

**Client autonomy in treatment decisions.** Clients have the fundamental right to choose for themselves what kinds of mental health treatment they will participate in. While there are exceptions to this, such as for clients who present an imminent danger to themselves or others and thus can be involuntarily hospitalized, most clients can choose their treatment type, treatment provider, and treatment goals as they see fit. (Some goals would be considered inappropriate for therapy, such as a parent bringing their child into therapy in hopes of changing the child's sexual orientation. While a parent is certainly free to pursue this goal, it would not be appropriate for a therapist to attempt to offer this treatment.) Consistent with this principle, clients can also discontinue treatment or change treatment provider at any time. Even when treatment is taking place by court order, clients typically can choose their provider. MFTs respect clients' rights to choose whether to start therapy and whether to leave it at any time. Of course, we can and should discuss such decisions with clients, but we cannot require them to remain in therapy, or to remain in therapy with us, if they do not wish to do so.

**Culturally and developmentally appropriate methods.** MFTs should gain consent for treatment in a manner that is culturally and developmentally appropriate. If a client is illiterate, does not read English, comes from a culture that promotes deference, or is otherwise unable to make sense of the informed consent document, their signature on it may not truly reflect informed consent. The informed consent process would be better served with a verbal discussion in language that the client can understand. MFTs also should be aware of the possibility that clients may be attending therapy against their wishes, at the demand of a family member or someone else; in such instances, it is important for the MFT to determine whether the client is truly providing voluntary consent for treatment.

**Guardians and representatives.** When clients are unable to make informed decisions on their own, their guardians and legal representatives have the right and responsibility to make choices on the client's behalf. Most commonly, this happens when a parent or legal guardian consents to the treatment of a minor. However, it can also apply when a client under conservatorship is put into treatment by their conservator, or when a court-appointed *guardian ad litem* seeks treatment for minors involved in a custody dispute. In these and other instances, guardians and legal representatives are responsible for making informed decisions about treatment that will be in the best interest of the client.

**Clients who can't provide voluntary consent.** When a client is unable to provide voluntary consent for treatment, the MFT remains responsible for protecting client welfare. Clients may be unable to voluntarily consent for treatment if they are under the influence of drugs or alcohol, if they have been involuntarily hospitalized as a danger to themselves or others, or if they are a child brought to treatment by their parents, as a few examples.

In these instances, the MFT would still take steps to promote client welfare and facilitate the client's ability to make decisions about treatment to the degree possible. In the case of a client under the influence of drugs or alcohol, the MFT may simply take steps to keep the client safe until the influence of the drug has worn off and the client can voluntarily consent to further treatment. A more thorough informed consent process may take place at that point. If a client has been involuntarily hospitalized, the MFT may remind them of their remaining rights. In the case of a minor, an MFT may utilize an assent agreement, which spells out the purpose, risks, and benefits of therapy in a way that is developmentally appropriate to the child and allows them to ask questions about the therapy.

Clients mandated to treatment by a court or other outside entity typically retain their right to choose their treatment provider and voluntarily consent to therapy. They may be required by a court to be in therapy, but typically, they don't have to be in therapy *with you*. MFTs working with mandated clients are ethically required to clarify the MFT's role and the limits of confidentiality that will apply to the mandated services. This clarification helps protect client rights, as they can choose whether to go forward in treatment under those rules.

# Concurrent psychotherapy K65-66

**Effects of concurrent treatment.** When done well, concurrent treatment can maximize therapeutic gains. Coordinated care among multiple therapists can mean that family members receive individual therapy to work on their individual concerns at the same time they are receiving family therapy to address relational issues. This may speed improvement by addressing multiple levels of concern at once, and by reducing the homeostatic processes in family systems that can keep symptoms locked in place.

Concurrent treatment can also cause problems, however, especially when the multiple therapists involved are not in communication with one another. It is not in the best interests of clients to go to one therapist who encourages the client to create distance from the client's mother, and then to go to another therapist who is working to develop a closer relationship between mother and client.

**Ethical guidelines for concurrent psychotherapy.** The CAMFT Code of Ethics allows MFTs to work with clients who are simultaneously working with other mental health providers. Such an arrangement is not unusual if the therapists are working with different treatment units (such as an individual therapist and a couple therapist) or different problems (such as one therapist treating substance use while another addresses trauma). Under the CAMFT code, therapists discuss potential confusion or conflicts with the client, including whether consulting or coordinating care with the other therapist would be appropriate.

# Working with multiple clients K67-72

**Identifying the "client."** MFTs are ethically obligated to clarify at the beginning of therapy which person or persons are considered clients, and the nature of the relationship the therapist will have with each person involved in treatment. There is a meaningful difference between a partner or family member *visiting* treatment, where they might offer input or moral support, and being *a part of* treatment, where they may be directly involved in therapeutic interventions.

When a couple, family, or group is considered the client, MFTs have an ethical responsibility to carefully balance the needs of the client with the needs of each individual who is part of the client unit.

**Confidentiality.** When working with couples or families, confidentiality becomes a key concern. If a client calls between sessions and informs the therapist of a secret, does the therapist have the right to bring that information up in a couple or family session? The AAMFT Code of Ethics takes a default position that MFTs maintain individual confidences unless given specific permission otherwise; the CAMFT code simply acknowledges that MFTs must respect the confidences of their clients, while also noting that the "client" may be more than one person, which brings "unique confidentiality responsibilities."

Most MFTs clarify at the beginning of therapy what the MFT's policy is regarding the holding of secrets. Some MFTs support a no-secrets policy, where individual confidences will not be upheld. Other MFTs prefer a limited secrets policy, believing this is better for accurate assessment of the couple or family. In either case, it is best for the MFT to have a clear, written policy that everyone participating in treatment has agreed to, and for the MFT to then stick to that policy.

In therapy groups, MFTs educate group members on the meaning and importance of confidentiality. MFTs may ask group members to sign an agreement that they will respect the privacy of the group.

**Preserving the therapeutic relationship.** Of course, it would not be possible to list all the factors that can influence the therapeutic relationship in family therapy. Nor is that necessary for an exam about legal and ethical practice. Lots of things can influence the relationship, not all of which are foreseeable. If the MFT keeps client welfare and the preservation of the therapeutic relationship paramount, the MFT will be able to manage most of these factors easily.

Consider two examples: In the first, an MFT doing couple therapy begins to feel hostility from one of the partners and is not sure why. The MFT asks the other partner whether it would be ok to meet alone with the hostile partner for a few minutes, and the other partner agrees. During this time, the hostile partner reveals that she is concerned the therapist is siding with her spouse over her. While this was not the MFT's intent, the MFT is able to change behavior moving forward, and offers and apology to the hostile partner.

In the second example, an MFT doing family therapy with a mother, father, and their two adolescent girls assesses that the girls' acting out behavior appears to be related to conflict in the parental subsystem. The MFT discusses with the family the possibility of changing the treatment modality to focus on couple work. While the MFT reminds the family that he enjoys having them all come in, he believes the girls have done their job, and now it is time for him to do his in treating the family's core issue.

In each of these cases, the therapist took steps to support client welfare and the therapeutic relationship, when it would have easily been possible for therapy to go down an unproductive path. An MFT should be able to address therapeutic issues related to their role, the modality of treatment, and the involvement of outsiders openly with clients.

**Potential conflicts.** When an MFT is providing concurrent therapy to multiple people in the same family system – for example, when the MFT is seeing members of a couple both individually and as a couple – conflicts can quickly emerge. Individuals in the same couple or family may have competing and even incompatible needs. An individual may want to talk with the MFT privately about something they don't want their family to know. More practically, scheduling and costs can become difficult in these situations. MFTs are ethically obligated to carefully consider potential conflicts in these situations, and to take steps to avoid or minimize those conflicts. Good ways to do so include having a clearly identified "client," maintaining a clear policy on secrets, regularly addressing confidentiality issues, and following a clear treatment plan.

**Treatment involving multiple systems or third parties.** The AAMFT Code of Ethics encourages MFTs to routinely revisit discussions of confidentiality with clients. This is especially important when treatment involves multiple systems or third parties. In some cases, treating an adolescent systemically may mean involving their teacher, their religious leader, their social worker, their physician, and others in the therapy all at once. If these third parties start attending the family's therapy sessions, everyone involved should be clear about what the third parties' roles are in the treatment, and what information may be shared with them. Managing privacy and confidentiality in these situations can be a complex task. Of course, clients should give permission before third parties are brought in to treatment, and they should be made aware that they can revoke this permission at any time.

# Managing confidentiality K73-74

**Ethical standards.** Both CAMFT and AAMFT have standards for MFTs to specifically inform clients of the limits of confidentiality at the beginning of treatment. (Technically, AAMFT requires such disclosures, while CAMFT simply encourages disclosure of "significant" exceptions to confidentiality.) Of course, this is not the only time when it may be relevant to discuss confidentiality. The AAMFT code notes that therapy may require multiple discussions of confidentiality and its limits.

In addition, throughout the course of therapy there are multiple standards that relate to therapists' responsibility to keep information from therapy private. Consultations, recordkeeping, telemedicine, supervision, teaching/presentation, and preparation for moving or closing a practice are *all* to be done in ways that protect client confidentiality, unless a specific exception applies or the client has granted permission for their information to be shared.

**Managing the impact of confidentiality issues.** Particularly if an MFT has been required to share information from therapy, a discussion with the client about what information was shared, with whom, and why can help minimize negative impacts on the therapeutic relationship. Such a discussion can also serve to remind the client of the limits of confidentiality, and of the therapist's commitment to protecting the safety of any others involved. For example, if a report of suspected child abuse has been made, the MFT may want to discuss the role that an MFT plays in larger society in protecting vulnerable populations from suspected abuse. Ultimately, a conversation like this can refocus client and therapist on the therapeutic process and may help repair any harm done to the therapeutic relationship.

# Managing crises K75-77

**Assessing level of risk.** When seeking to determine how much danger a client poses for potential violence, therapists tend to look most closely at a handful of issues:

- **History of violence or suicidality.** Previous suicide attempts are the strongest statistical predictor of a future attempt.
- **Plan.** Does the client have a plan for the harm they would inflict to themselves or others? Is it detailed and specific?
- **Means.** If the client is planning to engage in an act of violence, do they have the means to carry it out? Clients who consider gun violence who have guns in the home should be considered higher risk than those who do not.
- **Intent.** Some clients indulge in violent fantasies to manage their anger or other feelings.
- **Imminence.** Is the client intending to commit the violent act as soon as they can? Obviously, the client with a more immediate plan is a more immediate risk. However, a client with a detailed plan that is more distant may still be considered dangerous, as any instance of heightened impulsivity (from alcohol intoxication, a manic episode, or any other reason) could lead them to advance their timeline.
- **Risk and protective factors.** Clients with strong social connections, a sense of purpose, and other protective factors are lower risk than clients without these. And clients with meaningful risk factors, such as a history of violence or a recent significant loss, should be considered a higher potential danger.

The assessment of risk is a process that involves direct questioning of the client, observance of their behavior, gathering history and information on risk and protective factors, and involving any other available information: Assessment results, information from the client's physician or others you have permission to consult, prior records (medical, mental health, court, or other), and anything else that may be useful.

There is no magic formula for determining risk, and recent research suggests that screening instruments intended to quantify client risk level aren't especially effective on their own. When determining a client's risk level, consider the totality of their presentation.

If you intervene in a way that involves the sharing of client information, you should be prepared to support this action by documenting specific client statements, behaviors, and risk factors that led you to the conclusion that it was necessary to do so.

**Ethical obligations for protecting safety.** There are no standards in the CAMFT or AAMFT codes of ethics that are specific to the protection of client safety. However, several standards are indirectly related. Both codes speak to an MFT's responsibility to advance client welfare, which would include protecting their safety. The AAMFT code makes specific reference to honoring the public trust. And the professions are fundamentally guided by general ethical principles of beneficence (doing good), non-malfeasance (avoidance of harm), autonomy (clients' freedom to make their own choices), fidelity (honesty and loyalty), and justice. Among these, beneficence, non-malfeasance, and justice all would suggest that an MFT has an ethical responsibility to protect the safety of both clients and the public.

**Procedures for managing safety needs.** Safety needs should be addressed through the least intrusive means necessary to resolve the concern. You wouldn't hospitalize a mildly depressed patient, after all. Here are a few procedures for managing safety needs, ranging from the least to the most intrusive. This is not a complete list, and the options here are not mutually exclusive; it may be appropriate to develop a safety plan *and* increase the frequency of contact, for example.

- **Continue to assess.** In the absence of any specific safety concerns, the therapist would simply continue assessing for safety in future interactions with the client, documenting the process.
- **More detailed assessment.** If a client suggests that their depression is deepening or that their hostility to others is increasing, but does not discuss any specific danger or threat, the therapist should assess the area of concern in more detail.
- **Development of a safety plan.** If a client has a history of safety issues or is currently showing non-specific safety concerns (for example, a client with mild passive suicidality, but no plan or intent to harm themselves), a therapist may develop a safety plan. This plan lays out specific steps the client can take if their symptoms worsen. Steps usually follow a progression if early steps are unavailable or do not solve the problem. Steps may include contacting loved ones, contacting the therapist, contacting

another on-duty therapist, and if these steps are unsuccessful, contacting a 24-hour crisis hotline or calling 988 or 911.

- **Increasing frequency of contact.** If you have been seeing a client weekly and you begin to have concerns about their safety, but those concerns do not rise to the level where more immediate intervention is needed, you may ask to see them more often, or for the client to check in by phone more regularly.
- **Refer to a higher level of care.** Clients whose symptoms get worse or who become dangerous during outpatient psychotherapy may be better served through inpatient treatment.
- **Voluntary hospitalization.** Clients who pose an imminent danger to themselves or others and are willing to be assessed and treated voluntarily at a hospital will not be held there against their will. When a therapist is firm with a client that hospitalization is necessary, most clients will choose voluntary hospitalization over involuntary hospitalization.
- **Involuntary hospitalization.** If a client presents a major safety risk and is not willing to be hospitalized, an MFT may initiate the process of involuntary hospitalization. While most MFTs cannot invoke involuntary hospitalization, they can demand that a client be evaluated for a possible 72-hour hold.

Of course, if the safety concern is that the client poses an immediate danger of severe bodily harm to a reasonably identifiable victim, the appropriate procedure would be to notify the victim and law enforcement.

# Best interests of the client K78-80

**How legal and ethical obligations impact therapy.** Our legal and ethical obligations exist primarily to protect the best interests of clients. They can have the side effect of protecting therapists, by setting clear standards of professional behavior (and thus protecting us from accusations of being unprofessional when we are not), but they fundamentally exist to protect clients *from* us.

Sometimes, our legal and ethical obligations can create an inconvenience for therapist and client alike. Clients may not read every word of a long informed consent document, and therapists may not want to spend time in therapy discussing the limits of confidentiality. However, failing to meet our obligations can place clients at risk in a variety of ways. We fulfill these obligations because it is good for clients, even when it isn't convenient.

**Conflicts between legal and ethical obligations.** There are many times when there is not a direct conflict between law and ethics, but they set different standards. For example, the law may offer a stricter standard than the ethics codes, or vice versa. In these instances, an MFT should follow the stricter standard, regardless of which set of rules it comes from.

If there is a direct conflict between the code of ethics and the law – that is, if the law says that you *must* do one thing, while the code of ethics says that you *must* do something that is different from and incompatible with what the law requires – the law wins. MFTs should follow the law, and practice in accordance with the code of ethics to the greatest extent possible.

**Conflicts between agency and ethical obligations.** It is also common for MFTs to work in settings where ethics codes conflict with workplace policy. The AAMFT and CAMFT codes both require MFTs who face such conflicts to make their obligation to ethical standards known to the organization, and to take reasonable steps to resolve the issue in a way that allows the MFT to practice in keeping with their ethical responsibilities. The overriding principle is clear: Agency policy does not provide an excuse for MFTs to ignore their ethical duties.

# Diversity and nondiscrimination K81-84

**Ethical standards for non-discrimination.** The CAMFT and AAMFT codes of ethics both prohibit discrimination in professional services based on the following factors:

- Race
- Age
- Gender
- Gender identity
- Religion
- National origin
- Sexual orientation
- Disability
- Socioeconomic status
- Marital or relationship status

The AAMFT code adds health status to this list; the CAMFT code adds ethnicity, indigenous heritage, immigration status, and gender expression.

While the AAMFT code simply says that MFTs "provide professional assistance to persons without discrimination" based on the factors above, the CAMFT code notes that MFTs do not "condone or engage in" discrimination, nor do we refuse services based on any of the above.

**Diversity factors in therapy.** Virtually any area of difference between client and therapist has the potential to impact the therapy process. While discussions of diversity in the US tend to center on issues of race, ethnicity, sexual orientation, and gender identity, a wide variety of other factors can impact a client's identity and cultural norms. In addition to all of the factors listed in the non-discrimination standards above, therapy can be impacted by differences between client and therapist in urban versus rural setting, educational level, regional identity, and many more.

The impacts of diversity factors can be far-reaching. Misunderstandings are common. Differences in diversity factors can also lead to misdiagnosis of clients, microaggressions, and even the continued marginalization of historically marginalized groups. This is why it is so important for therapists to understand how their own backgrounds impact their work, including awareness of (and active efforts to reduce) bias.

**Ethical standards for providing services to diverse groups.** Therapists are ethically obligated to be mindful of all forms of historical and social prejudice, as this prejudice can lead to misdiagnosing clients or pathologizing culturally accepted behavior. In addition, MFTs "actively strive to identify and understand the diverse backgrounds of their clients/patients by obtaining knowledge, gaining personal awareness, and developing sensitivity and skills pertinent to working with a diverse client/patient population" (CAMFT Code of Ethics principle 5.7).

**Improving knowledge, skills, awareness, and sensitivity.** So what can a therapist do when approached by a client who is different from the therapist in ways that impact the therapy process? While postmodern models of therapy encourage MFTs to allow clients to inform the therapist about the client's life and circumstances, it is likely to be inadequate for a therapist to take no other action to improve their knowledge and skills around the relevant diversity issues. The MFT could:

- Attend a continuing education training on working with the client's population
- Seek consultation or supervision from other therapists who identify as part of, or regularly work with, the client's population
- Seek out greater exposure to the client's population
- Read articles and other literature on the client's population
- Attend their own therapy to address issues of bias

# Client autonomy K85-86

**Collaborative relationship between client and therapist.** It is the role of the MFT to *assist* clients in making important life decisions, not to make those decisions for the client. In fact, MFTs are ethically prohibited from making major decisions for their clients, such as decisions about entering or leaving a relationship. Instead, we specifically inform clients that such decisions are up to them, and we respect their right to make those decisions as they see fit. In our roles as MFTs, we help clients to understand the consequences of various decisions they may be considering, while the ultimate decision-making is up to the client.

This sometimes gets misunderstood as a ban on advice-giving. Many MFTs directly advise their clients, and this can be consistent with models of therapy that place the MFT in a directive, expert role. Even the assigning of homework, which is a common intervention in many therapeutic models, can be considered giving advice, and it is certainly ethically acceptable to suggest that clients try out specific new skills in the week ahead.

**Methods to assist client decision-making.** There are many ways an MFT can assist a client in decision-making without interfering with the client's autonomy in making those decisions. The therapist can help the client list various courses of action they could take in a difficult time, often expanding the possibilities beyond those the client may see on their own. The therapist can help the client foresee possible consequences of each of the possible courses of action, using current research as well as the therapist's knowledge of the client's specific context. The therapist can assess the client's readiness to act. The therapist can reflect and validate the client's excitement about some possibilities and anxiety about others. Each of these tasks facilitates the client making an important decision on their own, with the therapist's guidance and support.

# Third-party reimbursement K87-88

**Ethical standards for interacting with payors.** Whenever you provide client information to a third-party payor, you need to make sure that the information you are providing is truthful and accurate. As is the norm when sharing any confidential information, you should only provide the information necessary for that particular interaction.

**Advocacy with third-party payers.** Some clients are more able than others to navigate the complex bureaucracy of their insurance company. MFTs advocate for their clients with payors when necessary and appropriate, so that the clients receive the care they need. MFTs can help clients in challenging an insurer's denials of coverage or denials of payment, and may be able to assist clients in gathering needed information about their coverage or reimbursement processes.

# Termination and referrals K89-94

**Ethical considerations with interrupting or terminating.** There are times when interrupting or terminating therapy is appropriate or necessary even when the goals of therapy have not been reached. You as the therapist may become seriously ill or need to step away from your practice to care for loved ones. The client may suddenly be called to a military deployment or a new job out of state. The clinic where you are seeing the client may lose its funding. While we all hope these situations will not occur, the reality is that they often do, and an MFT is ethically required to be ready for such abrupt shifts. An MFT also must take appropriate steps when this kind of situation does happen.

MFTs are ethically required to have emergency procedures in place in the event that they become suddenly incapacitated or otherwise unavailable. These procedures may include emergency contact numbers where clients may reach the therapist or others able to take over client care. MFTs are also ethically required to be prepared for their own potential absence from (or inability to continue) care, which is typically addressed in private practice settings through what is called a *professional will*. This document lays out issues like who will take over client care in the event of the therapist's serious injury or death. The person assigned to take over client care must be given access to records so that they can contact clients to let them know of the change; for this reason, many MFTs include an authorization in their informed consent agreement letting clients know that a professional will exists and having clients agree that their records may be forwarded when necessary.

Having these plans in place minimizes the harm that may come to clients when a therapist is suddenly unavailable. However, treatment interruptions or sudden terminations are not always due to something happening to the therapist. MFTs are allowed to terminate therapy for client non-payment of fees, though termination should not be the first step you take in such an instance; we usually try first to develop a plan that provides continuity of care while the client pays down their balance.

Whenever treatment must be interrupted or terminated, regardless of whether it is because of something happening to the client, the therapist, the clinic, or the larger social context, MFTs have ethical responsibilities to *non-abandonment* and appropriate *continuity of care*. Non-abandonment simply means that clients in need of continued services cannot be left to fend for themselves; if treatment with the current MFT must be interrupted or ended, the MFT still has a responsibility to ensure that crisis needs are addressed and that the change in treatment does not result in harm. Continuity of care means that the client can receive continued care with another provider appropriate to their needs; most commonly, this means providing referrals that are local to the client, within their financial means, and able to treat the client's specific problem type and severity.

These standards are sometimes misunderstood. A therapist may sometimes need to leave their practice, or they may need to discontinue treating a specific client. The ethical standards here require that a client's needs for crisis care and for continuity of care are met, but not that those needs are necessarily met by the same therapist remaining the treatment provider. If you arrange appropriate referrals and take reasonable steps to provide crisis care and continuity of care, that is typically sufficient to resolve your ethical obligations.

**Knowledge of referrals/resources to provide continuity of care.** In order to make those referrals when necessary, an MFT must be aware of local resources that can provide consistency of care to clients if therapy is suddenly stopped. Many MFTs maintain referral lists that include local hospitals and crisis resources, low-fee mental health clinics, psychiatrists, other providers whose services are like those of the MFT, and additional community resources.

**Indicators of need to terminate.** The clearest indication that it is time to terminate therapy is, of course, when the client has reached their treatment goals, and no new goals have emerged. Even in the absence of having reached the goals of treatment, termination may be appropriate if the client regularly comes in appearing to no longer be in distress, and sessions are spent on ordinary social conversation. Termination may also be appropriate if the client is behaving toward the therapist in a manner that is aggressive, threatening, or harassing. Finally, termination (and referral) is appropriate if the client's symptoms are not appropriate for continued outpatient therapy – in other words, if they need a higher level of care.

**Client is not benefiting.** Even if the goals of therapy have not been reached, it is appropriate to terminate therapy if it is clear that the client is not benefiting from treatment. Further deterioration of functioning is a clear indication of treatment failure. A lack of improvement in symptoms may or may not indicate a lack of benefit from treatment; if a client entered therapy on a downward trend, simply stabilizing them and keeping them out of hospitalization can be considered a benefit. Ultimately, though, clients should experience a benefit from being in therapy. If, by their own report or by therapist or other observation of client behavior, they are not benefiting, termination should be considered – with referrals given if appropriate.

**Managing termination.** A good termination process starts at the beginning of therapy, with therapist and client reaching clear agreement on what the goals of therapy are and what improvements will lead to a determination that therapy can end. Discussions of progress toward termination should be a regular part of therapy. Once it is clear that termination is appropriate, a responsible MFT will provide advance notice of termination, take steps to prevent a relapse of symptoms, recognize the gains the client has made in therapy, and provide appropriate referrals for any additional needed care. The number of sessions needed for a formal termination may vary by client, but the process should not be needlessly prolonged.

**Preventing abandonment or neglect.** A termination process that is done too quickly or without appropriate referrals can be considered client abandonment. There may be times when a therapist does need to end therapy abruptly, due to a medical illness, client job transfer or deployment, inappropriate client behavior, or for other reasons. In such circumstances, the MFT (or, in the case of the MFT's illness, someone designated by the MFT) should offer as much advance notice of termination as reasonably possible, make appropriate referrals, and to the degree appropriate, follow up to ensure the clients are able to obtain continued services.

# Sample Questions
See the next page for answers and rationales

1. The client of an LMFT has health insurance, but the insurance carrier is refusing to cover the client's therapy because she is seeing the LMFT for couple therapy and does not, in the therapist's assessment, qualify for a diagnosis of mental illness. The LMFT should:

    a.  Assess the client's ability to advocate on her own behalf with the insurance company

    b.  Offer to include an "insurance diagnosis" on the client's paperwork to facilitate coverage

    c.  Work with the client to develop an alternative plan for payment

    d.  Discontinue therapy

2. An LMFT is working with a same-sex couple. One partner expresses that he is feeling hostile toward the LMFT. The LMFT asks to meet briefly with that partner alone. During the individual discussion, the partner says that he feels the LMFT is siding against him, interrupting him, and generally not respecting his complaints about the relationship. The LMFT is surprised by this, and begins to wonder what else the LMFT has been missing in session. How should the LMFT handle their responsibilities in this case?

    a.  Recognize each individual as a unique client, and offer to see the partners individually if they prefer

    b.  Discontinue treatment, as the therapeutic relationship has been corrupted, and refer to at least three therapists competent in working with same-sex couples

    c.  Conceptualize the client's reaction as paranoia, as it is inconsistent with the therapist's experience. Integrate this into the LMFT's understanding of the dynamics of the relationship

    d.  Work to restore the therapeutic relationship with the partner, and consider finding consultation or supervision for this case

# Sample Questions: Answers and Rationales

1. The client of an LMFT has health insurance, but the insurance carrier is refusing to cover the client's therapy because she is seeing the LMFT for couple therapy and does not, in the therapist's assessment, qualify for a diagnosis of mental illness. The LMFT should:

   a. **Incorrect.** Assess the client's ability to advocate on her own behalf with the insurance company.
   b. **Incorrect.** Offer to include an "insurance diagnosis" on the client's paperwork to facilitate coverage.
   c. **CORRECT.** Work with the client to develop an alternative plan for payment.
   d. **Incorrect.** Discontinue therapy.

It is legal and fairly common for insurers to provide coverage for therapy only in the presence of a diagnosed mental illness. As such, the LMFT will need to work with the client on an alternative plan for payment. A is incorrect because the client's ability to advocate is not relevant; the insurance carrier is within the rules to refuse coverage. B is incorrect as the creation of a diagnosis solely for the purposes of insurance coverage, when the therapist does not believe the client actually qualifies for the diagnosis, would likely be considered insurance fraud. D is incorrect because a sudden discontinuation of therapy could be considered abandonment. While termination due to unpaid fees is ethically acceptable, in this case the client may be able to simply pay out of pocket. Choosing to discontinue therapy would be premature.

2. An LMFT is working with a same-sex couple. One partner expresses that he is feeling hostile toward the LMFT. The LMFT asks to meet briefly with that partner alone. During the individual discussion, the partner says that he feels the LMFT is siding against him, interrupting him, and generally not respecting his complaints about the relationship. The LMFT is surprised by this, and begins to wonder what else the LMFT has been missing in session. How should the LMFT handle their responsibilities in this case?

    a. **Incorrect.** Recognize each individual as a unique client, and offer to see the partners individually if they prefer.

    b. **Incorrect.** Discontinue treatment, as the therapeutic relationship has been corrupted, and refer to at least three therapists competent in working with same-sex couples.

    c. **Incorrect.** Conceptualize the client's reaction as paranoia, as it is inconsistent with the therapist's experience. Integrate this into the LMFT's understanding of the dynamics of the relationship.

    d. **CORRECT.** Work to restore the therapeutic relationship with the partner, and consider finding consultation or supervision for this case.

Maintaining the therapeutic relationship becomes a complex task with couples and families. Here, the LMFT is surprised by a partner feeling ganged up on. The LMFT should not respond by defensively discontinuing treatment (B) or dismissing the client's experience as evidence of pathology (C). Since the unit of treatment is the couple, splitting them on the basis of this exchange (A) is premature at best, and raises its own set of ethical concerns. A more appropriate first step would be to resolve this rift in the therapeutic relationship without otherwise compromising the established therapeutic process.

# ETHICS
# Business Practices and Policies

**Scored exam questions (approximate): 7-8**

## Advertising K95-97

**Accurate representation.** Ethically, you can only advertise those degrees or credentials you have actually earned (honorary degrees should not be advertised), and which are relevant to the practice of marriage and family therapy. If you have a master's degree in family therapy and a doctorate in English, you could not include your doctorate as a professional qualification. Even though you do have a doctorate, it would be a misrepresentation of the credentials you hold relative to your clinical work.

**Testimonials.** The AAMFT Code of Ethics does not have standards related to testimonials in advertising. The most recent CAMFT code allows MFTs to solicit (that is, ask for) testimonials from both current and former clients, so long as the person is not "vulnerable to undue influence." Such requests for testimonials risk exploiting the therapist's role and the client's vulnerability if the person perceives the solicitation as more of a demand than a request. Of course, you're also free to solicit testimonials from colleagues, supervisors, and others who may be familiar with your work.

This issue has gotten more complicated in the age of apps and websites designed for patients to share their experiences with health care professionals. Clients sometimes provide testimonials on such sites without being prompted to by therapists. MFTs should be aware that *responding* to any online testimonial may be considered a breach of client confidentiality, even when the client is openly discussing their treatment.

**Recruiting clients through affiliations.** As you would expect, MFTs cannot advertise themselves as being partners or associates of a group that they don't actually belong to. As with other rules about how you represent yourself, even *implying* an affiliation that doesn't exist, without outright saying it, would still be a violation.

# Documentation K98-100

**Documentation of services.** Recall from earlier that neither state law nor professional ethical codes define the specific *content* that needs to be in treatment records, and there are a wide variety of formats for things like assessments and progress notes. However, all MFTs are legally required to keep records that are consistent with the standards of the profession, and professional ethical codes demand that treatment and financial records be accurate and adequate. The AAMFT and CAMFT codes of ethics both demand that MFTs document the following:

- Authorization to release confidential information
- Precautions taken regarding multiple relationships
- When client requests for records are refused, the request and reasons for refusal should both be documented
- Specific consent for recording sessions or third-party observation (must be in writing)
- Consent to share confidential and identifiable information in consultations (must be in writing)
- Consent from subjects of evaluations (must be in writing)
- Consent for use of clinical materials in teaching, writing, or presenting, unless client identities are protected

The CAMFT code also requires MFTs to document their treatment decisions and encourages MFTs to document any agreements made by members of a therapy group to respect the confidentiality of the group.

Records should be released when legally required or permitted, when the MFT is the subject of a lawsuit or disciplinary action arising from the therapy, or when a client specifically authorizes the release in writing.

Whenever records are released, the information released should be limited to just that which is necessary to address the specific reason for release.

**Protecting the confidentiality of records.** MFTs have an ethical responsibility to store, transfer, exchange, and dispose of records in ways that protect the confidentiality of those records. Methods for protecting the confidentiality of records include:

- Keeping paper records in a secure, locked file cabinet
- Keeping electronic records in a secure, encrypted format
- Carefully controlling who has access to client files
- When the time comes, shredding paper files to dispose of them (an MFT should never simply throw old client files in the trash)

# Other professional roles K101-103

**Responsibility to clarify role.** MFTs often serve in professional capacities that are different from being a therapist or supervisor. For example, MFTs may serve as custody evaluators, expert witnesses, consultants, or in other roles. When doing so, it is important that MFTs be clear (with themselves, clients, courts, and anyone else directly involved) about what their role is, how it is different from therapy, and how information from clients may be used and shared with the court or with other professionals.

**Conflicting roles.** MFTs are responsible for clearly distinguishing between the roles of therapist and evaluator. In the therapist role, an MFT is working clinically with clients to help them achieve therapeutic goals. In an evaluator role, the MFT is to remain objective, simply assessing an individual or family's functioning.

MFTs are specifically discouraged from serving as both therapist and evaluator for the same clients unless the therapist is required to do so by a court or other legal authority. The most common example of this is custody evaluation: An MFT can be the treating therapist for a family, or be a custody evaluator for them, but not both. The AAMFT Code of Ethics prohibits MFTs from providing "evaluations for custody, residence, or visitation" for minors that the MFT has treated.

Of course, MFTs who have proper releases of information can inform the court of a minor's or family's progress in therapy. The MFT just needs to be very careful to not include statements that might be considered as evaluative statements related to custody, visitation, or whatever legal proceeding is underway.

**Legal proceedings.** MFTs who take part in legal proceedings have an ethical responsibility to remain impartial and objective. If your client has given you permission to testify on their behalf in a court case, you are testifying as a fact witness – someone directly involved with one of the parties in the case. Your role is not to advocate on the client's behalf, it is to accurately and objectively answer the questions put before you.

If someone has hired you solely for the purpose of providing expert knowledge to the court, but you do not have any knowledge of the people directly involved in the case, you are testifying as an expert witness. When an MFT testifies as an expert witness, the MFT must base their conclusions on sound clinical judgment and appropriate data, and must acknowledge the limitations of their data and conclusions.

When an MFT gives any professional opinion in a legal proceeding, regardless of what type of witness they role the MFT is in, their testimony must be truthful and not misleading.

Many MFTs have gotten into trouble for writing letters to courts, or testifying in court, in ways that can be construed as assessing or diagnosing someone the MFT has never actually met. For example, MFTs have been disciplined for making evaluative statements about one parent's fitness for custody when the therapist only ever met with the other parent. The ethical guidelines for MFTs are clear that MFTs involved in court cases are not to offer opinions about people the MFT has not personally evaluated.

# Technology K104-106

**Ethical standards.** The 2015 AAMFT Code of Ethics added several specific requirements for therapists providing services via telemedicine, and the current CAMFT code is largely consistent with these requirements.

Remember that these obligations operate *on top of* all regular ethical requirements for therapy, not in place of them. Therapists providing services via telemedicine are ethically obligated to:

- Ensure that their use of technology is legally compliant
- Determine that the use of technology is clinically appropriate, considering client needs and abilities
- Inform clients of the risks and benefits of telemedicine, including risks related to confidentiality, clinical limitations, emergency response, and technology failure
- Ensure the security of the communication medium
- Only use telemedicine if the MFT has appropriate training, education, or supervision in the technology being used

Note that clients do not have the ability to waive any of these requirements. So even if a client is comfortable using an unsecured video platform for sessions, an MFT would still be violating their professional ethics by using such a platform.

**Limitations of telemedicine**. The use of technology to connect with clients over great distances comes with some natural risks and limitations, some of which are directly addressed in the ethical requirements listed above. Some clients (and some therapists) lack the technical skills needed to use technology in the delivery of mental health services. The technology may not be sufficient for the MFT to pick up on subtle cues that would otherwise be important to assess. The client may need services beyond what the therapist can provide through telemedicine. And of course, there is always the possibility that the technology will simply fail, leaving client and therapist disconnected. While technology may be a suitable method for working with many clients, MFTs must carefully assess whether telemedicine services are appropriate to the client's needs and abilities.

**Potential for harm**. Taking these concerns a step further, the use of technology in therapy has the potential to harm the client or the therapeutic relationship. Direct harm may come to the client if the MFT is unable to accurately assess the nature or severity of client symptoms, or changes to those symptoms, when seeing a client by phone or online. The client also may be harmed if the therapist is unable to provide needed local resources in an emergency, or if a session taking place by phone or Internet leads to breaches of confidentiality. Even when the client is not directly harmed, the relationship between therapist and client can be damaged when technology is not used responsibly. Clients may perceive that the therapist is not as attendant to their needs, or unable to intervene with them in the ways they would in person. Unless a client is well-motivated for technology-based services, the MFT should consider whether seeing the client in person would be a better fit.

# Setting and collecting fees K107-111

**Determining fees.** There are many factors you can consider when setting fees, such as a client's income, the fees generally charged for services in your area, your own qualifications, and so on. There are three things you *can't* do when determining fees:

- You can't enter into an agreement with other independent practitioners or clinics to set a common fee (or common minimum fee) in your area. This would be a violation of federal antitrust law.
- You can't set different fees based on race, national origin, or any other protected class in anti-discrimination rules.
- You can't set fees that are exploitive (i.e., high fees that take advantage of clients' vulnerability or wealth).

You can raise or lower fees whenever you wish, even for existing clients. You simply need to make sure that your fee changes are within the rules listed above, and that clients have been given adequate notice of the change. There is no specific standard for how long is "adequate."

You have an ethical requirement to inform clients in advance of fees that will be charged for non-therapy services, like copying records, testifying in court, or missed appointments. Remember that you also have a legal requirement to inform clients of fees and their basis prior to starting treatment.

**Fees for referrals.** In addition to the legal prohibition noted earlier, MFTs are also ethically prohibited from giving or receiving payment for referrals. It doesn't matter whether those fees come from the client or from the person you are making the referral to (or receiving the referral from) – both would be considered unethical. Referrals should always be made solely based on the best interests of the client. If you are receiving payment for referrals, it gives the appearance that you might be giving or receiving specific referrals because there's a financial incentive for you.

**Bartering.** Bartering – that is, exchanging clinical services for some other product or service, rather than money – comes with a lot of potential problems. There is risk of exploitation if the market value of the goods or services the client offers as payment exceeds the usual fee the MFT charges. There is also the risk that the therapy relationship will be impacted, if the therapist particularly likes or dislikes the goods or services received, or if they hold strong sentimental value for the client.

Despite those problems, bartering is not completely prohibited. While MFTs ordinarily do not exchange goods or services from clients in return for the MFT's clinical services – that word, "ordinarily," is used in both the AAMFT and CAMFT codes – it may be ethically acceptable in very limited circumstances. Under both the AAMFT and CAMFT Codes of Ethics, bartering with clients is *only* acceptable if all these conditions are met:

1, The client requests it
2, The bartering is not exploitive
3, The professional relationship is not negatively impacted, and
4, A clear written bartering agreement is established.

Therapists are also encouraged to consider the cultural issues involved, such as whether bartering is an accepted practice in the community. Generally, you should not enter into a bartering arrangement with clients. However, under the limited circumstances described above, there may be times when bartering for services is preferable to interrupting, discontinuing, or otherwise not providing treatment.

**Collecting unpaid balances.** MFTs are within their legal rights and ethical boundaries to collect unpaid balances, and to use collection agencies or courts when necessary to do so. The ethics codes require that MFTs simply give clients reasonable notice before referring for collection or filing a legal claim. Naturally, the collection agency or court should not be given any clinical information about the client. The CAMFT code also requires MFTs to "exercise care" in choosing what collection agency they work with, though this is not further defined.

**Continuation of treatment.** The CAMFT Code of Ethics specifically *allows* termination of therapy based on non-payment of fees, so long as the termination is handled in a manner that is clinically appropriate. As mentioned earlier, MFTs working with clients with unpaid balances typically attempt first to resolve the balance without terminating, through a payment plan, reduction in fee, or other means. But when an MFT is unable or unwilling, for any reason, to provide continued care to a client, the MFT must assist the client in arranging for continuation of treatment. You cannot withhold referrals or treatment records simply because a client has an unpaid balance.

# Services paid for by a third party K112

**Ethical standards for providing services when interacting with third-party payors.** MFTs are ethically obligated to be truthful and accurate in documentation submitted to third-party payors. Additional ethical rules around MFTs' interactions with third-party payors include:

- Disclose to clients what information is likely to be shared with third-party payors, and obtain consent for information sharing where needed
- Explain at the beginning of therapy what the process is for collecting payment if third-party coverage is denied
- Do not withhold records or information simply because you have not yet been paid for services
- Do not limit discussions of treatment alternatives to only those alternatives that will be covered by insurance or other third-party payors

When considering these standards, it is worth bearing in mind that insurance companies are not the only third-party payors with whom you may interact. Other family members sometimes pay for services. The client's workplace, another person's liability insurance (after a car accident where that other person was at fault, for example), a charitable organization, or some other person or organization may be paying for your client's treatment. The ethical rules around third-party payors apply to all third-party payors, not just the client's insurance company.

# Gifts K113-114

While some ethical standards have gotten stricter over time, the standards around giving and receiving gifts have actually grown more flexible. This is due largely to increased recognition of the cultural significance of gifts in many populations. Refusing a small gift may be culturally insensitive, and harm the clinical relationship. MFTs should be mindful of cultural norms when considering whether to give gifts to clients or accept gifts from clients. We consider the value of the gift, the effect of giving or receiving the gift on the client, and the potential impact of the gift on the therapy process.

Giving a gift to a client, or accepting a gift from a client, does come with some risks. The client might perceive that the gift changes the nature of their relationship with you to a more personal one. They might hold an expectation that any gift should be reciprocated. They might expect preferential treatment in scheduling or other elements of therapy. In each of these instances (and surely many others you could come up with), the integrity of the therapeutic process can be impacted. Whether you accept or reject a client gift, it is good practice to document your decision-making.

# Research ethics K115-118

**Procedures for safeguarding research participants.** The most important safeguard for research participants is the process of informed consent. Just as a client should be fully informed of the processes, risks, and potential benefits of therapy, a research participant should be fully informed of the processes, risks, and benefits of their participation in a study. Most studies are overseen by some form of Institutional Review Board, which reviews the protocols and protections the researchers have in place. The MFT codes of ethics also require MFTs to seek the advice of qualified colleagues in designing and conducting research, and to observe appropriate research safeguards.

**Necessary disclosures to research participants.** Research participants need to be informed of all elements of the research that might reasonably influence the participant's willingness to participate. This would include potential risks or negative effects from participating, and discomfort that the participant might be expected to go through in the study. The AAMFT Code of Ethics also requires that research participants be specifically informed of:

- Purpose of the research
- Expected length of study participation
- Study procedures
- Potential research benefits
- Limits of confidentiality
- Whom to contact with any questions about the study or their rights

**Client rights when participating in research.** In addition to the right to be informed about the study they are participating in, clients also have the right to decline or withdraw their participation in a study at any time. They also have a right to confidentiality unless they sign a waiver specifically authorizing the release of information from their participation. (If the study is a study involving therapy services, the same limits of confidentiality would apply as ordinarily apply in therapy, and the clients should be informed of this as part of the informed consent process.)

**Confidentiality of research data.** Unless clients provide a written waiver, MFTs consider any information they learn about a research participant to be confidential, subject to the exceptions to confidentiality outlined earlier. If a participant's family members or others may be able to gain access to a participant's research data, the MFT must explain this possibility at the beginning of the study and share their plan for protecting confidentiality.

# Unethical or incompetent colleagues K119-120

**Situations that can impair the integrity or effectiveness of therapy.** MFTs not only need to be able to recognize when their own ability to provide therapy is compromised. We also must be aware of times when a colleague's ability to provide ethical and effective therapy is compromised. Such situations include multiple relationships (subject to the boundaries previously described); therapist substance abuse, mental illness, or emotional disturbance; bias or discrimination by the therapist; exploitation; and many more.

**Guidelines for addressing unethical or incompetent conduct by colleagues.** Unlike some other states, California does not have any rules allowing practitioners to directly report colleagues who are behaving in unethical or incompetent ways. When a client tells you about bad behavior on the part of their previous therapist, you are typically required to keep this information confidential. Reporting it to the board yourself, or directly confronting the colleague, would be an illegal and unethical breach of confidentiality. If a client grants permission for you to talk with the other therapist (through a written release of information), you could then address the other therapist, but it would be important to treat the client's report as their own experience, rather than objective fact. There are often two very different sides to such stories, sometimes clients and therapists misunderstand each other, and therapists are expected to treat each other with respect.

If you learn of another therapist's illegal or incompetent behavior *directly from that therapist*, it can be more complicated. For example, if you learn that a colleague in your clinic is struggling with an alcohol abuse problem, you could encourage your colleague to seek treatment and to discontinue seeing clients until the problem is under control. The CAMFT Code of Ethics encourages MFTs to offer assistance to colleagues who are impaired by substance abuse or mental or emotional problems. Doing so would certainly be in the best interests of their clients. If the other therapist refuses, though, there is no law or ethical standard that requires or even allows you to report the colleague to the board. In fact, the CAMFT Code of Ethics requires therapists to respect the confidences of colleagues when in the context of their professional relationship.

There is only one situation that calls for specific action on your part based on another therapist's incompetence. As described in the law section, when your client tells you they had a sexual relationship with their former therapist, you are legally required to provide your client with the state-authored brochure called *Therapy Never Includes Sexual Behavior.*

What is most important in a situation like this is that you take appropriate action to promote the welfare of clients. While you typically cannot report it yourself when a client tells you that another therapist is behaving unethically or incompetently, you can (and often should) encourage the client to report that behavior themselves. You can't *require* the client to make that report – that would be putting your wishes above the client's – but you can encourage it.

# Supervision K121

Supervisors have several specific responsibilities defined in the CAMFT Code of Ethics. In brief, supervisors are required to:

- Maintain their supervision skills, getting consultation when needed
- Stay up to date in their knowledge of the practice of MFT
- Stay aware of changes to legal and ethical guidelines
- Keep supervisees aware of changes to legal and ethical guidelines
- Address cultural and diversity issues in supervision
- Have clear policies and procedures that are given to supervisees at the beginning of supervision
- Regularly evaluate supervisees, identifying concerns
- Follow the law regarding business and employment practices
- Guide supervisees in getting assistance for problems that might be hurting their work
- Document decisions to let go of supervisees
- Review trainee agreements with universities

The AAMFT Code of Ethics further requires that supervisees be specifically informed of the risks and benefits of technology when supervision is going to involve the use of technology.

Supervisees, meanwhile, also have a few specific responsibilities defined in the CAMFT code:

- Understand that the clients the supervisee sees are considered clients of their employer
- Know the laws and regulations governing MFT practice and licensing
- Function within the limits of a supervisee's role as defined by law
- Maintain registration as required by law

# Sample Questions

See the next page for answers and rationales

1. An LMFT wishes to advertise that the services she provides in her private practice are based on a solid scientific foundation and are offered at a sliding fee scale to accommodate clients with lower incomes. Which of the following would be an appropriate way for her to advertise her services?

    a.   "Rates as low as $35 per session."
    b.   "You will have a better life *and* a fatter wallet."
    c.   "The most effective therapy available."
    d.   "Pick up the phone and call now!"

2. An LMFT learns of a new cross-referral group on a popular social media site. The group is open to all health care professionals. To remain in the group, each person must agree to provide at least one referral a month to at least one other member of the group. A group administrator collects information about these referrals to ensure members are meeting the requirement. That information only includes the member making the referral, the members referred to, and the date, without any client information. The LMFT believes joining this group will help build her practice. The LMFT should:

    a.   Join and make referrals in the group, as confidentiality is protected
    b.   Join the group and agree to the requirement, but explain to the group administrator that the LMFT cannot provide any information on when referrals are made or to whom
    c.   Join the group, make her commitment to her professional ethics known, and participate in the group in a manner most adherent to the ethics code possible given the group's requirements
    d.   Not join the group as it runs counter to her ethical responsibilities

# Sample Questions: Answers and Rationales

1. An LMFT wishes to advertise that the services she provides in her private practice are based on a solid scientific foundation and are offered at a sliding fee scale to accommodate clients with lower incomes. Which of the following would be an appropriate way for her to advertise her services?

   a. **Incorrect.** "Rates as low as $35 per session." *State law requires advertising that includes prices to be specific, in order to avoid what is known as "bait and switch" advertising. This statement would violate the law as well as being considered ethically inappropriate.*

   b. **Incorrect.** "You will have a better life *and* a fatter wallet." *This appears to present a guarantee to consumers, and for that reason it would be considered misleading. If "will" were replaced with "could," it would be more acceptable.*

   c. **Incorrect.** "The most effective therapy available." *Any claims of effectiveness must be supported with peer-reviewed scientific studies. At present, there is not a specific model that would qualify as the "most effective therapy available," making this statement also misleading.*

   d. **CORRECT.** "Pick up the phone and call now!" *This kind of call to action is not prohibited.*

2. An LMFT learns of a new cross-referral group on a popular social media site. The group is open to all health care professionals. To remain in the group, each person must agree to provide at least one referral a month to at least one other member of the group. A group administrator collects information about these referrals to ensure members are meeting the requirement. That information only includes the member making the referral, the members referred to, and the date, without any client information. The LMFT believes joining this group will help build her practice. The LMFT should:

    a.   **Incorrect.** Join and make referrals in the group, as confidentiality is protected. *The protection of confidentiality does not change the concern about the LMFT receiving payment for referrals (see below) and making referrals based on her own interests rather than those of the client.*

    b.   **Incorrect.** Join the group and agree to the requirement, but explain to the group administrator that the LMFT cannot provide any information on when referrals are made or to whom. *By agreeing to the requirement, the LMFT is promising to make referrals that may not be clinically appropriate.*

    c.   **Incorrect.** Join the group, make her commitment to her professional ethics known, and participate in the group in a manner most adherent to the ethics code possible given the group's requirements. *The group itself is fundamentally not in keeping with the ethics code. While this language can be useful for LMFTs figuring out what to do when an **employer's** practice conflicts with the ethics code, here the group is not an employer.*

    d.   **CORRECT.** Not join the group as it runs counter to her ethical responsibilities. *The LMFT would be, in effect, receiving payment for referrals, which is a violation of both law and professional ethics. The payment would come in the form of continued group membership, which is a tangible benefit. Furthermore, this scenario suggests that the LMFT would be making referrals based in part on* her own *interests (in remaining part of the group), rather than making referrals based on what is in* the client's *best interests. The LMFT should not join the group.*

# Mini-Mock Exam

# Mini-mock exam

The real exam will not simply ask you to recount facts from the preceding pages. Instead, it will ask you to *apply and integrate* the legal and ethical standards that govern the field. That's why the sample questions so far, like questions on the real test, have taken the form of case vignettes instead of simple memorization. Over the next few pages, you'll get some more practice.

What makes these questions a bit different (and, indeed, a bit tougher) from the ones you've seen already is that in many cases, they ask you to *combine multiple areas of knowledge* when determining the correct answer. You may need to pull from several content areas to rule out incorrect responses and determine the correct one.

These next 25 questions can help give you a sense of how knowledge might be organized and applied to arrive at the right answers here. Remember that, as is the case on the test itself, questions may be complex, and they may require careful reading – but they aren't designed to trick. There's a single, best answer for each question.

# Mini-Mock Exam:
# Answer Sheets

# California MFT Law & Ethics

# Mini-Mock Exam

1. _____    11. _____    21. _____

2. _____    12. _____    22. _____

3. _____    13. _____    23. _____

4. _____    14. _____    24. _____

5. _____    15. _____    25. _____

6. _____    16. _____

7. _____    17. _____

8. _____    18. _____

9. _____    19. _____

10. _____   20. _____

# California MFT Law & Ethics

# Mini-Mock Exam

1. _____     11. _____     21. _____

2. _____     12. _____     22. _____

3. _____     13. _____     23. _____

4. _____     14. _____     24. _____

5. _____     15. _____     25. _____

6. _____     16. _____

7. _____     17. _____

8. _____     18. _____

9. _____     19. _____

10. _____    20. _____

**The mini-mock exam begins when you turn the page.**

If you are timing your mini-mock exam, start the timer, and then turn the page to begin.

*Throughout this test, unless stated otherwise, any references to a
"therapist," "MFT," or "LMFT" refer to a California Licensed Marriage and
Family Therapist. "BBS" means the California Board of Behavioral Sciences.*

1. An LMFT is providing services to an individual client through the client's
insurance plan, which the LMFT serves as an in-network provider. The
LMFT provides the client with treatment for major depressive disorder and
for substance use disorder, but comes to find that the insurer is only paying
for claims related to the depressive disorder treatment and not the
substance use treatment. How should the LMFT address the legal elements
of this case?

    a. Inform the client that they will be fully responsible for fees related to
substance abuse treatment
    b. Resubmit the billing and advocate for the insurer to pay for all
services the LMFT provided
    c. Ask the client to provide a copy of their policy's specific exclusions
and limitations
    d. Continue billing under the depressive disorder diagnosis regardless
of which actual problem is being worked on, to facilitate payment

2. A family experiencing high conflict and homelessness seeks the services
of an LMFT in private practice. The LMFT has published a book explaining
their belief that "radical confessions" will change family patterns and resolve
long-standing problems. Though the process has not been studied, the
family is interested in attempting this process in family therapy. Ethically,
how should the LMFT proceed?

    a. Inform the family that the LMFT cannot provide this treatment until it
develops a more significant scientific basis
    b. Inform the family that the treatment should be considered
experimental and may not work
    c. Inform the family that if they go ahead with the treatment, they will
be considered research participants and not therapy clients, and
may have different rights and protections
    d. Inform the family that the LMFT is able to provide the treatment, but
cannot charge a fee for it

3. An LMFT working for a nonprofit agency launches a side business making T-shirts and other low-cost merchandise. The LMFT sees many clients through the agency who would benefit from jobs with flexible hours, and needs employees to grow the side business. The LMFT is interested in helping these clients in any way the LMFT can. Considering the LMFT's ethical responsibilities, how could the LMFT proceed?

    a.   Hire a business manager to run the day-to-day operations of the side business, including decisions about whom to hire, and then refer clients to potential job openings there

    b.   Turn the structure of the side business into a nonprofit organization

    c.   Sell the side business to someone who shares the LMFT's commitment to hiring those in need

    d.   Discontinue therapy for any client who is referred to a job opening with the side business

4. Six months after the disclosure of an affair, a married heterosexual couple tells the LMFT who has been providing them with couple therapy that they are planning to change the structure of their relationship. The couple says that they will have an open marriage going forward. The husband, who had the affair, says he strongly believes this is the best way for the couple to heal. The wife expresses skepticism, but says she is willing to try it in hopes of rebuilding trust. The LMFT is deeply concerned about this choice, as the LMFT believes the couple has not fully recovered from the affair, and that opening the relationship when the wife appears hesitant only creates the possibility of further damage to their marriage. How should the LMFT address this situation, considering the LMFT's ethical responsibilities?

    a.   Inform the clients that they should not open their marriage at this time

    b.   Inform the clients that couple therapy cannot move forward if they open their relationship, as it is contrary to the treatment plan

    c.   Inform the clients that the decision is theirs to make, while expressing concern about its potential impacts

    d.   Inform the clients that the LMFT profession is generally opposed to open relationships, and encourage them to restore trust within the previous boundaries of their marriage

5. After maintaining an in-person practice for many years, an LMFT in private practice is planning to end the lease on their physical office and transition to a fully telehealth practice. Some clients have expressed reservations about the change, as they find the LMFT's office to be a welcoming and familiar environment. Three of the LMFT's clients have at least some history of crisis. Considering the LMFT's ethical obligations, how should they proceed with the transition to telehealth?

    a.  Continue in-person care only for those clients who have expressed reservations about the transition

    b.  Continue in-person care only for those three clients who have history of crisis

    c.  Evaluate each client for their appropriateness for telehealth care

    d.  Continue in-person care with all pre-existing clients, engaging new clients via telehealth until the point at which the LMFT's practice has fully transitioned

6. An LMFT is working with a client on issues of anxiety and body image. The client gives the LMFT permission to consult with the client's physician, but asks the LMFT not to discuss the client's recent weight gain with the physician. The client explains that they felt shamed by the physician and pressured to lose weight despite the client being in overall good health. The LMFT contacts the physician and explains that the client appears to be learning to manage their anxiety effectively without medication. The physician asks whether the client is losing weight as instructed. How should the LMFT respond?

    a.  Say yes to satisfy the physician, and redirect the conversation

    b.  Inform the physician of the client's weight gain, considering the potential medical concerns

    c.  Explain that the client's weight is not part of their therapy

    d.  Without directly answering the question, inform the physician that the client has experienced pressure to lose weight and that such pressure may worsen the client's anxiety

7. An LMFT is meeting with a family seeking therapy for issues of family conflict. The parents in the family are starting a business, and they report that they cannot afford to pay for therapy at this time, but they believe therapy is necessary for the family to get along together in ways that will make the business a success. They offer to pay the LMFT by giving the LMFT a small ownership stake in the family's business, which the LMFT could later share at a large profit if the business is successful. The family offers the LMFT a 10% share of the business to cover the full course of therapy for as many sessions as may be needed in the next 12 months. They note that bartering is common and accepted in their culture. Ethically, the LMFT should:

    a.   Ask the family whether they have other products or services that they may consider using as part of a bartering arrangement instead

    b.   Consider the fair market value of the ownership stake, and if the LMFT later sells that stake for a profit, return that profit to the family

    c.   Consider the fair market value of the ownership stake, and offer to contract for a specific number of sessions rather than an unlimited number over a year

    d.   Consider whether addressing family conflict in ways that will help a family business is consistent with the LMFT's scope of competence

*Question 8 is on the next page.*

8. An LMFT is working with a 16-year-old boy and his mother in therapy. The mother has discovered that the boy and his girlfriend, also 16, have been sending each other naked photos of themselves. The mother says that she does not know, and does not want to know, whether the couple is having sex. The boy is angry that his mother was looking at his phone messages, and perceives this as an invasion of privacy. Considering the LMFT's legal obligations, how should the LMFT proceed?

    a.   Report suspected child abuse, with the mother as the perpetrator and the girlfriend as the victim

    b.   Assess for potential child abuse, and encourage the mother to support her son's autonomy

    c.   Assess for potential child abuse, and educate the boy about the dangers of sending personal images

    d.   Report suspected child abuse, with the boy and his girlfriend as both perpetrators and victims

9. A prospective client contacts an LMFT who offers therapy services via telehealth through a secure video platform. The client identifies themselves only as "Jose" and informs the LMFT that they are 27 years old and interested in receiving treatment for childhood trauma. The client is willing to attest that they live in California and will complete any intake paperwork the therapist sends, as long as they can sign as just "Jose." They say they are ashamed of what they experienced as a child, and this will make it easier for them to discuss it. Considering the LMFT's legal responsibilities, what must the LMFT do?

    a.   Require the client to provide prepayment for all services

    b.   Refuse to conduct sessions via telehealth unless the client is willing to provide their full name

    c.   Locate the hospital and crisis house closest to the client's geographic location

    d.   Document the client's request and the LMFT's reasons for agreeing to it

10. An LMFT is closing their private practice and planning to start a full-time job with a county mental health agency. They have been using an electronic health record (EHR) system to maintain records of their private practice cases. They plan to stop paying the monthly fee for this system in two weeks, when they begin their new job. Once they stop paying the fee, they would lose access to the EHR system. Considering their legal responsibilities, what should the LMFT do with their private practice records?

    a.  Continue paying the monthly fee for at least 5 years so that records can be accessed as needed

    b.  Once the LMFT stops paying the fee, inform all current and past private practice clients that the EHR company becomes the custodian of their records

    c.  Download all client records from the EHR and transfer them to the system used by the county to ensure ongoing access as needed

    d.  Download all client records and store them securely in a manner and location separate from the county's system

11. An LMFT is working with an elderly client from another country. The client frequently complains of headaches and other body aches, but rarely discusses emotions directly. The LMFT also notices that the client rarely makes eye contact, and waits to be asked specific questions before speaking. How should the LMFT proceed?

    a.  Seek to better understand the client's cultural background

    b.  Refer the client to a physician to rule out possible medical issues

    c.  Remind the client that they are safe and reinforce boundaries

    d.  Consider the client's history of intergenerational trauma

12. An LMFT is in the process of termination with an individual from Ghana who has successfully completed individual therapy for issues of depression and loneliness. During therapy, it became clear that the client wanted greater connection with their culture, and as they achieved it, their symptoms lifted. The LMFT is interested in writing a case study about the successful treatment, for publication in a peer-reviewed journal. Considering their ethical obligations, the LMFT should:

    a.   Ensure that specific information that could be used to identify the client, such as their age, culture, occupation, and any direct quotes, is fully removed from the article

    b.   Inform the client of the potential benefits of being featured in a scholarly journal

    c.   Seek the client's informed consent to have their case included in research

    d.   Choose a different case to write about, since research participation was not agreed upon in advance of therapy beginning

13. An LMFT has been providing individual therapy to a 33-year-old Chinese woman who reported conflict with her sibling's partner. The client was concerned that the conflict may stem from cultural differences between the two of them, and the client was hopeful that they could improve their relationship in the event that the sibling and the partner eventually married. The client comes to therapy and informs the LMFT that the sibling and the partner have broken up, with no expectation that they will reconcile. The client expresses empathy for her sibling, and relief for herself. Considering the LMFT's ethical responsibilities, the LMFT should:

    a.   Seek the client's permission to contact the sibling and offer to bring them into session

    b.   Inquire as to the reasons for the breakup, if known

    c.   Ask the client for more information on their cultural norms

    d.   Move toward termination

14. An LMFT receives a referral from a psychiatrist. The client tells the LMFT that she meets regularly with the psychiatrist to manage psychotic symptoms. After the client's initial session, she calls the LMFT and sounds disoriented. She blames a recent medication change. The LMFT is concerned and wants to discuss this with the psychiatrist, but the client has not signed a release of information. Considering the LMFT's obligations under HIPAA, the LMFT should:

   a. Understand that the client is in crisis and refer for an immediate medication monitoring appointment with the psychiatrist
   b. Inquire as to possible extrapyramidal symptoms of the medication, and suggest the client stop taking the medication if necessary
   c. Mail the client a Release of Information form and ask the client to bring it with them to the next session
   d. Contact the psychiatrist to discuss the client's diagnosis and treatment planning

15. A 15-year-old girl is seeing an LMFT individually for issues related to body image and self-esteem. Her parents provided consent for the therapy and pay for her sessions, but do not participate. The girl tells the LMFT that she has been exploring her sexuality. While her parents were out of town, she had sexual intercourse with a friend's 19-year-old brother. A few days later, she had intercourse with another boy, an 18-year-old senior at her high school. The LMFT should manage their legal responsibilities by:

   a. Reporting child abuse to the local child protective service agency
   b. Investigating to ensure that the sexual activity was not coerced or while under the influence of drugs or alcohol
   c. Notifying the parents of their daughter's high-risk sexual behavior
   d. Maintaining confidentiality

16. An LMFT with a new private practice is considering how to market their practice. He wants to operate on a sliding fee scale based on client income. How can he best fulfill his legal and ethical responsibilities?

    a.  Develop a fee structure that is based on services provided, and not client income. Fee scales based on client income are prohibited in private practice settings

    b.  Advertise that services are offered "as low as" the lowest fee on his scale

    c.  Make no mention of fees in his advertising

    d.  Make his sliding fee scale a percentage of income, regardless of the income level

17. A married couple seeing an LMFT in hopes of improving their marriage tells the therapist that they are considering taking Ecstasy together. They report having heard about users experiencing moments of great bonding while using the drug. They ask the LMFT whether she would recommend the couple try it together, and make clear that they would be using the drug in their home without anyone else present. Ethically, the LMFT should:

    a.  Discourage all forms of lawbreaking, including illegal drug use

    b.  Review with the clients how they perceive the possible risks and benefits

    c.  Refer all discussion of drug effects to a physician

    d.  Update the diagnosis of one or both partners to include Substance Use Disorder

18. In a rural community, an LMFT is treating a client whose daughter is good friends with the LMFT's children. Toward the end of a session, the client mentions that the client's daughter will be having a birthday party in a couple of weeks. The client says that they would love for the LMFT's children to attend but they are nervous about the LMFT coming. "I'm sure I'm just being silly," the client says, "but you know an awful lot about me, and it might be weird for my family to have you there." The LMFT should:

a. Address the client's projection onto their family, and consider it to be the client's discomfort, rather than their family's
b. Offer to discuss the party at another time, as it would not be appropriate to do so during a therapy session
c. Discuss the client's concern directly, describing the steps the LMFT will take to protect the client's confidentiality
d. Reassure the client that the LMFT will not attend the party, and discuss the benefits and risks of having the LMFT's children attend

19. An LMFT encounters a former client from many years ago at a party. They enjoy catching up socially, and are each impressed with the other. In the time since therapy, the former client has been married and divorced. The LMFT, also now divorced, finds herself seeing the former client as an equal. She also finds herself attracted to the former client. Ethically, the LMFT should:

a. Provide the former client with a copy of the brochure *Therapy Never Includes Sexual Behavior*
b. Assess whether the former client also sees the LMFT as an equal, and if so, consider initiating a romantic relationship
c. Review the reasons why the client sought therapy years ago, and determine whether the former client has truly resolved those concerns
d. Limit her social contact with the former client

20. An elder client tells an LMFT working in hospice care that the client was recently taken to a local religious gathering against her will by her 50-year-old daughter. The daughter is a member of the religious group. By the client's report, the daughter told her mother that "this might be good for you, being around people with good values" and did not bring the mother home when the mother said she was uncomfortable there. Furthermore, the daughter donated the cash in the client's purse to the religious group, despite the client's repeated statements to her daughter that the client did not support the group. How should the LMFT respond to their legal obligations in this case?

    a.  Report suspected elder abuse (specifically, kidnapping)
    b.  Report suspected elder abuse (specifically, financial abuse)
    c.  Report suspected elder abuse (specifically, emotional abuse)
    d.  Report suspected elder abuse (specifically, isolation)

21. An LMFT has been working with a couple in therapy after discovering that their children's behavioral problems showed up primarily when the couple was arguing. Treatment has progressed well, and the LMFT has built trust with the couple by insisting on a "no secrets" policy where neither partner is allowed to communicate individually with the therapist. As they transition to family therapy within the same treatment plan, the parents ask the therapist not to share certain information from the couple therapy with their children. How should the LMFT manage the ethical issues in this case?

    a.  Continue to insist on a "no secrets" policy to build trust throughout the family
    b.  Close the couple therapy file and start a new file for each individual participant in family therapy
    c.  Determine and have the family agree to a new policy on individual secrets in family therapy
    d.  Push the parents to disclose to the children what happened in couple therapy

22. The adult client of an LMFT calls the therapist from a police station. The client is filing a police report after their roommate physically attacked the client in an argument over housework. The client asks to reschedule the next planned session and reports that they do not feel safe going home, as the roommate is still there and the client believes the roommate is still very angry. How should the LMFT proceed?

   a. Ask the client for permission to speak to the police officer taking the report
   b. Ensure that the client has a safe place they can go
   c. Develop a plan for what to do if the roommate becomes violent or threatening again
   d. Assess the client for suicidality

23. An LMFT receives a court order to testify in a case involving a former client. The LMFT cannot determine from the order much of what the case is about, though it appears to be a criminal case where the former client is charged with a crime. The order is signed by a judge and requires the LMFT to appear in court the following week, and to provide a copy of the client file. How should the LMFT proceed, considering their legal obligations?

   a. Consult with an attorney, and plan to appear in court at the date and time shown on the order, with a copy of the client's file
   b. Contact the client to determine their wishes, and appear in court or provide records only if the client is first willing to sign a release allowing the therapist to do so
   c. Inquire with the court about whether questions of privilege have been addressed
   d. Agree to testify, but withhold documentation, citing section 56.10 of the Civil Code

24. An LMFT is conducting a home visit with a 16-year-old client who lives with their 43-year-old mother and 70-year-old grandmother. The family is poor and lives in a small apartment. The LMFT had previously met the mother when the mother provided consent for the daughter's treatment, but had not previously met the grandmother. When the client introduces the LMFT to the grandmother, the LMFT notices that the grandmother is in bed in the middle of the afternoon, appears to have an unbandaged infection on her arm, and the bed smells strongly of urine. The client apologizes for the mess in the apartment and says that she is working an after-school job to help her mother, who works two full-time jobs, so that they can save up for a caregiver for the grandmother, who has dementia. How should the LMFT proceed?

   a.  Report suspected elder neglect
   b.  Refer the family to programs that provide in-home health care at reduced costs
   c.  Consider the family's socioeconomic context and their good faith efforts
   d.  Report suspected elder and child neglect

25. In a rural community, an LMFT supervisor has been close friends for more than 20 years with a local attorney. The attorney's daughter is an associate MFT, and inquires with the LMFT supervisor about the possibility of coming to work for the LMFT supervisor's private practice. Considering the LMFT supervisor's ethical responsibilities, the LMFT supervisor should:

   a.  Consider their level of friendship with the associate MFT, independent from the LMFT supervisor's relationship with the attorney
   b.  Refer the associate to other prospective supervisors
   c.  Consult with the attorney for guidance in managing the complexities of the relationship
   d.  Agree to supervise the associate, and meet with both the attorney and the associate to discuss how the relationship will be managed

# - STOP HERE -

# Mini-Mock Exam:
# Quick Answer Key

# Mini-Mock Exam: Quick Answer Key

| | | |
|---|---|---|
| 1. B | 11. A | 21. C |
| 2. B | 12. C | 22. B |
| 3. C | 13. D | 23. A |
| 4. C | 14. D | 24. A |
| 5. C | 15. D | 25. B |
| 6. C | 16. C | |
| 7. A | 17. B | |
| 8. D | 18. C | |
| 9. B | 19. D | |
| 10. D | 20. B | |

# Mini-Mock Exam:
# Answers and Rationales

1. An LMFT is providing services to an individual client through the client's insurance plan, which the LMFT serves as an in-network provider. The LMFT provides the client with treatment for major depressive disorder and for substance use disorder, but comes to find that the insurer is only paying for claims related to the depressive disorder treatment and not the substance use treatment. How should the LMFT address the legal elements of this case?

    a. **Incorrect.** Inform the client that they will be fully responsible for fees related to substance abuse treatment

    b. **CORRECT.** Resubmit the billing and advocate for the insurer to pay for all services the LMFT provided

    c. **Incorrect.** Ask the client to provide a copy of their policy's specific exclusions and limitations

    d. **Incorrect.** Continue billing under the depressive disorder diagnosis regardless of which actual problem is being worked on, to facilitate payment

Parity law demands that insurers who provide mental health care coverage do so on a level parallel to their coverage for physical health treatment, and that the mental health care coverage includes substance use treatment. The insurer is obligated to pay these claims. The LMFT can best demonstrate their knowledge of parity law by resubmitting the claims and advocating for payment. Simply billing under the depression code when that is not the actual issue being treated could be considered misleading.

2. A family experiencing high conflict and homelessness seeks the services of an LMFT in private practice. The LMFT has published a book explaining their belief that "radical confessions" will change family patterns and resolve long-standing problems. Though the process has not been studied, the family is interested in attempting this process in family therapy. Ethically, how should the LMFT proceed?

    a. **Incorrect.** Inform the family that the LMFT cannot provide this treatment until it develops a more significant scientific basis

    b. **CORRECT.** Inform the family that the treatment should be considered experimental and may not work

    c. **Incorrect.** Inform the family that if they go ahead with the treatment, they will be considered research participants and not therapy clients, and may have different rights and protections

    d. **Incorrect.** Inform the family that the LMFT is able to provide the treatment, but cannot charge a fee for it

LMFTs are allowed to develop new and innovative treatments, and to try interventions that may have a sound basis in theory but have not been the focus of direct scientific research. They can charge normal fees for such services. When offering experimental treatments, clients should be informed of the risks, including the possibility that the treatment will fail. Clients who are undergoing experimental treatments may or may not be participating in a research study at the time, but in either case are still considered clients.

3. An LMFT working for a nonprofit agency launches a side business making T-shirts and other low-cost merchandise. The LMFT sees many clients through the agency who would benefit from jobs with flexible hours, and needs employees to grow the side business. The LMFT is interested in helping these clients in any way the LMFT can. Considering the LMFT's ethical responsibilities, how could the LMFT proceed?

  a.  **Incorrect.** Hire a business manager to run the day-to-day operations of the side business, including decisions about whom to hire, and then refer clients to potential job openings there

  b.  **Incorrect.** Turn the structure of the side business into a nonprofit organization

  c.  **CORRECT.** Sell the side business to someone who shares the LMFT's commitment to hiring those in need

  d.  **Incorrect.** Discontinue therapy for any client who is referred to a job opening with the side business

Hiring a client is specifically defined in the CAMFT Code of Ethics as a problematic dual relationship. It presents the LMFT with a clear conflict of interests, as what is good for the client's treatment may not be good for the side business. This remains true regardless of the structure of the side business. The therapist should not terminate therapy just to engage in an improper dual relationship. The best way forward here, that allows the clients to seek flexible employment while also ensuring they receive continuity of mental health care, is for the LMFT to sell the side business to someone with a similar worldview. Then the business hiring the LMFT's clients would not present dual relationship concerns.

4. Six months after the disclosure of an affair, a married heterosexual couple tells the LMFT who has been providing them with couple therapy that they are planning to change the structure of their relationship. The couple says that they will have an open marriage going forward. The husband, who had the affair, says he strongly believes this is the best way for the couple to heal. The wife expresses skepticism, but says she is willing to try it in hopes of rebuilding trust. The LMFT is deeply concerned about this choice, as the LMFT believes the couple has not fully recovered from the affair, and that opening the relationship when the wife appears hesitant only creates the possibility of further damage to their marriage. How should the LMFT address this situation, considering the LMFT's ethical responsibilities?

a. **Incorrect.** Inform the clients that they should not open their marriage at this time

b. **Incorrect.** Inform the clients that couple therapy cannot move forward if they open their relationship, as it is contrary to the treatment plan

c. **CORRECT.** Inform the clients that the decision is theirs to make, while expressing concern about its potential impacts

d. **Incorrect.** Inform the clients that the LMFT profession is generally opposed to open relationships, and encourage them to restore trust within the previous boundaries of their marriage

The primary ethical responsibilities of the LMFT here are to support client autonomy while also giving weight to what is likely to be in their best interests. While the LMFT profession takes no overall stance on the appropriateness of open relationships, the specific circumstances of this case suggest that such an arrangement could indeed invite additional problems into an already-strained marriage. The LMFT should express this concern, but avoid making demands or imposing a specific relationship structure or other values onto the clients.

5. After maintaining an in-person practice for many years, an LMFT in private practice is planning to end the lease on their physical office and transition to a fully telehealth practice. Some clients have expressed reservations about the change, as they find the LMFT's office to be a welcoming and familiar environment. Three of the LMFT's clients have at least some history of crisis. Considering the LMFT's ethical obligations, how should they proceed with the transition to telehealth?

    a. **Incorrect.** Continue in-person care only for those clients who have expressed reservations about the transition

    b. **Incorrect.** Continue in-person care only for those three clients who have history of crisis

    c. **CORRECT.** Evaluate each client for their appropriateness for telehealth care

    d. **Incorrect.** Continue in-person care with all pre-existing clients, engaging new clients via telehealth until the point at which the LMFT's practice has fully transitioned

The LMFT is not obligated to personally continue offering in-person services to any client or group of clients. They should, however, assess each client for their appropriateness for the transition to telehealth, and take steps to refer out any clients who would be better served through ongoing in-person care.

6. An LMFT is working with a client on issues of anxiety and body image. The client gives the LMFT permission to consult with the client's physician, but asks the LMFT not to discuss the client's recent weight gain with the physician. The client explains that they felt shamed by the physician and pressured to lose weight despite the client being in overall good health. The LMFT contacts the physician and explains that the client appears to be learning to manage their anxiety effectively without medication. The physician asks whether the client is losing weight as instructed. How should the LMFT respond?

    a.  **Incorrect.** Say yes to satisfy the physician, and redirect the conversation
    b.  **Incorrect.** Inform the physician of the client's weight gain, considering the potential medical concerns
    c.  **CORRECT.** Explain that the client's weight is not part of their therapy
    d.  **Incorrect.** Without directly answering the question, inform the physician that the client has experienced pressure to lose weight and that such pressure may worsen the client's anxiety

The LMFT should respect the client's request for their weight to not be discussed with the physician. At the same time, the LMFT does not need to lie or argue with the physician to accomplish this. Best to simply explain that the client's weight is not part of their therapy and move on in the conversation. This protects the client's rights while preserving the LMFT's role.

7. An LMFT is meeting with a family seeking therapy for issues of family conflict. The parents in the family are starting a business, and they report that they cannot afford to pay for therapy at this time, but they believe therapy is necessary for the family to get along together in ways that will make the business a success. They offer to pay the LMFT by giving the LMFT a small ownership stake in the family's business, which the LMFT could later share at a large profit if the business is successful. The family offers the LMFT a 10% share of the business to cover the full course of therapy for as many sessions as may be needed in the next 12 months. They note that bartering is common and accepted in their culture. Ethically, the LMFT should:

   a. **CORRECT.** Ask the family whether they have other products or services that they may consider using as part of a bartering arrangement instead
   b. **Incorrect.** Consider the fair market value of the ownership stake, and if the LMFT later sells that stake for a profit, return that profit to the family
   c. **Incorrect.** Consider the fair market value of the ownership stake, and offer to contract for a specific number of sessions rather than an unlimited number over a year
   d. **Incorrect.** Consider whether addressing family conflict in ways that will help a family business is consistent with the LMFT's scope of competence

The proposed bartering agreement would create an ongoing business relationship between the LMFT and the family, and presents the possibility of conflicting roles as well as the potential for exploitation. For example, the LMFT could profit more off of their share in the company if the family pays themselves lower salaries, even though higher salaries may help the family function more effectively. Bartering in and of itself is acceptable here, but the specific arrangement the family has proposed is not. As it relates to scope of competence, any LMFT should have family conflict within their competence to address clinically.

8. An LMFT is working with a 16-year-old boy and his mother in therapy. The mother has discovered that the boy and his girlfriend, also 16, have been sending each other naked photos of themselves. The mother says that she does not know, and does not want to know, whether the couple is having sex. The boy is angry that his mother was looking at his phone messages, and perceives this as an invasion of privacy. Considering the LMFT's legal obligations, how should the LMFT proceed?

    a.  **Incorrect.** Report suspected child abuse, with the mother as the perpetrator and the girlfriend as the victim

    b.  **Incorrect.** Assess for potential child abuse, and encourage the mother to support her son's autonomy

    c.  **Incorrect.** Assess for potential child abuse, and educate the boy about the dangers of sending personal images

    d.  **CORRECT.** Report suspected child abuse, with the boy and his girlfriend as both perpetrators and victims

Sending, or intentionally downloading, such images qualifies as child abuse and is a mandated report. In this instance, as the boy and the girlfriend have both been sending the images (and both appear to be welcoming images from each other), both would be considered perpetrators of abuse as well as victims.

9. A prospective client contacts an LMFT who offers therapy services via telehealth through a secure video platform. The client identifies themselves only as "Jose" and informs the LMFT that they are 27 years old and interested in receiving treatment for childhood trauma. The client is willing to attest that they live in California and will complete any intake paperwork the therapist sends, as long as they can sign as just "Jose." They say they are ashamed of what they experienced as a child, and this will make it easier for them to discuss it. Considering the LMFT's legal responsibilities, what must the LMFT do?

    a. **Incorrect.** Require the client to provide prepayment for all services

    b. **CORRECT.** Refuse to conduct sessions via telehealth unless the client is willing to provide their full name

    c. **Incorrect.** Locate the hospital and crisis house closest to the client's geographic location

    d. **Incorrect.** Document the client's request and the LMFT's reasons for agreeing to it

A legal requirement for LMFTs at each telehealth session is that they verbally obtain and document the client's full name and current location. If the client is not willing to provide their full name, the LMFT would be violating the law by conducting the session. Prepayment is not legally required under any circumstances, and LMFTs offering telehealth must document the reasonable efforts made to locate crisis resources local to the client; that does not necessarily require them to locate the closest hospital and crisis house, especially if the client does not present concerns about risk.

10. An LMFT is closing their private practice and planning to start a full-time job with a county mental health agency. They have been using an electronic health record (EHR) system to maintain records of their private practice cases. They plan to stop paying the monthly fee for this system in two weeks, when they begin their new job. Once they stop paying the fee, they would lose access to the EHR system. Considering their legal responsibilities, what should the LMFT do with their private practice records?

a. **Incorrect.** Continue paying the monthly fee for at least 5 years so that records can be accessed as needed

b. **Incorrect.** Once the LMFT stops paying the fee, inform all current and past private practice clients that the EHR company becomes the custodian of their records

c. **Incorrect.** Download all client records from the EHR and transfer them to the system used by the county to ensure ongoing access as needed

d. **CORRECT.** Download all client records and store them securely in a manner and location separate from the county's system

It is the responsibility of the clinician to ensure that records are securely maintained for at least seven years after the last professional contact. This is not the responsibility of the EHR if the therapist stops paying for it, and is not the responsibility of the county. At the same time, the therapist is not obligated to keep paying the EHR fee; they can download records for secure storage, so long as they maintain both security and appropriate access. Transferring records onto the county's system could make them available to county staffers who should not have access to them, and would thus not be appropriate.

11. An LMFT is working with an elderly client from another country. The client frequently complains of headaches and other body aches, but rarely discusses emotions directly. The LMFT also notices that the client rarely makes eye contact, and waits to be asked specific questions before speaking. How should the LMFT proceed?

    a.  **CORRECT.** Seek to better understand the client's cultural background

    b.  **Incorrect.** Refer the client to a physician to rule out possible medical issues

    c.  **Incorrect.** Remind the client that they are safe and reinforce boundaries

    d.  **Incorrect.** Consider the client's history of intergenerational trauma

The client's behavior may be common and understood as polite in the client's culture. Before assuming intergenerational trauma or a medical condition, the therapist should seek to better understand the client's culture, and how their behavior may reflect cultural norms. This will improve the therapist's ability to properly assess for relevant treatment needs. There is no indication of boundary concerns in the question.

12. An LMFT is in the process of termination with an individual from Ghana who has successfully completed individual therapy for issues of depression and loneliness. During therapy, it became clear that the client wanted greater connection with their culture, and as they achieved it, their symptoms lifted. The LMFT is interested in writing a case study about the successful treatment, for publication in a peer-reviewed journal. Considering their ethical obligations, the LMFT should:

    a.   **Incorrect.** Ensure that specific information that could be used to identify the client, such as their age, culture, occupation, and any direct quotes, is fully removed from the article

    b.   **Incorrect.** Inform the client of the potential benefits of being featured in a scholarly journal

    c.   **CORRECT.** Seek the client's informed consent to have their case included in research

    d.   **Incorrect.** Choose a different case to write about, since research participation was not agreed upon in advance of therapy beginning

The benefits of research largely confer to the researcher and the profession, not to the research participant who has already been successfully helped by the therapy. The LMFT should seek the client's consent to have their case written about. While de-identification is useful in some research contexts, case studies and qualitative research often rely on direct quotes and other information about clients in order to provide the most useful descriptions. The LMFT, like other researchers, must balance the risk of participant identification against the benefits of rich descriptions of client experiences. And the client should be informed of the risk of identification.

13. An LMFT has been providing individual therapy to a 33-year-old Chinese woman who reported conflict with her sibling's partner. The client was concerned that the conflict may stem from cultural differences between the two of them, and the client was hopeful that they could improve their relationship in the event that the sibling and the partner eventually married. The client comes to therapy and informs the LMFT that the sibling and the partner have broken up, with no expectation that they will reconcile. The client expresses empathy for her sibling, and relief for herself. Considering the LMFT's ethical responsibilities, the LMFT should:

a. **Incorrect.** Seek the client's permission to contact the sibling and offer to bring them into session
b. **Incorrect.** Inquire as to the reasons for the breakup, if known
c. **Incorrect.** Ask the client for more information on their cultural norms
d. **CORRECT.** Move toward termination

The reason for therapy has resolved, and nothing in the question suggests additional clinical needs. Continuing treatment would be ethically inappropriate.

14. An LMFT receives a referral from a psychiatrist. The client tells the LMFT that she meets regularly with the psychiatrist to manage psychotic symptoms. After the client's initial session, she calls the LMFT and sounds disoriented. She blames a recent medication change. The LMFT is concerned and wants to discuss this with the psychiatrist, but the client has not signed a Release of Information. Considering the LMFT's obligations under HIPAA, the LMFT should:

    a.   **Incorrect.** Understand that the client is in crisis and refer for an immediate medication monitoring appointment with the psychiatrist. *The client's disorientation may or may not be a crisis, and consultation with the psychiatrist is allowed under HIPAA (see option D below).*

    b.   **Incorrect.** Inquire as to possible extrapyramidal symptoms of the medication, and suggest the client stop taking the medication if necessary. *A suggestion to stop taking medication is medical advice and is outside of the LMFT's scope of practice.*

    c.   **Incorrect.** Mail the client a Release of Information form and ask the client to bring it with them to the next session. *The client's disorientation may suggest a more urgent problem, one that can be resolved quickly without violating HIPAA. See option D below.*

    d.   **CORRECT.** Contact the psychiatrist to discuss the client's diagnosis and treatment planning. *HIPAA specifically allows two people who are both actively providing treatment to a client to communicate without a release for the purposes of diagnosis and treatment planning.*

15. A 15-year-old girl is seeing an LMFT individually for issues related to body image and self-esteem. Her parents provided consent for the therapy and pay for her sessions, but do not participate. The girl tells the LMFT that she has been exploring her sexuality. While her parents were out of town, she had sexual intercourse with a friend's 19-year-old brother. A few days later, she had intercourse with another boy, an 18-year-old senior at her high school. The LMFT should manage their legal responsibilities by:

    a.  **Incorrect.** Reporting child abuse to the local child protective service agency

    b.  **Incorrect.** Investigating to ensure that the sexual activity was not coerced or while under the influence of drugs or alcohol

    c.  **Incorrect.** Notifying the parents of their daughter's high-risk sexual behavior

    d.  **CORRECT.** Maintaining confidentiality

The age combination of the partners, in both instances of sexual activity, does not require reporting (a). If either boy were 21 or over, or under 14, these combinations would be reportable. While it may be clinically relevant to explore the context of the sexual activity in more detail, the LMFT is not obligated to do so, and in fact should not position themselves as an investigator (b). While the parents may be able to access their daughter's treatment records, the LMFT does not have a responsibility to proactively inform them of sexual behavior; further, there is not enough information in the vignette to determine whether the girl's behavior indeed qualifies as "high-risk" (c). In the absence of a legal requirement or allowance for disclosure, the LMFT is legally obligated to maintain confidentiality.

16. An LMFT with a new private practice is considering how to market their practice. He wants to operate on a sliding fee scale based on client income. How can he best fulfill his legal and ethical responsibilities?

   a. **Incorrect.** Develop a fee structure that is based on services provided, and not client income. Fee scales based on client income are prohibited in private practice settings.
   b. **Incorrect.** Advertise that services are offered "as low as" the lowest fee on his scale.
   c. **CORRECT.** Make no mention of fees in his advertising.
   d. **Incorrect.** Make his sliding fee scale a percentage of income, regardless of the income level.

Sliding scales are allowed in private practice, making (A) incorrect. Note that some insurance carriers have terms in their contracts effectively prohibiting such scales, which makes the "cash-pay" distinction important. An "as low as" advertisement (B) is considered misleading in state law. And a scale that is a percentage of income *regardless of income level* (D) could be considered exploitive of high-income clients, considering the high fees that could result. Option C is the best answer here; while LMFTs are allowed to state fees in their advertising, they are not required to do so. Since each other option is clearly incorrect, this approach – removing fees from advertising – is the best one of the choices available.

17. A married couple seeing an LMFT in hopes of improving their marriage tells the therapist that they are considering taking Ecstasy together. They report having heard about users experiencing moments of great bonding while using the drug. They ask the LMFT whether she would recommend the couple try it together, and make clear that they would be using the drug in their home without anyone else present. Ethically, the LMFT should:

    a. **Incorrect.** Discourage all forms of lawbreaking, including illegal drug use. *LMFTs are neither required nor encouraged to discourage all forms of lawbreaking. Some lawbreaking, in some contexts, may be consistent with the client's morals. It would not be appropriate for the LMFT to impose their morality, which might place a higher priority on following the law, onto the client.*

    b. **CORRECT.** Review with the clients how they perceive the possible risks and benefits. *This best preserves client autonomy and the LMFT's role.*

    c. **Incorrect.** Refer all discussion of drug effects to a physician. *While advising on drugs would be outside of the LMFT's scope of practice, the discussion in this case does not need to involve the LMFT providing medical advice. The clients can tell the LMFT how the clients perceive possible risks and benefits.*

    d. **Incorrect.** Update the diagnosis of one or both partners to include Substance Use Disorder. *Simple use is not the same as a use disorder, and in this case, the couple has not yet even advanced to use. A change in diagnosis is not called for.*

18. In a rural community, an LMFT is treating a client whose daughter is good friends with the LMFT's children. Toward the end of a session, the client mentions that the client's daughter will be having a birthday party in a couple of weeks. The client says that they would love for the LMFT's children to attend but they are nervous about the LMFT coming. "I'm sure I'm just being silly," the client says, "but you know an awful lot about me, and it might be weird for my family to have you there." The LMFT should:

a. **Incorrect.** Address the client's projection onto their family, and consider it to be the client's discomfort, rather than their family's
b. **Incorrect.** Offer to discuss the party at another time, as it would not be appropriate to do so during a therapy session
c. **CORRECT.** Discuss the client's concern directly, describing the steps the LMFT will take to protect the client's confidentiality
d. **Incorrect.** Reassure the client that the LMFT will not attend the party, and discuss the benefits and risks of having the LMFT's children attend

This is fundamentally a question about maintaining boundaries in the presence of a dual relationship. Such relationships are common in rural areas (and in some communities within urban areas as well), and are not necessarily problematic. The LMFT should actively address boundary concerns (C). Refusing to attend the party (D) may be more conspicuous and thus more problematic than attending it, considering the closeness of the children's friendship; perhaps more to the point, there's nothing here that demands such a reaction. Refusing to discuss the issue (B) places the boundary in the wrong place, suggesting that dual relationship and boundary concerns are somehow not appropriate for the client to bring up in therapy. Conceptualizing the client's concern (A) is a clinical determination, not a legal or ethical one.

19. An LMFT encounters a former client from many years ago at a party. They enjoy catching up socially, and are each impressed with the other. In the time since therapy, the former client has been married and divorced. The LMFT, also now divorced, finds herself seeing the former client as an equal. She also finds herself attracted to the former client. Ethically, the LMFT should:

a. **Incorrect.** Provide the former client with a copy of the brochure *Therapy Never Includes Sexual Behavior. This is a legal requirement when a client informs a therapist that the client had a sexual relationship with a prior therapist.*

b. **Incorrect.** Assess whether the former client also sees the LMFT as an equal, and if so, consider initiating a romantic relationship. *The AAMFT Code of Ethics now makes the prohibition against sexual relationships with former clients a lifetime prohibition. The CAMFT Code of Ethics, while keeping the absolute prohibition at two years, goes on to acknowledge that such relationships remain problematic even after that timeframe.*

c. **Incorrect.** Review the reasons why the client sought therapy years ago, and determine whether the former client has truly resolved those concerns. *This is not relevant to consideration of whether to initiate a romantic relationship.*

d. **CORRECT.** Limit her social contact with the former client. *Of the options available, only this option recognizes the potential for harm in a sexual relationship with a former client and acts in response to that potential.*

20. An elder client tells an LMFT working in hospice care that the client was recently taken to a local religious gathering against her will by her 50-year-old daughter. The daughter is a member of the religious group. By the client's report, the daughter told her mother that "this might be good for you, being around people with good values" and did not bring the mother home when the mother said she was uncomfortable there. Furthermore, the daughter donated the cash in the client's purse to the religious group, despite the client's repeated statements to her daughter that the client did not support the group. How should the LMFT respond to their legal obligations in this case?

   a. **Incorrect.** Report suspected elder abuse (specifically, kidnapping)
   b. **CORRECT.** Report suspected elder abuse (specifically, financial abuse)
   c. **Incorrect.** Report suspected elder abuse (specifically, emotional abuse)
   d. **Incorrect.** Report suspected elder abuse (specifically, isolation)

All four options share reporting, so it is safe to presume that reporting is a requirement here. The differences relate to the *type* of abuse being reported. The law surrounding kidnapping (a) requires that the elder have been taken across state lines, which is not stated in the question. Emotional abuse (c) is not a specific category of elder abuse in statute, though the elder abuse rules do provide wide latitude for therapists to report anything they find to be abusive to an elder. Isolation (d) is perhaps most clearly not appropriate here, as the daughter took the client to a social event. Financial abuse (b) is most appropriate here, given that the client states her daughter took her money against her will and spent it on a cause she would not have supported on her own.

21. An LMFT has been working with a couple in therapy after discovering that their children's behavioral problems showed up primarily when the couple was arguing. Treatment has progressed well, and the LMFT has built trust with the couple by insisting on a "no secrets" policy where neither partner is allowed to communicate individually with the therapist. As they transition to family therapy within the same treatment plan, the parents ask the therapist not to share certain information from the couple therapy with their children. How should the LMFT manage the ethical issues in this case?

   a. **Incorrect.** Continue to insist on a "no secrets" policy to build trust throughout the family
   b. **Incorrect.** Close the couple therapy file and start a new file for each individual participant in family therapy
   c. **CORRECT.** Determine and have the family agree to a new policy on individual secrets in family therapy
   d. **Incorrect.** Push the parents to disclose to the children what happened in couple therapy

The unit of treatment impacts confidentiality considerations. In this case, the "no secrets" policy that the couple preferred for their treatment may not be appropriate when it comes to information being shared with their children. We do not know the age of the children, but many children do not need, want, or benefit from learning their parents' secrets. Best to set a new policy that the family agrees to.

22. The adult client of an LMFT calls the therapist from a police station. The client is filing a police report after their roommate physically attacked the client in an argument over housework. The client asks to reschedule the next planned session and reports that they do not feel safe going home, as the roommate is still there and the client believes the roommate is still very angry. How should the LMFT proceed?

    a. **Incorrect.** Ask the client for permission to speak to the police officer taking the report

    b. **CORRECT.** Ensure that the client has a safe place they can go

    c. **Incorrect.** Develop a plan for what to do if the roommate becomes violent or threatening again

    d. **Incorrect.** Assess the client for suicidality

There is an immediate and potentially ongoing risk to the client if they return home. When managing risks to safety, immediate physical safety is the highest priority. The LMFT should start by ensuring that the client has a safe place to go.

23. An LMFT receives a court order to testify in a case involving a former client. The LMFT cannot determine from the order much of what the case is about, though it appears to be a criminal case where the former client is charged with a crime. The order is signed by a judge and requires the LMFT to appear in court the following week, and to provide a copy of the client file. How should the LMFT proceed, considering their legal obligations?

    a. **CORRECT.** Consult with an attorney, and plan to appear in court at the date and time shown on the order, with a copy of the client's file

    b. **Incorrect.** Contact the client to determine their wishes, and appear in court or provide records only if the client is first willing to sign a release allowing the therapist to do so

    c. **Incorrect.** Inquire with the court about whether questions of privilege have been addressed

    d. **Incorrect.** Agree to testify, but withhold documentation, citing section 56.10 of the Civil Code

While a subpoena can be considered a request for records or testimony, a court order signed by a judge is a demand. The LMFT does not need the client's permission, and the LMFT cannot summarily withhold the client's file. The LMFT should plan to appear in court and provide records as ordered. Consulting with an attorney will ensure that the LMFT is well-prepared to testify within the bounds set by law.

24. An LMFT is conducting a home visit with a 16-year-old client who lives with their 43-year-old mother and 70-year-old grandmother. The family is poor and lives in a small apartment. The LMFT had previously met the mother when the mother provided consent for the daughter's treatment, but had not previously met the grandmother. When the client introduces the LMFT to the grandmother, the LMFT notices that the grandmother is in bed in the middle of the afternoon, appears to have an unbandaged infection on her arm, and the bed smells strongly of urine. The client apologizes for the mess in the apartment and says that she is working an after-school job to help her mother, who works two full-time jobs, so that they can save up for a caregiver for the grandmother, who has dementia. How should the LMFT proceed?

    a.  **CORRECT.** Report suspected elder neglect
    b.  **Incorrect.** Refer the family to programs that provide in-home health care at reduced costs
    c.  **Incorrect.** Consider the family's socioeconomic context and their good faith efforts
    d.  **Incorrect.** Report suspected elder and child neglect

There is no evidence in the question to suggest that the child is being neglected, but the grandmother's untreated infection and urine smell suggest that she is. While the LMFT should be sensitive to the family's circumstances, reporting in this case is an obligation. Doing so can help ensure that the grandmother receives the care she needs. Rather than attempting to punish the child or mother, the most likely outcome would be that the local adult protective service agency would connect the family with appropriate services.

25. In a rural community, an LMFT supervisor has been close friends for more than 20 years with a local attorney. The attorney's daughter is an associate MFT, and inquires with the LMFT supervisor about the possibility of coming to work for the LMFT supervisor's private practice. Considering the LMFT supervisor's ethical responsibilities, the LMFT supervisor should:

a. **Incorrect.** Consider their level of friendship with the associate MFT, independent from the LMFT supervisor's relationship with the attorney

b. **CORRECT.** Refer the associate to other prospective supervisors

c. **Incorrect.** Consult with the attorney for guidance in managing the complexities of the relationship

d. **Incorrect.** Agree to supervise the associate, and meet with both the attorney and the associate to discuss how the relationship will be managed

Both the AAMFT and CAMFT codes of ethics note that close relationships between a supervisor and a supervisee's family member can constitute unethical dual relationships. The best option here is to refer to another supervisor. If no other supervisor is available – a highly unlikely scenario considering the legality and availability of video-based supervision – the supervisor should weigh the relevant interests involved, rather than simply agreeing and only then giving consideration to how it might work.

How did you do? If you struggled a bit with these, don't worry. It's most important at this stage that you are able to understand *why* any questions you got wrong were incorrect. If you are interested in taking a full-length practice test, well, that's up next.

# You've got this.

Good luck!

# Practice Test

# Taking the practice test

This test is 75 questions, the same length as the actual test. Use them as you see fit! There are a few different ways you could use these items to help you prepare:

1. **Focus on understanding.** In this study method, you would take a practice test untimed, focusing on carefully examining the question and thinking through the available responses. You would then spend a fair amount of time with the *rationale* for each correct answer, making sure that you are deeply understanding the underlying concepts. While of course you hope to get a good score, your score on the practice exam is not terribly important when understanding is your goal. Any question you answer incorrectly is simply a chance to expand your knowledge and better prepare you for the real test. After all, while the actual test will cover the same content areas as this practice exam, it is unlikely they will ask the same questions in the same ways. You need to be able to understand and *apply* the key legal and ethical concepts across different clinical situations.

2. **Focus on timing.** In this study method, you would time yourself on the test, making sure you finish within the 90-minute time limit. This also gives you an opportunity to practice any anxiety management techniques you may need, and to practice time management skills like skipping questions you may want to come back to later. Many examinees have reported that they spent more time on the actual test than they did on practice tests, so it's good if you have at least some amount of time left over when you complete the test here.

3. **Focus on performance.** In this study method, a good score is the only goal. As is the case in method 1 above, you still want to make sure you understand why you answered incorrectly on any items you got wrong, but this method is more about confidence-building leading up to your test day. One thing to note if you're focused on your score: Because cycles of the real exam vary in difficulty, it is

not safe to presume that a score on any given practice test (the one here, or anyone else's) equates with roughly the same score on the real thing. If you're getting a significant majority of the items on a practice test right, your scores have been steadily improving, and you can understand why any incorrect answers you gave were incorrect, that is probably a better measure of preparedness than any specific score.

There are other, more creative ways you can use the material here as well, such as:

- Quizzing others in a study group
- Dividing the questions into three "mini-exams" of 25 questions each
- Using the book as a study guide, going through questions and rationales one at a time

I'm a big believer in being pragmatic where studying for an exam is concerned. Do what you know works best for you.

# A few cautionary notes

While these questions and responses are written to help prepare you for the California MFT Law and Ethics Exam, it is important to bear in mind that the practice test here (like all practice tests) is an *approximation* of the style and format of the exam itself. The actual exam changes with each 90-day test cycle; some exam cycles have a difficult exam, while others have an easier exam. This is why the passing score changes with each cycle, to ensure that examinees aren't disadvantaged by happening into a tougher cycle of the test.

It's also worth noting that, while every effort has been made here to tie these questions with specific and identifiable legal and ethical principles, ethical decision-making isn't always clear-cut. Even on questions where these is a clear correct answer, reasonable arguments can sometimes be made for some of the other response choices. If you find yourself arguing with the rationale on a question, focus your efforts on understanding why the correct response was identified as such.

If you are using multiple practice tests from different sources (for example, if you are using this book alongside practice tests provided by a test prep company), you may find that in some instances, the different sources suggest different answers for similar questions. That can be confusing and anxiety-provoking, but usually has a good explanation. You may be able to find that even minor, technical differences between the questions account for the differences in the best answers. You may also find that one source or another has something wrong – either because the law or ethical standard has changed, or because it has been misinterpreted. All of us (myself included) make mistakes on occasion. Rest assured that for the actual exam, every item must be keyed to an objective standard, so there will always be a current, justifiable best answer. If you find yourself disagreeing with a practice item from any source, and you have a clear legal or ethical rationale supporting your response choice, you're probably in good shape for the actual test. And of course, if you'd like to discuss anything in this book that you think I may have incorrect, please email my team at
support@BenCaldwellLabs.com and let us know.

Finally, you may find that some questions here resemble situations that you have actually encountered in your practice. Hopefully it would go without saying, but nothing here should be construed as legal advice or as a substitution for consulting with a qualified attorney. The kinds of case vignettes that are written for an exam are (by design) reductionist, focusing on only a few features of a case. Real-life decision-making is often more complex.

# Practice Test:
# Answer Sheets

# California MFT Law & Ethics

| | | | |
|---|---|---|---|
| 1. ____ | 21. ____ | 41. ____ | 61. ____ |
| 2. ____ | 22. ____ | 42. ____ | 62. ____ |
| 3. ____ | 23. ____ | 43. ____ | 63. ____ |
| 4. ____ | 24. ____ | 44. ____ | 64. ____ |
| 5. ____ | 25. ____ | 45. ____ | 65. ____ |
| 6. ____ | 26. ____ | 46. ____ | 66. ____ |
| 7. ____ | 27. ____ | 47. ____ | 67. ____ |
| 8. ____ | 28. ____ | 48. ____ | 68. ____ |
| 9. ____ | 29. ____ | 49. ____ | 69. ____ |
| 10. ____ | 30. ____ | 50. ____ | 70. ____ |
| 11. ____ | 31. ____ | 51. ____ | 71. ____ |
| 12. ____ | 32. ____ | 52. ____ | 72. ____ |
| 13. ____ | 33. ____ | 53. ____ | 73. ____ |
| 14. ____ | 34. ____ | 54. ____ | 74. ____ |
| 15. ____ | 35. ____ | 55. ____ | 75. ____ |
| 16. ____ | 36. ____ | 56. ____ | |
| 17. ____ | 37. ____ | 57. ____ | |
| 18. ____ | 38. ____ | 58. ____ | |
| 19. ____ | 39. ____ | 59. ____ | |
| 20. ____ | 40. ____ | 60. ____ | |

# California MFT Law & Ethics

| | | | |
|---|---|---|---|
| 1. _____ | 21. _____ | 41. _____ | 61. _____ |
| 2. _____ | 22. _____ | 42. _____ | 62. _____ |
| 3. _____ | 23. _____ | 43. _____ | 63. _____ |
| 4. _____ | 24. _____ | 44. _____ | 64. _____ |
| 5. _____ | 25. _____ | 45. _____ | 65. _____ |
| 6. _____ | 26. _____ | 46. _____ | 66. _____ |
| 7. _____ | 27. _____ | 47. _____ | 67. _____ |
| 8. _____ | 28. _____ | 48. _____ | 68. _____ |
| 9. _____ | 29. _____ | 49. _____ | 69. _____ |
| 10. _____ | 30. _____ | 50. _____ | 70. _____ |
| 11. _____ | 31. _____ | 51. _____ | 71. _____ |
| 12. _____ | 32. _____ | 52. _____ | 72. _____ |
| 13. _____ | 33. _____ | 53. _____ | 73. _____ |
| 14. _____ | 34. _____ | 54. _____ | 74. _____ |
| 15. _____ | 35. _____ | 55. _____ | 75. _____ |
| 16. _____ | 36. _____ | 56. _____ | |
| 17. _____ | 37. _____ | 57. _____ | |
| 18. _____ | 38. _____ | 58. _____ | |
| 19. _____ | 39. _____ | 59. _____ | |
| 20. _____ | 40. _____ | 60. _____ | |

**The practice test begins when you turn the page.**

If you are timing your practice test, start the timer, and then turn the page to begin.

*Throughout this test, unless stated otherwise, any references to a "therapist," "MFT," or "LMFT" refer to a California Licensed Marriage and Family Therapist. "BBS" means the California Board of Behavioral Sciences.*

1. A family consisting of a 25-year-old man, his 19-year-old nonbinary sibling, and their 50-year-old mother presents to an LMFT for family therapy. The man has been recently diagnosed with schizophrenia, and at the direction of his physician has begun taking medication for it. He also has started seeing an individual therapist. The family is seeking family therapy to manage their interactions around the son and provide support. The LMFT should:

   a.  Avoid providing family-based treatment while the man is also seeing an individual therapist
   b.  Agree to provide treatment to the family only if the LMFT also takes over individual therapy, to ensure consistency between the two therapies
   c.  Discuss how family treatment would differ from individual therapy, and determine whether to seek the man's permission to consult with the individual therapist
   d.  Advise the family to wait 90 days for the medication to take its full effect prior to proceeding with either individual or family-based psychotherapy

*Question 2 is on the next page.*

2. An LMFT is serving as the individual therapist for an adult client who is a well-known artist. The LMFT has implemented processes of collaborative documentation in the LMFT's practice in an effort to reduce hierarchy. The client proposes that, starting with the following week's session, the LMFT and the client spend the last 10 minutes of each session on a small watercolor painting, which would serve as their documentation of both the content and experience of the session. Ethically, the LMFT should:

    a.  Consider the client's cultural background in assessing the appropriateness of the request

    b.  Insist that each watercolor be marked with the session date, time, length, and location

    c.  Consider the cost of supplying paint, brushes, and paper or canvases appropriate to this purpose

    d.  Consider the potential therapeutic benefit of this process, while ensuring that typical written documentation also continues

3. A 29-year-old client being treated by an LMFT in a community mental health agency reports sleeping outside and refusing food, because the client is hearing voices telling them that their family is trying to poison them. The client has been prescribed medication but believes that this, too, is an effort to poison them. The client appears underweight and dehydrated, and the LMFT learns that the client has a sister who has been appointed by the court to protect the client's legal rights. How should the LMFT address the situation, considering their legal obligations?

    a.  Contact the sister to coordinate treatment

    b.  Connect the client with services offering housing and food assistance

    c.  Report the client's suspicion that their family is attempting to poison them

    d.  Report suspected dependent adult neglect

4. An adult client with an extensive history of gambling seeks couple therapy with his wife of 14 years. Despite the best efforts of an LMFT, the treatment fails, and the couple chooses to divorce. The man's gambling worsens, eventually leaving him bankrupt. He sues the LMFT, claiming that the LMFT's misconduct negatively impacted his mental health, causing him to lose his job and ultimately run out of money. The LMFT believes that records of the case will ultimately lead a court to rule in the LMFT's favor, but the client refuses to release the records. Instead, the client goes on television, where he discloses his gambling and therapy history and again accuses the therapist of misconduct. Legally, how should the LMFT proceed?

    a.  Disclose the client file to the public, as the client has waived confidentiality with his own disclosures to the media
    b.  Disclose the client file to the court
    c.  Through an attorney, move to submit the client file into evidence
    d.  Through an attorney, contact the client in a good-faith effort to have the records released

5. A recently-licensed LMFT is interested in helping others successfully navigate the licensure process. She posts to a closed group of licensed and prelicensed therapists on a popular social media platform about her experience taking her clinical exam. In her post, she encourages those about to take their tests to focus their diagnostic review on mood disorders and schizophrenia, as these came up multiple times on her test. Considering the LMFT's legal responsibilities, this post could result in:

    a.  No action against the LMFT, as she was not specific about the questions she was asked
    b.  No action against the LMFT, as the post was to a closed group and not the general public
    c.  Action against the LMFT's license
    d.  A jail sentence for the LMFT

6. A family of five comes to an LMFT to address family conflict surrounding the family's business. The parents own an auto body shop. Their children, ages 16, 19, and 22, are all working there but are interested in pursuing their own careers. The parents are concerned that the body shop cannot survive if it has to hire outside workers, and they want the shop to be a place the children can rely on. The children express love and support for their parents but openly wonder whether the business should survive if it is relying on their underpaid work. How should the LMFT proceed with the family?

    a.  Allow the parents to set the goals of treatment, while recognizing that the 19-year-old and 22-year-old may choose not to participate
    b.  Attempt to define goals for therapy that all family members can agree upon
    c.  Separate the units of treatment to better support their specific interests, seeing the parents as a couple and each child individually
    d.  Refer out as this is outside of the LMFT's scope of practice

7. An LMFT is providing couple therapy to a separated couple with two young children. Both partners have given the LMFT permission to testify at an upcoming court hearing where the judge may approve their temporary custody agreement. The LMFT has agreed to testify. As the hearing approaches, the LMFT notices that each partner seems to be trying to win the LMFT's favor, complimenting the LMFT on small changes in their office or offering small gifts. How should the LMFT manage their ethical responsibilities?

    a.  Clarify the LMFT's role as a treatment provider, and differentiate this from the role of a custody evaluator
    b.  Remind the couple that it is not legally appropriate to attempt to bribe a future witness
    c.  Draft a Testimony Agreement that clearly defines court testimony as a separate service with a separate fee
    d.  Rescind the LMFT's agreement to testify, as it should not have been given

8. An LMFT becomes concerned when a client who has been struggling with depression does not show for two consecutive sessions. The client does not respond to the LMFT's efforts to contact the client by phone and email. While the client has not signed any Releases of Information during the therapy process, they did list a friend's name and phone number in the "Emergency Contact" section of their intake paperwork. How should the LMFT proceed?

    a.  Attempt to contact the Emergency Contact solely to request that the person have the client contact the LMFT, without providing additional information
    b.  Consider the listing of someone as an "Emergency Contact" to be a limited authorization to release information in the event of an emergency, and contact them to request assistance
    c.  Continue attempting to contact the client by phone and email, and review client history for indicators of potential crisis or safety issues
    d.  Contact law enforcement or a local psychiatric emergency response team to perform a wellness check on the client

9. An LMFT has been learning about herbal medicine and its connections with overall health and wellness. The LMFT mentions this to some clients, and the clients respond with interest in learning how herbal medicine might be incorporated into their therapy processes. Some clients report difficulty with sleep and anxiety, and say they are hopeful that herbal remedies could work alongside talk therapy. How can the LMFT respond to the clients' inquiries?

    a.  Refer interested clients to external books, videos, or herbal medicine practitioners
    b.  Provide recommendations for herbal remedies only to target those issues also being addressed in therapy
    c.  Provide herbal teas, lotions, and other potential remedies specific to clients' presenting issues, noting that clients may use or apply those remedies themselves during sessions
    d.  Seek certification as an herbal wellness practitioner, and integrate herbal remedies into therapy only after receiving the appropriate certification

10. In family therapy, a single father reports that he raises his two children to be strong and silent. The children, ages 7 and 10, are not allowed to question the father's decisions, and cannot go to bed at night until their homework is completed, the house is clean, and they have chosen their clothes for the next day. The family therapy surrounds lingering grief over the death of the mother two years ago. The family reports that the mother did not share all of the father's beliefs, and sometimes balanced his more strict rules. How should the LMFT address the ethical issues present in this case?

    a. Urge the father to integrate the mother's memory in the family by loosening some rules

    b. Report suspected child abuse to the local child protective service agency

    c. Ask the father how he determined the rules he would set for the children

    d. Develop a transition plan to gradually loosen some rules as the children demonstrate their competence

11. A couple has been working with an LMFT as they consider whether to divorce. One spouse emails the LMFT and asks the LMFT to fantasize with them about the client and the LMFT sneaking away for a sexual encounter together. The spouse explains that they do not want to do this in real life, but that fantasizing about it simply is an outlet for their sexual frustration in their marriage. How should the LMFT proceed?

    a. Seek permission from the other spouse to engage in the email conversation

    b. Report the client email to the BBS, clarifying that no actual sexual encounter occurred

    c. Reaffirm therapeutic boundaries, and consider whether the exchange could serve as a meaningful component of the couple's therapy

    d. Explain to the client that such an exchange would not be appropriate

12. A supervisee expresses frustration to their LMFT supervisor that the supervisee is still having many of the same clinical challenges they were having a year ago when they started working under the supervisor. The supervisee explains to the supervisor that the supervisee has reviewed clinical records and session tapes, and still does not understand what they are doing wrong in therapy. While some of the supervisee's clients appear to be improving, many are not. Considering the supervisor's ethical obligations, how should the supervisor proceed?

    a.  Consider terminating the supervision relationship in light of the supervisee's lack of improvement

    b.  Provide a summary of the supervisee's strengths and weaknesses as the supervisor perceives them

    c.  Reassure the supervisee that therapeutic growth is sometimes slow and inconsistent

    d.  Utilize a substitute supervisor to provide the supervisee an alternate perspective on their work

*Question 13 is on the next page.*

13. A 25-year-old Mexican-American man has been seeing an LMFT individually for several months to address auditory hallucinations. The client has had some success in quieting his internal voices with medication, but does not like the side effects of his medication and so he does not take it every day. The client's mother calls the LMFT and expresses concern that the client has not taken his medication for several days, has had worsening hallucinations telling him to kill himself, and left this morning to go for a hike armed with a large knife. The mother believes the client is planning to die by suicide. The mother lives with the client, but the LMFT does not have a release to share information with the mother. How should the LMFT address the issues presented in this case?

    a. Do not acknowledge that the client is a client; attempt to contact the client to assess risk

    b. Ask the mother for the client's last known location and direction of travel; contact law enforcement to initiate involuntary hospitalization

    c. Do not acknowledge that the client is a client; review prior treatment records for evidence of risk

    d. Ask the mother for the client's last known location and direction of travel; contact park rangers to notify other hikers who may be in the area

14. An individual client who typically gets along well with an LMFT arrives to session visibly angry. The client explains that they searched for the LMFT online, and found that the LMFT is active in political causes that the client strongly disagrees with. The client says they are unsure whether they can continue in therapy, with the knowledge of this difference in their views. How should the LMFT proceed?

    a. Pause therapy to give both the client and the LMFT time to reflect on their positions

    b. Consult with a supervisor or therapist on the appropriateness of the LMFT's political involvement

    c. Reinforce boundaries and remind the client that the LMFT's personal politics do not in any way impact therapy

    d. Discuss the client's reasons for considering ending therapy entirely

15. An LMFT in private practice has chosen to specialize in working with "long-term married" couples, which the LMFT defines as having been married for at least 20 years. The LMFT notes that they are willing to make exceptions for same-sex couples who have been together for at least that long, as they may not have been legally able to marry when they got together. The LMFT is approached by an unmarried couple with four children, ranging in ages from 4 to 19. The couple explains that they are seeking treatment for their relationship, and they are fully committed to each other, they simply chose never to marry. The LMFT believes that marriage creates bonds and obligations for a couple that cannot be replicated outside of marriage. How should the LMFT address the ethical issues present?

    a.   Offer treatment to the couple, and build competency in committed, non-marital relationships

    b.   Refer the couple to qualified therapists who do not share the LMFT's beliefs about marriage

    c.   Accept the couple for treatment on a probationary basis, to assess whether their relationship is meaningfully similar to a marriage

    d.   Clarify the reasoning behind the policy and its connections to the LMFT's religious belief

16. An LMFT is working with a family consisting of a mother and her three daughters, when the LMFT develops reasonable suspicion that the oldest daughter was physically abused by her sixth-grade teacher. The family is undocumented and has actively sought to avoid any involvement with government systems other than the girls' school for fear of deportation or the family being forcibly broken up. How should the LMFT manage the potential impact of reporting on the clinical relationship?

    a.   Make the report of suspected child abuse anonymously

    b.   Not disclose to the family that the LMFT is making the report of suspected child abuse

    c.   Inform the family about the report and attempt to address their fears

    d.   Balance the potential benefits of reporting against the potential risks when determining whether to make the report

17. While browsing a popular mobile phone app where people can share short videos, an LMFT is shocked to see a former client from 10 years ago holding up the LMFT's picture and repeatedly saying "This psychologist saved my life." The former client explains how they had struggled with depression and suicidality, and came through it thanks to the therapy process. The video ends with the client saying, "If you're a client now, you're lucky. Next time you go to session... say thanks for me, ok?" The LMFT no longer has records from the client's treatment, but sees that they can contact the former client through the app. Ethically, how should the LMFT proceed?

    a. Contact the app's support team to request that the video be taken down, without revealing why

    b. Contact the former client to request that they change the word "psychologist" since the LMFT is not one

    c. Contact the former client to ask that they take down the video, as it would be considered a testimonial

    d. Post a response video thanking the former client, providing the therapist's contact information, and including all legally required disclosures

18. An LMFT is in the process of leaving the agency where they have worked for the past five years. The agency has honored some client requests to be reassigned to other therapists in the agency, but some clients have been referred to outside providers if the client had a preference to be referred out or if their specific needs suggested that an external referral would be preferable. The LMFT's last day at the agency is one week away. How can the LMFT best assure continuity of care to clients who are being transferred?

    a. Contract with the external providers to ensure that transferred clients will continue to pay the same fee

    b. For clients who authorize it, speak directly with each client's new provider, and provide copies of records to external providers

    c. Consult with a supervisor

    d. Check back in with all transferring clients in 30 days to ensure they are satisfied with the transfer

19. An LMFT attends a weeklong workshop focused on understanding human behavior in its social and cultural context. The LMFT returns to working with clients the next week, and finds that the LMFT's views of many clients have changed dramatically. Though she stands by her assessment of specific client symptoms and her observations of client behaviors, she no longer believes that most of the diagnoses she had given should be included in the clients' records, as she has come to see diagnosis as a fundamentally oppressive act. Clients express confusion at the change, and become frustrated when their insurance will no longer cover therapy. How should the LMFT proceed?

a. Evaluate herself for impairment, and consider whether diagnosis can be given in a manner that facilitates treatment without being oppressive

b. Explain for clients the rationale behind the decision, and reframe their behaviors as adaptive

c. Inform clients of their right to include a supplementary statement in their files if they wish

d. Advocate on behalf of clients for insurers to pay for treatment without a diagnosis present

*Question 20 is on the next page.*

20. A client has cancelled three of the last seven scheduled sessions with an LMFT, and been a no-show for the other four. Each time, the client has promised to pay any balance charged, and to come in for a session the following week. The LMFT finds herself irritated with the client's behavior, going so far as to warn the client two weeks ago that she would simply close the client's case and refer out if the client didn't come in. The client was a no-show for the next two scheduled sessions. Even before this long series of missed appointments, the LMFT found herself personally disliking the client. How should the LMFT manage her ethical responsibilities in this case?

    a. Meaningfully assess for crisis, and continue as the client's treatment provider if necessary

    b. Close the case, providing the client with appropriate referrals to other providers

    c. Provide the client at least two additional warnings, one of which must be in writing, prior to terminating therapy

    d. Seek consultation to address countertransference, and continue to work toward the client more regularly attending therapy

21. A client requests and receives a copy of her clinical record from the LMFT who has been providing her with therapy. The client reviews the record and becomes visibly angry, demanding that the LMFT change the diagnosis in her file. The LMFT should:

    a. Remind the client that treatment records are the property of the therapist

    b. Remind the client that the LMFT was not required to turn over the record at all

    c. Remind the client that she may submit a written statement disputing the diagnosis and have that statement included in the file

    d. Remind the client that the diagnosis is used simply to facilitate payment for services

22. As a client leaves an LMFT's office, the LMFT believes the client poses a serious danger to the client's spouse. (The client had been making threats in session about what he would do to her.) The LMFT, knowing the couple lives roughly 30 minutes from the LMFT's office, calls the client immediately, and is able to resolve the danger. The client disavows any continued plan to harm his spouse, and apologizes to the LMFT for "getting so out of hand." What does the LMFT need to do to resolve the LMFT's legal responsibility?

    a.   Notify the spouse and law enforcement immediately
    b.   Notify the spouse immediately
    c.   Notify law enforcement within 24 hours
    d.   Notify the local child protective services agency

23. A 14-year-old client consented to her own treatment at a nonprofit agency, which agreed to treat her for $5/session. The client tells the therapist (an LMFT) that the client has been abusing a friend's prescription painkillers. Legally, the LMFT should:

    a.   Notify the local child protective service agency
    b.   Notify the client's parent or guardian, as the behavior is considered high-risk
    c.   Work with the client to develop a plan to gradually reduce dosage and ultimately stop the client's drug use
    d.   Document the discussion and refer the client to a physician

24. An LMFT is working with a client in a different part of the state, one the LMFT is not familiar with, via telemedicine. During a session taking place via videoconference, the client informs the therapist that he recently lost his job and is struggling to navigate the complex web of social services in his area. He fears losing his home in a matter of weeks. Ethically, the LMFT should:

a. Volunteer to serve as the client's case manager to better coordinate his services
b. Travel to where the client is located to provide services in person on a temporary basis
c. Reconsider whether telemedicine services are appropriate for this client
d. Assess for suicidality and substance use

25. An LMFT is brought in as an expert witness in a criminal case where a woman was accused of violently beating her 8-year-old daughter. The LMFT is asked by the court to speak on the long-term effects of child abuse, as well as on factors that can lead mothers to become abusive. The LMFT has expertise in these areas. The LMFT also finds the behavior that the woman is accused of repugnant. The LMFT should:

a. Speak solely about what the LMFT knows about the specific case being tried, and avoid speaking in generalities
b. Speak solely from her knowledge and expertise in the field, and avoid saying anything about the specific case being tried
c. Clarify for the court that no explanatory factors for abuse should be understood as making child abuse acceptable
d. Investigate the merits of the case before determining how to testify

26. An LMFT turns away a prospective client after the client suggests the LMFT overbill the client's employer, who is paying for treatment through an Employee Assistance Program. The client was hoping to split the money with the therapist. Months later, the former prospective client is on trial for fraud, accused of engaging in a similar scheme with a different therapist. The LMFT is called to testify against the client. The LMFT should:

a. Advocate on behalf of the former prospective client
b. Prepare to testify
c. Inform the prosecutors and the court that the LMFT cannot testify
d. The LMFT has no obligation to respond or testify, as the person never formally became a client

27. The client of an LMFT notices that before her session, as the LMFT is escorting her previous appointment out of the office, the LMFT and the person she is escorting out are discussing plans to have coffee together later. The client asks the LMFT about this at the beginning of her session. The client tells the LMFT that she, too, would like to have a more personal and social relationship with the therapist that involves meeting outside of the office. What should the LMFT do to manage her ethical responsibilities in this case?

a. Consider whether the earlier appointment was confidential
b. Inform the client that the existing relationship is not unethical as it has no negative impact on client care. Consider whether a similar relationship is possible with the current client
c. Scold the client for inquiring about the therapist's relationships
d. Cancel the coffee plan by phone with the client in the room, to acknowledge and take responsibility for her mistake

28. An online business aims to make therapy more affordable for telehealth clients by using what they call a "reverse auction" process. When a prospective client signs up with the business, the business creates a de-identified summary of client information (such as location, demographics, and presenting problem), and then allows participating therapists to "bid" on the client by posting what they would agree to charge that client per 50-minute therapy session. The therapist who has offered the lowest "bid" when the auction closes pays the business a nominal fee, and then receives the client's full information, including their name, phone number, and email address. The client is told which therapist won the auction, what fee the therapist committed to, and the therapist's contact information. How should LMFTs interact with this service?

    a.  LMFTs should not participate in this service
    b.  LMFTs should ensure that no actual therapy information is shared with the service
    c.  LMFTs should only participate in this service if the fees they charge auction clients are in line with fees they would charge to the general public
    d.  LMFTs should demand that the business do additional screening on potential clients, to address potential crisis issues

*Question 29 is on the next page.*

29. In the client's second session, the individual client of an LMFT requests a letter that would allow the client to have an emotional support dog in their apartment. The client reports that their apartment building does not typically allow dogs, but their pet dog who is currently in the care of a family member helps the client to manage their panic attacks. Considering the LMFT's legal obligations, the LMFT is required to:

   a. Seek records from the client's prior treatment to support the need for an emotional support animal, prior to issuing such a letter
   b. Observe the animal directly in order to be able to attest to the animal's safety
   c. Observe the animal and the client together to directly assess the animal's impact on the client
   d. Establish at least a 30-day clinical relationship with the client, including a full clinical assessment

30. An LMFT is providing individual therapy to a young adult who is planning her wedding. The client and her partner are both part of a tight-knit religious community, and the LMFT believes that other members of the community could benefit from the LMFT's services, as the LMFT is familiar with this community despite not being a part of it. The client expresses that she and her partner are building the guest list for the wedding, and are struggling with the question of whether to invite guests from outside the religious community. Considering the LMFT's ethical obligations, what would be the most appropriate course of action for the LMFT to take?

   a. Inquire further about the reasons behind the couple's struggle
   b. Directly request an invitation to the wedding, while ensuring the couple that their confidentiality will be protected
   c. Discuss the potential benefits to the community of inviting outsiders as guests, potentially but not necessarily including the LMFT
   d. Express the LMFT's belief that the therapist's services could be of benefit to the community, and ask the client what the best way would be for the LMFT to support the wedding while building community connections

31. An LMFT is working with a family that chooses not to vaccinate their children or to receive most medical care because of the family's religious beliefs. Though the parents take their children to a physician for annual checkups, they otherwise avoid what they describe as the "toxic western medical establishment." The LMFT has not encountered these beliefs before, but largely dismisses them as irrelevant to the treatment being provided. The family is working in therapy on the father's anger, one child's difficulty in social relationships, and another child's regressed behavior. Considering the LMFT's ethical responsibilities, the LMFT should:

a. Report suspected child neglect
b. Seek out additional information on the family's religion
c. Provide the family with information about the benefits of vaccination, while supporting their decision-making autonomy
d. Inquire about any possible connections between the family's religion and the maladaptive behaviors of its individual members

32. An LMFT is diagnosed with a serious illness and told that they need to immediately discontinue their clinical practice. The illness is not contagious, but the LMFT's doctor believes that the LMFT cannot provide competent care due to the illness, and will need to focus all of their energy on treatment. Most clients are successfully transferred to other clinicians, but one of the LMFT's clients goes into crisis and threatens suicide if they cannot continue seeing the LMFT. The client offers to meet by telehealth instead of in-person, in hopes that this will allow for continued services. Considering their ethical responsibilities, how should the LMFT proceed?

a. Given the risks involved, continue seeing this one client via telehealth, while discontinuing all other clinical practice
b. Discontinue all contact with the client, as they have been notified of the transition and further contact may only further escalate them
c. Provide two sessions on an emergency basis, but make clear that the LMFT cannot provide any further treatment
d. Contact the client to apologize for the transition and attempt a warm handoff to another clinician

33. An LMFT in private practice is planning to raise her fees and limit her schedule in order to spend more time with her family. For most clients, she is charging $100 per session, and would like to double this to $200. She is seeing some reduced-fee clients for $50 per session, and would like to double this to $100. Considering her ethical responsibilities, what is the LMFT's best path forward in regard to raising her rates?

   a. Provide significant advance notice of the change to ongoing clients who will be impacted
   b. Limit the fee increase to no more than 10% per year until her fees are where she would like them to be
   c. Apply the increase only to full-fee clients, and not to reduced-fee clients, as they are the ones most likely to experience hardship as a result of higher fees
   d. See what fees are being charged in the local market, to ensure that her new fees are not exploitive

34. A wealthy celebrity client continues working with an LMFT via telehealth whenever the client is traveling within California. The LMFT agrees to accommodate the client's travel schedule by arranging a telehealth session on a Saturday, when the LMFT normally does not see clients. A short time after the session concludes, the LMFT sees that the client has paid triple their usual fee, with a note that the client attached to the payment simply saying "Thank you for making time in your weekend for me." Ethically, the LMFT should:

   a. Refund the client's overpayment and explain that making it was inappropriate
   b. Discuss the meaning of the client's overpayment with them at the next session
   c. Donate the client's overpayment to a charity of the LMFT's choosing
   d. Apply the client's overpayment as a credit toward future session fees

35. An LMFT is testifying in a court case involving a 15-year-old who is accused of sexually assaulting a 14-year-old classmate. The LMFT has been seeing the 15-year-old for individual therapy, and in that process has learned that the 15-year-old was raped when they were 12. The LMFT believes this is a critical factor in the court and the victim understanding the 15-year-old's actions, but the client has been insistent that the LMFT not share this information, even though the client otherwise has given permission for the LMFT to testify. Considering state law, how should the LMFT address this situation?

    a. Seek a private meeting with the judge to explain that the minor is the victim of a crime, and that in the eyes of the LMFT, disclosure of that fact is in the client's interests

    b. Maintain confidentiality around the rape, as the client has specifically requested that information not be shared

    c. Include information about the rape in the LMFT's testimony despite the client's wishes

    d. Submit a friend-of-the-court brief, separate from the LMFT's courtroom testimony, noting that many minors who engage in inappropriate sexual behaviors have themselves been victimized

36. An LMFT is preparing to transition from working for a nonprofit organization to launching the LMFT's own private practice. The LMFT is planning to see clients under the clients' insurance, and to submit claims electronically. In preparing for the transition, the LMFT has joined the panels of three popular insurance networks. Considering the LMFT's legal obligations, the LMFT must:

    a. Conduct a formal risk analysis regarding how client data will be gathered, stored, and shared

    b. Obtain from each insurance company their list of denial and exclusion criteria, and provide this to each insured client prior to beginning therapy services

    c. Offer a sliding fee scale to clients who have other insurances or are paying out of pocket for mental health care

    d. Review the insurance contracts to ensure that the LMFT is receiving the same per-session fee from each insurance company

37. A same-sex couple contacts an LMFT to arrange couple therapy. The LMFT informs the couple that, as part of the LMFT's standard couple assessment process, the LMFT will meet with the couple together first, and then with each partner individually. The couple agrees and schedules a session at the therapist's office. As the clients are walking into the office, one partner pulls the LMFT back, and quietly asks whether it is possible to tell the LMFT about "some things" that the client does not want their partner to know about. Considering the LMFT's ethical obligations, how can the LMFT best manage this situation?

    a.   Inform the client that the LMFT cannot hold individual secrets in couple therapy

    b.   Establish a policy that both partners agree to regarding how individual secrets will be handled

    c.   Ask the client to further define "some things" so that the LMFT can determine whether they would undermine the overall course of therapy

    d.   Explain that individual confidentiality is absolute, so the client can feel safe in sharing this information at the appropriate time

38. An associate marriage and family therapist is working under the supervision of an LMFT in private practice. The LMFT encourages the associate to take clients who are on the LMFT's waiting list and have an insurance plan that the LMFT participates in. For billing, the LMFT encourages the associate to use the LMFT's standard claim template, showing the LMFT as the provider. The LMFT explains that this is so that payments will be made to the LMFT and not the associate. Considering their legal obligations, the associate should:

    a.   Add a note or comment onto billing documents that identifies the associate as the person who performed the therapy

    b.   Adjust any billing documents to reflect the associate's name and the LMFT's license number for sessions conducted by the associate

    c.   Form a separate business entity that can bill for services rendered by the associate, while still designating the LMFT as the payee

    d.   Avoid billing insurance for any sessions provided by the associate

39. An LMFT is working with an 8-year-old girl and her mother in therapy. In their first session after the 8-year-old returned from visiting her grandparents out of state, she is shifting and squirming in her seat. Her mother tells the LMFT that the child has taken a sudden interest in learning about sex, and that the daughter has made vague statements about "learning things" on the trip but refuses to be more specific. How should the LMFT proceed?

   a. Refer the family to the child's pediatrician to assess for possible sexual abuse
   b. Interview the child alone to establish specific facts from the visit and investigate the likelihood that abuse took place
   c. Report suspected child abuse to the LMFT's local child protective service agency
   d. Because any possible abuse would have taken place outside of California, encourage the mother to report possible abuse to the appropriate agency where the grandparents are located

40. The client of an LMFT has been engaged in a difficult custody battle over her two sons. The client has shown the LMFT photos, emails and text messages her husband has sent her, where he regularly talks about being drunk and often appears intoxicated. Though the children are all healthy, the client expresses fear for her children's safety around the father, and asks the LMFT to inform the court that her husband may have a substance use disorder. The LMFT should:

   a. Consider whether a report of child neglect is appropriate
   b. Refuse to review these photos, emails, and text messages in the future, focusing instead on the client's reaction to them
   c. Provide the court with a letter stating that, based on the limited information available, the LMFT believes the husband may have a substance use disorder and should be further assessed
   d. Refuse the client's request

41. A couple is seeing an LMFT as the couple considers whether to divorce. The couple is expecting their first child, and they invite the LMFT to a party where they will reveal the baby's sex to friends and family. The couple explains to the LMFT that they do not want others to know they are in therapy, but they are worried about their conflict and anger coming up during the party, and if that happens they may need the LMFT to mediate. How should the LMFT proceed, considering the LMFT's ethical obligations?

   a. Have the couple sign a release authorizing the LMFT to attend the party, understanding the risks to confidentiality involved
   b. Attend the party in a coach or consultant role
   c. See whether a compromise solution, such as the LMFT being on-call during the party for an emergency telehealth session, is available
   d. Reinforce therapeutic boundaries and urge the couple to reconsider whether the party is a good idea

42. An LMFT is working with a young adult client who operates a channel on a popular video sharing web site. The client tells the LMFT that the channel involves older people, some over 100 years old, "flashing" their breasts or genitals. The client insists that they have consent from all of the participants in their videos, and that most participants find the videos to be "harmless fun." Only one participant has ever objected, and that participant was edited out after the video that featured them was published. The client is paid by the web site for their videos, but the client does not share this revenue with the video participants. The LMFT finds the channel to be exploitive and potentially harmful to the video participants. Which statement best summarizes the LMFT's legal obligations?

   a. The LMFT may report suspected elder abuse, but is not required to
   b. The LMFT must investigate the videos further to determine whether abuse is occurring
   c. The LMFT must report suspected elder abuse
   d. The LMFT must maintain confidentiality

43. A client comes to therapy expressing concern about his 94-year-old mother. The client tells the therapist that his mother, who lives a few houses down from the client, has been refusing to eat and is unwilling to leave her home to see a doctor. She is losing weight and appears to be in declining health, but wants simply to be left alone. The client is unsure of how to help. The LMFT should:

    a. Encourage the client to openly discuss his concern with his mother
    b. Encourage the client to transport his mother to a doctor for evaluation even if it means doing so against her will
    c. Encourage the client to report the situation to his local adult protective service agency
    d. Report the situation to the local adult protective service agency

44. An LMFT takes notes during sessions in order to track key moments in session and important words or phrases used by various clients. The LMFT keeps these handwritten notes separate from clients' files. The LMFT receives a court order for all available treatment records on one of the LMFT's clients. That client has an extensive file, as the LMFT had seen the client for more than 100 sessions. The LMFT should:

    a. Respond to the court order by asserting privilege
    b. Respond to the court order by providing a treatment summary
    c. Respond to the court order by providing the full file for the client, without the handwritten notes that had been kept separately
    d. Respond to the court order by providing the full file for the client and all handwritten notes pertaining to the client's sessions

45. An LMFT is working with a religious family whose son has been diagnosed with a blood disorder. While not fatal, the disorder could impact the boy's growth and development. The family tells you that after meeting with multiple doctors, they have elected to use only spiritual healing for their son, and to put his health "in God's hands." The LMFT should:

    a.   Advise the clients to utilize Western medicine techniques known to treat the disorder

    b.   Report suspected child abuse

    c.   Report suspected child neglect

    d.   Discuss with the family how they reached their decision and what its possible impacts could be

46. A client comes to an LMFT and identifies himself as the victim of intimate partner violence. He describes instances of his wife physically assaulting him and threatening him with a gun. He tells the LMFT that his wife is a police officer who is skilled with technology and monitors their bank accounts closely. He asks the LMFT to see him on a cash-only basis with no physical receipts, and to not keep any records of her treatment, as he is worried those records could be used by his wife to discover where he is currently staying and to describe him in future divorce proceedings as mentally unfit for custody of their children. Considering the LMFT's ethical responsibilities, the LMFT should:

    a.   Agree to the client's requests

    b.   Inform the client that neither of his requests can be honored

    c.   Agree to the client's requests surrounding payment, and inform the client that records from treatment of intimate partner violence are not subject to subpoena

    d.   Agree to the client's requests surrounding payment, and inform him that clinical records must be kept, but that those records will not include any information about his mental health

47. A young adult seeks the services of an LMFT to help him determine his life path. He specifically asks the LMFT to help him learn how to perform household tasks like laundry and help with financial management, explaining that since he had spent many years in a series of foster homes as a child, he never learned these skills. The LMFT should:

a. Turn away the client and refer him to community resources
b. Turn away the client and refer him to three other therapists
c. Accept the client and focus on the skills he is asking to learn
d. Accept the client and focus on the trauma he suffered in the foster care system

48. An LMFT has been working with a client who describes himself as a computer hacker. Sessions have focused on his difficulty in building friendships and romantic relationships. In session, the client tells the therapist that he was easily able to obtain a great deal of personal information about her, including her home address, bank account balances, and social security number. He sees that the LMFT is unsettled by this, and assures her he has no intention of misusing the information. The LMFT should:

a. Contact law enforcement and report the data theft, without revealing that the person suspected is a client
b. Discontinue treatment and refer the client to at least three other therapists
c. Make it a condition of treatment that the client delete all of this data from any place where he has it stored
d. Consult with an attorney and monitor her accounts closely

49. A client who has expressed great concern about anyone knowing she is in therapy passes out in the middle of a session. The LMFT the client was seeing is able to wake her long enough to learn that she has recently been struggling with illness and has pain from a neck injury, and the LMFT knows from the client's intake paperwork that she has a blood disorder. The LMFT should:

    a.  Stay with the client and continue attempting to wake her
    b.  Call 911 and transport the client outside of the office into a public area to protect her privacy
    c.  Call 911 and summon paramedics without providing any information about the client or her illness
    d.  Call 911, summon paramedics, and inform them of the client's medical issues

50. A few days after a particularly difficult session, a client asks her therapist (an LMFT) to show her the information the LMFT wrote in the client's file about that session. The client had discussed childhood trauma and tells the LMFT she wants any information about that trauma removed immediately from the file. The LMFT empathizes with the client, but had included information about the trauma in progress notes and believes it is important to the client's treatment. Legally, the LMFT should:

    a.  Comply with the client's request by sharing the progress note and removing any offending information from the file within 15 days
    b.  Inform the client that the client is free to review the file but that the LMFT cannot comply with the client's request to change the note
    c.  Inform the client that she may replace the progress note from the session with a statement of up to 250 words that she has written herself
    d.  Refuse the client's request and process her reasons for wanting to keep the information secret

51. A client calls her therapist, an LMFT, from a train headed outside of California. The two have typically been working via video with the client's consent, so the LMFT is initially surprised that the client called in by phone. The client tells the LMFT that she expects the train will cross out of California in about 20 minutes, but that there is no way for her to know when exactly that happens. The LMFT should:

    a.  End the conversation within about 20 minutes
    b.  Continue the session for the fully scheduled time
    c.  Conduct a crisis assessment and then immediately end the call
    d.  Confirm the client's formal state of residency

52. A middle-aged man who is seeing a psychologist to work on his symptoms of anxiety inquires with an LMFT about the possibility of the man and his wife seeing the LMFT for couple counseling. The man explains that while some of his anxiety is about how others in his life perceive him, this is improving with treatment and he sees this as being markedly different from the work he and his wife would do with the LMFT. The couple have been together for eight years and have two children. The LMFT should:

    a.  Defer the request and ask the man to wait for couple counseling until the individual treatment is concluded.
    b.  Accept the man and his wife as a couple client, and encourage the man to discontinue individual therapy while the couple work is in progress.
    c.  Consider the potential conflicts involved in the man seeing two therapists simultaneously for treatment of issues that may be intertwined.
    d.  Refuse the request on the grounds that his anxiety is already being appropriately treated.

53. A client asks to use her insurance to pay for therapy with an LMFT, as she would not be able to pay out of pocket. The client's husband works for a large multinational corporation, and the client's insurance is provided through that corporation. The client tells the LMFT that she believes she may have Borderline Personality Disorder and Substance Use Disorder, and does not want her husband or the corporation to learn of these diagnoses. The LMFT should:

    a.  Provide referrals to low-fee clinics
    b.  Discuss what information is provided to insurers, and what the client's treatment options may be
    c.  Contact the insurer to advocate for the client
    d.  Advise the client to seek a court order that will seal her treatment records

54. A couple has been seeing an LMFT for premarital counseling. Toward the end of the counseling, they ask the LMFT whether she would be willing to attend the wedding and speak briefly at the reception about what makes the couple such a good fit. They say they have no problem with introducing the LMFT honestly and describing her role, saying she has been very helpful to them. They believe their families would be happy to meet her and to share their thanks as well. The LMFT should:

    a.  Politely refuse the request
    b.  Consider the cultural implications of the request and the potential impact on any future treatment
    c.  Attend the wedding, but decline to speak, and ask that she not be introduced as a therapist
    d.  Have the clients sign a release of information authorizing the LMFT to speak candidly, and then do so, consistent with the clients' request

55. An adolescent male client tells an LMFT that he is drawn to violent movies and video games, and spends a great deal of time fantasizing about what he would do if confronted with a situation where he would need to become violent to survive. Though he has no history of violence or substance use, the client is struggling in school and the family has guns in the home. The LMFT should:

   a. Assess for safety and for psychotic disorder
   b. Assess for substance use disorder
   c. Develop a safety plan
   d. Engage in discussion of what makes the games, movies, and fantasies so appealing

56. An Associate MFT has been working under supervision in a private practice setting for two years. The Associate achieves licensure, and informs the supervisor that the Associate will be starting their own private practice. The now-former Associate would like to bring their current clients along to the new practice. How can the Associate MFT best address their ethical responsibilities?

   a. Understand that the clients are ultimately clients of the supervisor, and allow the clients to determine how they wish to proceed
   b. Understand that the clients are ultimately clients of the supervisor, and allow the supervisor to determine which clients may follow the new licensee into their private practice
   c. Retain the files for all clients who wish to follow the new licensee into their private practice, allowing the supervisor to make copies if the supervisor wishes
   d. Allow the clients to determine whether to follow the new licensee into private practice, paying the supervisor a fee for each client who does so. This fee covers the supervisor's costs for marketing that brought the clients in to see the Associate originally

57. After consulting with an attorney and a colleague, an LMFT makes a child abuse report. The LMFT had learned from a family being seen together in treatment that the parents engage in physical punishment of their children. Three weeks after the report was made, the parents in the family ask directly in session whether the LMFT was the person who made the report. The parents have been frustrated and hope to confront the reporting party, as they do not believe their behavior is abusive and are embarrassed and angry that an investigator from the local child protective service agency visited their home and their child's school. The investigator was ultimately unable to substantiate the abuse report. Ethically, the LMFT should:

    a.  Acknowledge having made the report and share the specific reasons why the LMFT did so
    b.  Acknowledge having made the report, apologize for having done so, and work to repair the relationship
    c.  Deny having made the report, and empathize with their emotional response to the investigation
    d.  Deny having made the report, and guide the conversation back to the reasons why the family is in treatment

58. An LMFT receives a request from a former client for their complete therapy records. The client's treatment occurred four years ago. When the LMFT locates the former client's file, the LMFT finds that the file is disorganized, and consists mostly of brief, handwritten notes. The LMFT, whose current record-keeping is much improved, is embarrassed by the state of this old file. How should the LMFT address their legal responsibilities in this case?

    a.  Only agree to provide the client a written treatment summary in lieu of the full record
    b.  Recreate the handwritten notes in a more structured, typed format, adding details as needed. Discard the handwritten notes and provide the updated record within 10 days of the client's request
    c.  Refuse to release the file, on the grounds that it may be damaging to the LMFT's relationship with the former client
    d.  Release the file in its current form, and offer to address any questions the former client may have

59. In group supervision, several MFT associates and their supervisor (who is a licensed MFT) are discussing whether the client of one of the associates should make a report of suspected child abuse. The associate who has seen the client says she does not believe the situation warrants a report. The other associates believe there is enough information to form reasonable suspicion of abuse, based on what the associate who has seen the client has said in describing the case. The supervisor validates the arguments being made by both sides, and after a long discussion, their positions are unchanged. The Associate MFT who has seen the case should:

    a.   Make a report of suspected child abus
    b.   Defer a decision on reporting until she can conduct further assessment
    c.   Hold to her belief that a report is not warranted unless new information comes to light that would change her view
    d.   Consult with the local child protective service agency

60. An individual client tells an LMFT that she is in fear of her husband. The couple has a long history of severe intimate partner violence, and there are protective orders in place requiring that they couple stay away from each other except when meeting in supervised locations to hand off their children. Now that the couple is finally divorcing, the husband has begun leaving threatening voicemails. The client plays one such voicemail for the LMFT, who agrees that the client may be in danger. The LMFT should:

    a.   Notify law enforcement and warn the victim
    b.   Attempt to contact the husband to reduce the danger
    c.   Encourage the client to notify law enforcement
    d.   Notify the court that the husband is violating the protective order

61. An LMFT has been working with a family for several sessions and plans a session where the entire family will participate in a ceremony relieving the oldest daughter of the responsibility she has taken on as a co-parent. Shortly before the session, the mother informs the LMFT that she will be away on a business trip and asks whether she can participate in the session by phone or videoconferencing. The mother's frequent absences are part of the reason why the daughter felt obligated to take on parenting tasks. The LMFT should:

    a. Contact the BBS to see whether the LMFT can include the mother in session while she is on her trip
    b. Include the mother in the session and in the ceremony via phone or videoconference, and clarify that her involvement is consultation rather than therapy
    c. Refuse the mother's request and reschedule the ceremony for a time she can attend in person
    d. Contact the other family members to see whether they believe including the mother would be appropriate

62. An LMFT's new 34-year-old client recently moved to the US from another country. Though the LMFT not familiar with the other country's culture, the LMFT finds that they strongly like the client. The client appears intelligent and confident, and tells the LMFT that the client is also interested in becoming a therapist someday. The LMFT finds it difficult to develop concrete therapeutic goals with the client, as it seems the conversation in therapy over the first two sessions has been more social in nature. The LMFT should:

    a. Learn more about the other country's culture and social norms, to determine whether the client's behavior is normal
    b. Because the client is from a culture that is not familiar to the LMFT, refer the client to another therapist due to scope of competence
    c. Attend therapy to address the pathology that underlies the LMFT's immediate fondness for the client
    d. Assign the treatment goals the LMFT feels would be best, reminding the client that the client is free to participate or not participate in therapy as the client sees fit

63. A 37-year-old married client wishes to use their insurance to pay for substance use treatment provided by an LMFT. The LMFT is not in-network with the insurance company, but provides the client with superbills that the client then submits to the insurer. The insurance company contacts the LMFT to ask for more information on the client's treatment, including the client's diagnosis, the client's date of birth, and a copy of the treatment contract, before issuing payment. The LMFT attempts to contact the client but is unable to do so. Considering the LMFT's legal responsibilities, how may the LMFT address the insurance company's request?

    a. File a complaint with the state Department of Managed Health Care
    b. Contact the client's spouse to seek their permission to release records on the client's behalf
    c. Provide the requested documentation to the insurer
    d. Provide a copy of the client file, and a copy of the insurer's request, to an external licensed therapist to determine whether the insurer's request it reasonable under the circumstances

64. An LMFT is planning her retirement in a few months, and has agreed to sell her private practice to a local colleague. Several weeks before she turns the practice over, the LMFT should:

    a. Inform clients of her plans, and instruct them to continue as usual with the colleague as the colleague takes over
    b. Inform clients of her plans, and request that each client who wishes to continue treatment with the colleague sign a Release of Information form allowing their files to be transferred
    c. Inform clients of her plans, and offer to do a series of transitional sessions with each client while they are simultaneously starting therapy with the colleague
    d. Inform clients of her plans, and draft a transition document for the colleague

65. A client asks whether her 75-year-old mother can be part of her therapy. The mother speaks English, but can only read and write in her native language, which the LMFT is not familiar with. The LMFT believes that including the mother in the therapy may be helpful to the client. The LMFT should:

    a. Have the mother sign the informed consent form and join the therapy

    b. Verbally discuss the process, risks, and benefits of therapy with the mother to help her decide whether to join the therapy, and document the discussion and her response

    c. Refer the mother to a therapist who speaks her native language, and ask the client to sign a Release of Information form authorizing the LMFT to speak to that therapist

    d. Ask the mother to teach the LMFT her native language so that the LMFT can provide all appropriate paperwork in her language

66. A mother presents her 11-year-old child for treatment from an LMFT. The mother notes that the child has been struggling in school and in social relationships, and the mother is concerned that the child may be experimenting with drugs. The mother says she is willing to provide consent for treatment, and notes that she and the child's father were never married. Legally, the LMFT must:

    a. Have the mother provide consent for the child's treatment

    b. Seek consent from both the mother and the child's father

    c. Evaluate the 11-year-old's capacity to independently consent for treatment

    d. Report suspected child neglect based on the 11-year-old's potential drug use

67. An LMFT is working with an individual client who is contemplating moving out of the state. The client has twin 5-year-old children with her spouse, and the client says she is prepared to let her spouse have primary custody. The client explains that her marriage is failing and she cannot find work in California, but that her family in another state is prepared to give her a place to live and help connect her with possible jobs. She says she wants to be a good parent and maintain good relationships with her spouse and children. How should the LMFT proceed?

    a.  Help the client develop and consider possible outcomes of the move, and possible alternatives

    b.  Consider the family to be the client and support maintaining the family structure until instructed otherwise by the client

    c.  Offer to connect the client with a therapist in what will be their new state, including sending records if the client will allow

    d.  Inform the client that the therapist will listen and reflect as the client weighs their options, but that the LMFT will not guide the discussion in any way

68. An LMFT is working for a large nonprofit agency, which handles all aspects of client billing. The agency informs the LMFT that, as of one week from today, the agency will begin reporting unpaid balances to a collection agency when the balance is more than 30 days overdue. The LMFT objects, arguing that current and past clients with overdue balances have not been informed of this and that such reporting may have negative impacts on clients with both financial and mental health struggles. The agency insists that letters will be sent to all clients with overdue balances. How should the LMFT manage the ethical issues in this case?

    a.  Since the business relationship is between the client and the agency, not between the client and the LMFT, no action is required

    b.  Offer to personally take on the balances of clients who owe the agency, such that the therapist can collect balances as they see fit

    c.  Discontinue their employment at the agency, and seek alternative employment instead

    d.  Attempt to negotiate with agency administrators for more notice to potentially-impacted clients

69. To show support for the local high school basketball team, an LMFT advertises that new clients can receive their first six sessions at a per-session fee equal to the number of points scored by the basketball team's opponent in their most recent game. So, if the team plays great defense, new clients receive lower fees. After six sessions, clients who wish to continue therapy would do so at the LMFT's standard rate of $120 per session. Which best reflects the LMFT's legal obligations related to this promotion?

    a.  The LMFT cannot include a temporary or promotional fee in their advertising

    b.  The LMFT must include both the promotional rate and the standard rate in all advertisements

    c.  The LMFT must inform each new client, prior to the beginning of services, what their specific rate would be and why

    d.  The LMFT must set a minimum and maximum rate to protect both clients and the therapist from potential exploitation if basketball scores are unusually high or low

*Question 70 is on the next page.*

70. A couple in their 40s brings their 15-year-old child into therapy and expresses concern for the 15-year-old's safety and wellbeing. The parents report that the 15-year-old has begun identifying as a lesbian, and the parents are worried that this will cause problems in the family's conservative community. The parents say that they support their child, but are hopeful that the LMFT will help the child to also become more attracted to men, or at least to reduce attractions to women until such time as the child is old enough to move out. The LMFT expresses sensitivity to both the child's orientation and the parents' safety concerns, and is unsure of how to proceed. Considering the LMFT's ethical obligations, what should the LMFT do in this situation?

  a.  Provide services to the family under the banner of coaching or consulting, not as an LMFT
  b.  Seek articles and trainings related to adolescents who have faced similar situations
  c.  Work with the child toward a temporary identification as asexual, until such time as it is safe for them to identify openly as lesbian
  d.  Agree to provide services to the family as an LMFT only if doing so is consistent with every family member's religious beliefs, including the minor's

*Question 71 is on the next page.*

71. A 61-year-old individual client of an LMFT and the client's 66-year-old spouse were vacationing at a popular theme park when an argument between the spouses about what to get for lunch turned violent. They wrestled each other to the floor and had to be separated by park security. Both spouses were treated for their injuries and escorted out of the park. When the client tells this story at their next session, they tell the LMFT that the couple has been violent with one another for 10 years, since shortly after their youngest child moved out of the house. What must the LMFT do next?

    a.   Report the couple's extensive violence to local law enforcement
    b.   Report to the local adult protective service agency that the 66-year-old is a victim of suspected elder abuse
    c.   Require the partners to live in separate homes until they have established at least a 90-day window of nonviolence
    d.   Gather information from the theme park, including any notes and reports the park made about the incident, to determine whether any additional reporting is necessary

72. A 29-year-old woman brings her 19-year-old brother to an LMFT's office and explains that the brother needs therapy to address issues of grief and depression. The brother has some developmental delays and is illiterate, but is a legal adult and is not under conservatorship. The woman explains that she would be willing to provide consent for the brother's treatment and take financial responsibility for it, and could be in or out of the therapy based on the brother's preference and the LMFT's assessment. How should the LMFT fufill his ethical responsibilities?

    a.   Allow the sister to provide consent signatures for herself and her brother, and assess to determine the most appropriate unit of treatment
    b.   Ask the brother whether he is comfortable allowing his sister to consent to treatment on his behalf, and document his decision
    c.   Inform the sister that she can participate in therapy if the brother allows, but that he must be financially responsible for his treatment
    d.   Interview the brother individually to discuss risks and benefits of treatment, and assess his desire to participate

73. Six months after the end of their supervision relationship, an LMFT supervisor and their former supervisee encounter one another at a party. They express their attraction to each other and would like to develop a sexual relationship. The LMFT supervisor is still serving as therapist to a few clients that had previously been seen by the former supervisee. Which of the following best reflects the ethical obligations of both therapists?

    a.  The LMFT supervisor and the former supervisee may enter into a sexual relationship
    b.  The LMFT supervisor and the former supervisee may not enter into a sexual relationship until two years have elapsed since their last professional contact
    c.  The LMFT supervisor and the former supervisee may not enter into a sexual relationship until the LMFT supervisor has terminated therapy with all of the former supervisee's former clients
    d.  The LMFT supervisor and the former supervisee may not enter into a sexual relationship until the former supervisee is licensed, making the two professional equals

74. At a busy group practice, an LMFT observes that a colleague has been increasingly letting sessions go past their scheduled end time, and that the colleague's office has become disorganized. The colleague explains that they have been going through a divorce, and fighting for custody of their children. The colleague has been using cocaine to keep their energy up for client care, but feels "out of gas" to maintain client boundaries or organize their office. Considering the LMFT's ethical obligations, the LMFT should:

    a.  Pause referring clients to the colleague, and take no further action
    b.  Offer to connect the colleague with legal, substance use treatment, or other resources
    c.  Report the colleague's behavior to the BBS
    d.  To protect the interests of clients, threaten to inform the owners of the group practice about the colleague's behavior unless the colleague enters substance use treatment

75. During the assessment process in outpatient therapy, a 38-year-old woman describes to an LMFT the woman's long history of troubled romantic relationships. The woman carries a diagnosis of Borderline Personality Disorder. She reports that she was sexually abused as a child, had several difficult dating experiences, once had a threesome with the therapist she and her husband were seeing for couple therapy, later divorced that husband, and has had a series of brief romantic relationships with married people. She has been through a great deal of therapy, she says, but she asks the LMFT not to request prior treatment records. Considering the LMFT's legal responsibilities, the LMFT should:

    a.   Contact the client's prior clinicians to request records from prior treatment

    b.   Consider whether the client's statements are likely to be truthful, considering all relevant assessment data

    c.   Provide the client with a copy of the brochure *Therapy Never Includes Sexual Behavior*

    d.   Consider whether the client is in need of a higher level of care

# - STOP HERE -
# END OF TEST

# Practice Test:
# Quick Answer Key

# Quick Answer Key

| | | | |
|---|---|---|---|
| 1. C | 21. C | 41. C | 61. C |
| 2. D | 22. C | 42. A | 62. A |
| 3. D | 23. D | 43. D | 63. C |
| 4. C | 24. C | 44. D | 64. B |
| 5. C | 25. B | 45. D | 65. B |
| 6. B | 26. B | 46. B | 66. A |
| 7. A | 27. A | 47. A | 67. A |
| 8. C | 28. A | 48. D | 68. D |
| 9. A | 29. D | 49. D | 69. C |
| 10. C | 30. A | 50. B | 70. B |
| 11. D | 31. B | 51. A | 71. B |
| 12. B | 32. D | 52. C | 72. D |
| 13. B | 33. A | 53. B | 73. A |
| 14. D | 34. B | 54. B | 74. B |
| 15. A | 35. A | 55. D | 75. C |
| 16. C | 36. A | 56. A | |
| 17. B | 37. B | 57. A | |
| 18. B | 38. A | 58. D | |
| 19. A | 39. C | 59. A | |
| 20. B | 40. D | 60. C | |

# Subscale scoring

The numbers below refer to **question numbers** aligned with each of the major content areas in the exam. You can use these subscale scores to assess your strengths and weaknesses and guide additional study.

| Law | | | Ethics | | |
|---|---|---|---|---|---|
| Confidentiality, privilege, and consent | Limits to confidentiality, including mandated reporting | Legal standards for professional practice | Professional competence and preventing harm | Therapeutic relationship | Business practices and policies |
| 23 | 3 | 5 | 10 | 1 | 2 |
| 25 | 4 | 9 | 11 | 6 | 7 |
| 26 | 8 | 28 | 14 | 15 | 12 |
| 29 | 13 | 38 | 18 | 16 | 17 |
| 36 | 22 | 53 | 19 | 20 | 21 |
| 44 | 35 | 69 | 24 | 27 | 33 |
| 49 | 39 | 75 | 30 | 32 | 34 |
| 50 | 40 | | 31 | 37 | 56 |
| 58 | 42 | | 41 | 46 | 61 |
| 63 | 43 | | 45 | 48 | 73 |
| 66 | 59 | | 47 | 51 | 74 |
| | 71 | | 54 | 52 | |
| | | | 67 | 55 | |
| | | | 70 | 57 | |
| | | | | 60 | |
| | | | | 62 | |
| | | | | 64 | |
| | | | | 65 | |
| | | | | 68 | |
| | | | | 72 | |
| Total: ____ out of 11 | Total: ____ out of 12 | Total: ____ out of 7 | Total: ____ out of 14 | Total: ____ out of 20 | Total: ____ out of 11 |
| Law Total: ____ out of 30 | | | Ethics Total: ____ out of 45 | | |

# Practice Test:
# Answers and Rationales

1. A family consisting of a 25-year-old man, his 19-year-old nonbinary sibling, and their 50-year-old mother presents to an LMFT for family therapy. The man has been recently diagnosed with schizophrenia, and at the direction of his physician has begun taking medication for it. He also has started seeing an individual therapist. The family is seeking family therapy to manage their interactions around the son and provide support. The LMFT should:

a. **Incorrect.** Avoid providing family-based treatment while the man is also seeing an individual therapist

b. **Incorrect.** Agree to provide treatment to the family only if the LMFT also takes over individual therapy, to ensure consistency between the two therapies

c. **CORRECT.** Discuss how family treatment would differ from individual therapy, and determine whether to seek the man's permission to consult with the individual therapist

d. **Incorrect.** Advise the family to wait 90 days for the medication to take its full effect prior to proceeding with either individual or family-based psychotherapy

While LMFTs should be cautious about the possibility of providing duplicative treatment, it is possible to provide family-based therapy to someone who is also seeing an individual therapist. The LMFT simply needs to take steps to minimize possible confusion or conflict between the two therapies. Discussing the differences, and consulting with the other therapist, are good ways to do so.

2. An LMFT is serving as the individual therapist for an adult client who is a well-known artist. The LMFT has implemented processes of collaborative documentation in the LMFT's practice in an effort to reduce hierarchy. The client proposes that, starting with the following week's session, the LMFT and the client spend the last 10 minutes of each session on a small watercolor painting, which would serve as their documentation of both the content and experience of the session. Ethically, the LMFT should:

a. **Incorrect.** Consider the client's cultural background in assessing the appropriateness of the request
b. **Incorrect.** Insist that each watercolor be marked with the session date, time, length, and location
c. **Incorrect.** Consider the cost of supplying paint, brushes, and paper or canvases appropriate to this purpose
d. **CORRECT.** Consider the potential therapeutic benefit of this process, while ensuring that typical written documentation also continues

LMFTs are required to create and maintain records that are adequate and consistent with the standards of the profession. Using collaborative watercolors as treatment records would not be consistent with those standards. The LMFT should insist upon ongoing written documentation. The other options here each may be worthwhile considerations, but only the option for ongoing written documentation reflects an ethical obligation.

3. A 29-year-old client being treated by an LMFT in a community mental health agency reports sleeping outside and refusing food, because the client is hearing voices telling them that their family is trying to poison them. The client has been prescribed medication but believes that this, too, is an effort to poison them. The client appears underweight and dehydrated, and the LMFT learns that the client has a sister who has been appointed by the court to protect the client's legal rights. How should the LMFT address the situation, considering their legal obligations?

    a.  **Incorrect.** Contact the sister to coordinate treatment
    b.  **Incorrect.** Connect the client with services offering housing and food assistance
    c.  **Incorrect.** Report the client's suspicion that their family is attempting to poison them
    d.  **CORRECT.** Report suspected dependent adult neglect

The client qualifies as a dependent adult and is engaging in self-neglect. Reporting this may ultimately help the client receive the care they need. Offering the client housing and food services may or may not be helpful, considering their symptoms, but in either case is not a legal requirement.

4. An adult client with an extensive history of gambling seeks couple therapy with his wife of 14 years. Despite the best efforts of an LMFT, the treatment fails, and the couple chooses to divorce. The man's gambling worsens, eventually leaving him bankrupt. He sues the LMFT, claiming that the LMFT's misconduct negatively impacted his mental health, causing him to lose his job and ultimately run out of money. The LMFT believes that records of the case will ultimately lead a court to rule in the LMFT's favor, but the client refuses to release the records. Instead, the client goes on television, where he discloses his gambling and therapy history and again accuses the therapist of misconduct. Legally, how should the LMFT proceed?

    a.   **Incorrect.** Disclose the client file to the public, as the client has waived confidentiality with his own disclosures to the media
    b.   **Incorrect.** Disclose the client file to the court
    c.   **CORRECT.** Through an attorney, move to submit the client file into evidence
    d.   **Incorrect.** Through an attorney, contact the client in a good-faith effort to have the records released

The client's accusation of therapist breach of duty is an exception to privilege, but it is the role of the court, and not the therapist, to make that determination. The therapist should move to submit the client file into evidence, and the client can raise privilege claims in dispute of this if they wish. The file should not be disclosed unless and until a judge has determined that privilege does not apply.

5. A recently-licensed LMFT is interested in helping others successfully navigate the licensure process. She posts to a closed group of licensed and prelicensed therapists on a popular social media platform about her experience taking her clinical exam. In her post, she encourages those about to take their tests to focus their diagnostic review on mood disorders and schizophrenia, as these came up multiple times on her test. Considering the LMFT's legal responsibilities, this post could result in:

    a.   **Incorrect.** No action against the LMFT, as she was not specific about the questions she was asked

    b.   **Incorrect.** No action against the LMFT, as the post was to a closed group and not the general public

    c.   **CORRECT.** Action against the LMFT's license

    d.   **Incorrect.** A jail sentence for the LMFT

While the LMFT's post doesn't reveal specific test questions, it does provide detailed enough information to give those who see it an unfair advantage on their tests. Even though it is not open to the public, the social media group still includes prelicensed therapists who may soon be taking the test themselves. The LMFT's post would be considered unprofessional conduct. Unprofessional conduct can result in actions against one's license or registration, but these administrative actions are different from criminal charges that could result in jail time.

6. A family of five comes to an LMFT to address family conflict surrounding the family's business. The parents own an auto body shop. Their children, ages 16, 19, and 22, are all working there but are interested in pursuing their own careers. The parents are concerned that the body shop cannot survive if it has to hire outside workers, and they want the shop to be a place the children can rely on. The children express love and support for their parents but openly wonder whether the business should survive if it is relying on their underpaid work. How should the LMFT proceed with the family?

    a. **Incorrect.** Allow the parents to set the goals of treatment, while recognizing that the 19-year-old and 22-year-old may choose not to participate

    b. **CORRECT.** Attempt to define goals for therapy that all family members can agree upon

    c. **Incorrect.** Separate the units of treatment to better support their specific interests, seeing the parents as a couple and each child individually

    d. **Incorrect.** Refer out as this is outside of the LMFT's scope of practice

This is an example of a situation in which family treatment could present a conflict, as what the parents perceive as best for the family doesn't appear to align with what the kids perceive as best for the family. Rather than simply abandoning the idea of family treatment, the LMFT should first see whether there are shared goals that the family could align around.

7. An LMFT is providing couple therapy to a separated couple with two young children. Both partners have given the LMFT permission to testify at an upcoming court hearing where the judge may approve their temporary custody agreement. The LMFT has agreed to testify. As the hearing approaches, the LMFT notices that each partner seems to be trying to win the LMFT's favor, complimenting the LMFT on small changes in their office or offering small gifts. How should the LMFT manage their ethical responsibilities?

    a.   **CORRECT.** Clarify the LMFT's role as a treatment provider, and differentiate this from the role of a custody evaluator

    b.   **Incorrect.** Remind the couple that it is not legally appropriate to attempt to bribe a future witness

    c.   **Incorrect.** Draft a Testimony Agreement that clearly defines court testimony as a separate service with a separate fee

    d.   **Incorrect.** Rescind the LMFT's agreement to testify, as it should not have been given

Clarifying roles is the responsibility of the LMFT. A treatment provider's role is separate from that of a custody evaluator, and it is not clear what the parents hope they will achieve in court through their efforts.

8. An LMFT becomes concerned when a client who has been struggling with depression does not show for two consecutive sessions. The client does not respond to the LMFT's efforts to contact the client by phone and email. While the client has not signed any Releases of Information during the therapy process, they did list a friend's name and phone number in the "Emergency Contact" section of their intake paperwork. How should the LMFT proceed?

    a.   **Incorrect.** Attempt to contact the Emergency Contact solely to request that the person have the client contact the LMFT, without providing additional information

    b.   **Incorrect.** Consider the listing of someone as an "Emergency Contact" to be a limited authorization to release information in the event of an emergency, and contact them to request assistance

    c.   **CORRECT.** Continue attempting to contact the client by phone and email, and review client history for indicators of potential crisis or safety issues

    d.   **Incorrect.** Contact law enforcement or a local psychiatric emergency response team to perform a wellness check on the client

While a client with depression no-showing and not responding to attempted contacts is cause for concern, by itself the information here does not constitute an emergency. Nothing in the question suggests evidence of immediate risk for suicide or harm to others, and absent such evidence, the therapist should maintain confidentiality as they continue to attempt to contact the client. The client may be sick, traveling, uninterested in returning to therapy, or any number of other circumstances that do not justify breaking confidentiality. The LMFT should review the file for any potential crisis or safety issues they may have overlooked, but so far, none appear to be present at a level that would justify sharing client information without a release to do so. (Whether listing someone as an emergency contact serves as a release is debatable, but doesn't impact this question, as the situation is not an emergency.)

9. An LMFT has been learning about herbal medicine and its connections with overall health and wellness. The LMFT mentions this to some clients, and the clients respond with interest in learning how herbal medicine might be incorporated into their therapy processes. Some clients report difficulty with sleep and anxiety, and say they are hopeful that herbal remedies could work alongside talk therapy. How can the LMFT respond to the clients' inquiries?

    a.  **CORRECT.** Refer interested clients to external books, videos, or herbal medicine practitioners

    b.  **Incorrect.** Provide recommendations for herbal remedies only to target those issues also being addressed in therapy

    c.  **Incorrect.** Provide herbal teas, lotions, and other potential remedies specific to clients' presenting issues, noting that clients may use or apply those remedies themselves during sessions

    d.  **Incorrect.** Seek certification as an herbal wellness practitioner, and integrate herbal remedies into therapy only after receiving the appropriate certification

While they can have tremendous value, herbal remedies are not a psychotherapeutic technique. As such, they fall outside of the LMFT scope of practice, regardless of how much knowledge or training the LMFT may have on the subject. The LMFT can refer to external resources, but should not offer any remedies or specific recommendations for herbal remedies themselves.

10. In family therapy, a single father reports that he raises his two children to be strong and silent. The children, ages 7 and 10, are not allowed to question the father's decisions, and cannot go to bed at night until their homework is completed, the house is clean, and they have chosen their clothes for the next day. The family therapy surrounds lingering grief over the death of the mother two years ago. The family reports that the mother did not share all of the father's beliefs, and sometimes balanced his more strict rules. How should the LMFT address the ethical issues present in this case?

  a. **Incorrect.** Urge the father to integrate the mother's memory in the family by loosening some rules
  b. **Incorrect.** Report suspected child abuse to the local child protective service agency
  c. **CORRECT.** Ask the father how he determined the rules he would set for the children
  d. **Incorrect.** Develop a transition plan to gradually loosen some rules as the children demonstrate their competence

There is nothing in the question that suggests abuse, and nothing that even suggests the children are suffering because of the father's strict rules. For the LMFT to push for changes to those rules, in the absence of any evidence that the rules are proving harmful, is imposing the LMFT's personal values onto the family. The LMFT should instead demonstrate their clinical and cultural competence by learning more about how the rules were determined.

11. A couple has been working with an LMFT as they consider whether to divorce. One spouse emails the LMFT and asks the LMFT to fantasize with them about the client and the LMFT sneaking away for a sexual encounter together. The spouse explains that they do not want to do this in real life, but that fantasizing about it simply is an outlet for their sexual frustration in their marriage. How should the LMFT proceed?

    a.  **Incorrect.** Seek permission from the other spouse to engage in the email conversation

    b.  **Incorrect.** Report the client email to the BBS, clarifying that no actual sexual encounter occurred

    c.  **Incorrect.** Reaffirm therapeutic boundaries, and consider whether the exchange could serve as a meaningful component of the couple's therapy

    d.  **CORRECT.** Explain to the client that such an exchange would not be appropriate

There is no widely accepted form of couple therapy that would encourage the therapist to participate in a client's sexual fantasies. For the LMFT to respond (with or without the other spouse's permission) would be for the LMFT to engage in inappropriate sexual communications, which is an ethical violation. The LMFT should explain to the client why this is not appropriate, and work within the therapy process to strengthen the couple's relationship.

12. A supervisee expresses frustration to their LMFT supervisor that the supervisee is still having many of the same clinical challenges they were having a year ago when they started working under the supervisor. The supervisee explains to the supervisor that the supervisee has reviewed clinical records and session tapes, and still does not understand what they are doing wrong in therapy. While some of the supervisee's clients appear to be improving, many are not. Considering the supervisor's ethical obligations, how should the supervisor proceed?

    a.  **Incorrect.** Consider terminating the supervision relationship in light of the supervisee's lack of improvement

    b.  **CORRECT.** Provide a summary of the supervisee's strengths and weaknesses as the supervisor perceives them

    c.  **Incorrect.** Reassure the supervisee that therapeutic growth is sometimes slow and inconsistent

    d.  **Incorrect.** Utilize a substitute supervisor to provide the supervisee an alternate perspective on their work

While any of the options here could theoretically be useful and appropriate, only the evaluation of supervisees represents an ethical obligation.

13. A 25-year-old Mexican-American man has been seeing an LMFT individually for several months to address auditory hallucinations. The client has had some success in quieting his internal voices with medication, but does not like the side effects of his medication and so he does not take it every day. The client's mother calls the LMFT and expresses concern that the client has not taken his medication for several days, has had worsening hallucinations telling him to kill himself, and left this morning to go for a hike armed with a large knife. The mother believes the client is planning to die by suicide. The mother lives with the client, but the LMFT does not have a release to share information with the mother. How should the LMFT address the issues presented in this case?

    a.   **Incorrect.** Do not acknowledge that the client is a client; attempt to contact the client to assess risk

    b.   **CORRECT.** Ask the mother for the client's last known location and direction of travel; contact law enforcement to initiate involuntary hospitalization

    c.   **Incorrect.** Do not acknowledge that the client is a client; review prior treatment records for evidence of risk

    d.   **Incorrect.** Ask the mother for the client's last known location and direction of travel; contact park rangers to notify other hikers who may be in the area

Even without a release, therapists may break confidentiality if necessary to protect the life of a client threatening suicide. The therapist is allowed to treat information from the mother as trustworthy, and taking it at face value, the therapist should initiate involuntary hospitalization. Contacting park rangers to notify other hikers would be treating this as a Tarasoff situation, which is not appropriate as there is no evidence in the question that the client poses a threat to others. The danger is to himself.

14. An individual client who typically gets along well with an LMFT arrives to session visibly angry. The client explains that they searched for the LMFT online, and found that the LMFT is active in political causes that the client strongly disagrees with. The client says they are unsure whether they can continue in therapy, with the knowledge of this difference in their views. How should the LMFT proceed?

    a.  **Incorrect.** Pause therapy to give both the client and the LMFT time to reflect on their positions

    b.  **Incorrect.** Consult with a supervisor or therapist on the appropriateness of the LMFT's political involvement

    c.  **Incorrect.** Reinforce boundaries and remind the client that the LMFT's personal politics do not in any way impact therapy

    d.  **CORRECT.** Discuss the client's reasons for considering ending therapy entirely

The LMFT is free to engage in political activities as they see fit, however, clients may become aware of that involvement. The LMFT might understandably see their personal politics as unrelated to the client's therapy, but in this case those politics are actively impacting therapy, and to argue otherwise would be to engage in a needless power struggle. Pausing therapy could be seen as punishing the client for raising the issue, and may be inconsistent with the client's clinical needs. The best option would be to discuss the differences between the client and the LMFT in a non-defensive manner that allows for an informed decision about whether their relationship can continue.

15. An LMFT in private practice has chosen to specialize in working with "long-term married" couples, which the LMFT defines as having been married for at least 20 years. The LMFT notes that they are willing to make exceptions for same-sex couples who have been together for at least that long, as they may not have been legally able to marry when they got together. The LMFT is approached by an unmarried couple with four children, ranging in ages from 4 to 19. The couple explains that they are seeking treatment for their relationship, and they are fully committed to each other, they simply chose never to marry. The LMFT believes that marriage creates bonds and obligations for a couple that cannot be replicated outside of marriage. How should the LMFT address the ethical issues present?

a. **CORRECT.** Offer treatment to the couple, and build competency in committed, non-marital relationships

b. **Incorrect.** Refer the couple to qualified therapists who do not share the LMFT's beliefs about marriage

c. **Incorrect.** Accept the couple for treatment on a probationary basis, to assess whether their relationship is meaningfully similar to a marriage

d. **Incorrect.** Clarify the reasoning behind the policy and its connections to the LMFT's religious belief

Refusing to treat the couple, or accepting them on a probationary basis when a married couple would simply be accepted into treatment, would be discriminating on the basis of marital status. That is expressly prohibited by LMFT ethical standards, and any connections to the LMFT's religious belief would not change that. The only ethically acceptable option here is to accept the couple and ensure competence in treating them.

16. An LMFT is working with a family consisting of a mother and her three daughters, when the LMFT develops reasonable suspicion that the oldest daughter was physically abused by her sixth-grade teacher. The family is undocumented and has actively sought to avoid any involvement with government systems other than the girls' school for fear of deportation or the family being forcibly broken up. How should the LMFT manage the potential impact of reporting on the clinical relationship?

 a. **Incorrect.** Make the report of suspected child abuse anonymously
 b. **Incorrect.** Not disclose to the family that the LMFT is making the report of suspected child abuse
 c. **CORRECT.** Inform the family about the report and attempt to address their fears
 d. **Incorrect.** Balance the potential benefits of reporting against the potential risks when determining whether to make the report

Reporting here is a legal obligation, and the therapist must include their name in the reporting in order to fulfill their mandated reporting obligations. Informing clients about the required sharing of otherwise-confidential information is generally preferable to not informing them, especially when their fears about the information sharing can potentially be addressed. Here, the best path is to inform the family about the therapist's reporting mandate, and attempt to directly address the family's fears.

17. While browsing a popular mobile phone app where people can share short videos, an LMFT is shocked to see a former client from 10 years ago holding up the LMFT's picture and repeatedly saying "This psychologist saved my life." The former client explains how they had struggled with depression and suicidality, and came through it thanks to the therapy process. The video ends with the client saying, "If you're a client now, you're lucky. Next time you go to session... say thanks for me, ok?" The LMFT no longer has records from the client's treatment, but sees that they can contact the former client through the app. Ethically, how should the LMFT proceed?

    a.   **Incorrect.** Contact the app's support team to request that the video be taken down, without revealing why

    b.   **CORRECT.** Contact the former client to request that they change the word "psychologist" since the LMFT is not one

    c.   **Incorrect.** Contact the former client to ask that they take down the video, as it would be considered a testimonial

    d.   **Incorrect.** Post a response video thanking the former client, providing the therapist's contact information, and including all legally required disclosures

Clients and former clients are free to speak of their therapy as they see fit. Testimonials themselves are not prohibited; LMFTs are only prohibited from seeking them if the client is "vulnerable to undue influence." However, the client is misrepresenting the LMFT's licensure by calling them a Psychologist, and LMFTs do have an ethical obligation to attempt to correct such misrepresentations. Contacting the former client is the best way to do so. Contacting the app's support team to request that a video be taken down, without explaining why, is unlikely to be successful, and in any case could leave the former client making similarly misleading statements on the app and elsewhere.

18. An LMFT is in the process of leaving the agency where they have worked for the past five years. The agency has honored some client requests to be reassigned to other therapists in the agency, but some clients have been referred to outside providers if the client had a preference to be referred out or if their specific needs suggested that an external referral would be preferable. The LMFT's last day at the agency is one week away. How can the LMFT best assure continuity of care to clients who are being transferred?

    a.   **Incorrect.** Contract with the external providers to ensure that transferred clients will continue to pay the same fee

    b.   **CORRECT.** For clients who authorize it, speak directly with each client's new provider, and provide copies of records to external providers

    c.   **Incorrect.** Consult with a supervisor

    d.   **Incorrect.** Check back in with all transferring clients in 30 days to ensure they are satisfied with the transfer

The LMFT cannot check back in with transferring clients in 30 days unless the transferring clients have specifically authorized this contact, as the LMFT will no longer be employed by the agency at that point. The LMFT does not need to ensure that the clients are paying a consistent fee, and it is not clear what consultation with a supervisor may accomplish. But contacting new providers directly and providing records does meaningfully ensure continuity of care.

19. An LMFT attends a weeklong workshop focused on understanding human behavior in its social and cultural context. The LMFT returns to working with clients the next week, and finds that the LMFT's views of many clients have changed dramatically. Though she stands by her assessment of specific client symptoms and her observations of client behaviors, she no longer believes that most of the diagnoses she had given should be included in the clients' records, as she has come to see diagnosis as a fundamentally oppressive act. Clients express confusion at the change, and become frustrated when their insurance will no longer cover therapy. How should the LMFT proceed?

    a. **CORRECT.** Evaluate herself for impairment, and consider whether diagnosis can be given in a manner that facilitates treatment without being oppressive

    b. **Incorrect.** Explain for clients the rationale behind the decision, and reframe their behaviors as adaptive

    c. **Incorrect.** Inform clients of their right to include a supplementary statement in their files if they wish

    d. **Incorrect.** Advocate on behalf of clients for insurers to pay for treatment without a diagnosis present

The LMFT's judgment is impaired. If the LMFT stands by the observations and symptom assessments that led to the diagnoses she issued, then the diagnoses themselves should still be valid, and her refusal to continue with them is about her, not the clients. By removing the diagnoses, she is eliminating the mechanism that allows insurance to pay for clients' treatment, and is not acting in the clients' best interests. There are legitimate questions to pursue about the purpose, history, and impacts of DSM diagnosis, but simply removing the diagnoses for active clients is not the best way to pursue or address those questions. Insurers pay on the basis of medical necessity for treatment, and that necessity is established through diagnosis.

20. A client has cancelled three of the last seven scheduled sessions with an LMFT, and been a no-show for the other four. Each time, the client has promised to pay any balance charged, and to come in for a session the following week. The LMFT finds herself irritated with the client's behavior, going so far as to warn the client two weeks ago that she would simply close the client's case and refer out if the client didn't come in. The client was a no-show for the next two scheduled sessions. Even before this long series of missed appointments, the LMFT found herself personally disliking the client. How should the LMFT manage her ethical responsibilities in this case?

  a. **Incorrect.** Meaningfully assess for crisis, and continue as the client's treatment provider if necessary
  b. **CORRECT.** Close the case, providing the client with appropriate referrals to other providers
  c. **Incorrect.** Provide the client at least two additional warnings, one of which must be in writing, prior to terminating therapy
  d. **Incorrect.** Seek consultation to address countertransference, and continue to work toward the client more regularly attending therapy

LMFTs can terminate therapy for almost any reason, so long as that reason is not discriminatory in nature, any evident crisis issues are addressed, and the client is provided with appropriate referrals. In this case, the client has a pattern of non-attendance and was warned that this would lead to termination. There is no legal or ethical responsibility to provide redundant warnings (C). While assessing for crisis is generally a good idea (A), even if crisis issues were present, this would not necessarily obligate the therapist to remain the client's treatment provider. If anything, evidence of crisis combined with non-attendance in therapy might suggest a need for coordinated transfer to a higher level of care. While the LMFT's response to the client may indeed indicate countertransference (D), therapists are not legally or ethically required to continue working with clients they don't like. Termination is appropriate here.

21. A client requests and receives a copy of her clinical record from the LMFT who has been providing her with therapy. The client reviews the record and becomes visibly angry, demanding that the LMFT change the diagnosis in her file. The LMFT should:

    a. **Incorrect.** Remind the client that treatment records are the property of the therapist. *While it is accurate that records are the property of the therapist or their employer, that fact does not address the issue at hand.*

    b. **Incorrect.** Remind the client that the LMFT was not required to turn over the record at all. *The LMFT does have an obligation to release a client's records unless the LMFT believes that doing so will be harmful, which triggers a number of further legal obligations.*

    c. **CORRECT.** Remind the client that she may submit a written statement disputing the diagnosis and have that statement included in the file. *This is a legal right of any client who disagrees with something in their record.*

    d. **Incorrect.** Remind the client that the diagnosis is used simply to facilitate payment for services. *Diagnosis serves many purposes beyond facilitating payment, including the facilitation of emergency treatment and helping professionals communicate with one another.*

22. As a client leaves an LMFT's office, the LMFT believes the client poses a serious danger to the client's spouse. (The client had been making threats in session about what he would do to her.) The LMFT, knowing the couple lives roughly 30 minutes from the LMFT's office, calls the client immediately, and is able to resolve the danger. The client disavows any continued plan to harm his spouse, and apologizes to the LMFT for "getting so out of hand." What does the LMFT need to do to resolve the LMFT's legal responsibility?

    a.  **Incorrect.** Notify the spouse and law enforcement immediately
    b.  **Incorrect.** Notify the spouse immediately
    c.  **CORRECT.** Notify law enforcement within 24 hours
    d.  **Incorrect.** Notify the local child protective services agency

While warning an intended victim in a *Tarasoff* situation grants the LMFT certain additional legal protections, it is not always necessary or appropriate to do so. In this case, the LMFT was able to fully resolve the threat on their own, before notifying the intended victim or law enforcement. Still, under state law, the fact that the LMFT's *Tarasoff* responsibilities were triggered *at all* means that the LMFT must report the threatening person to law enforcement within 24 hours, even if notifying law enforcement was not necessary to resolve the initial threat. As noted in the study guide, the idea of this law is to prevent potentially dangerous individuals from buying guns.

23. A 14-year-old client consented to her own treatment at a nonprofit agency, which agreed to treat her for $5/session. The client tells the therapist (an LMFT) that the client has been abusing a friend's prescription painkillers. Legally, the LMFT should:

a. **Incorrect.** Notify the local child protective service agency
b. **Incorrect.** Notify the client's parent or guardian, as the behavior is considered high-risk
c. **Incorrect.** Work with the client to develop a plan to gradually reduce dosage and ultimately stop the client's drug use
d. **CORRECT.** Document the discussion and refer the client to a physician

Drug use, in and of itself, is not considered child abuse (a). No such report is needed. Since the client consented to treatment on their own, the parents do not have a right to the client's records; even a high-risk behavior would not be disclosed (b) unless doing so was to prevent imminent danger. Advising the client on reducing prescription drug dosage would be considered giving medical advice and is out of an LMFT's scope of practice. A referral to a physician (d) is appropriate.

24. An LMFT is working with a client in a different part of the state, one the LMFT is not familiar with, via telemedicine. During a session taking place via videoconference, the client informs the therapist that he recently lost his job and is struggling to navigate the complex web of social services in his area. He fears losing his home in a matter of weeks. Ethically, the LMFT should:

a. **Incorrect.** Volunteer to serve as the client's case manager to better coordinate his services. *Taking on a case manager role might be appropriate if the LMFT knows resources local to the client, but that is not the case here.*

b. **Incorrect.** Travel to where the client is located to provide services in person on a temporary basis. *This would be unreasonable to ask of the therapist, who is certainly not obligated to do so.*

c. **CORRECT.** Reconsider whether telemedicine services are appropriate for this client. *This best summarizes the LMFT's specific ethical responsibility in this case. We are required to evaluate whether telemedicine services are appropriate to the client's needs. In this case, the client's needs have changed, and so a reassessment of that question is appropriate.*

d. **Incorrect.** Assess for suicidality and substance use. *Assessing for suicidality may be appropriate given the job loss and potential loss of the home, but this is a clinical consideration and not an ethical one. The question is asking specifically for ethical considerations. Nothing in the question suggests substance use.*

25. An LMFT is brought in as an expert witness in a criminal case where a woman was accused of violently beating her 8-year-old daughter. The LMFT is asked by the court to speak on the long-term effects of child abuse, as well as on factors that can lead mothers to become abusive. The LMFT has expertise in these areas. The LMFT also finds the behavior that the woman is accused of repugnant. The LMFT should:

 a.  **Incorrect.** Speak solely about what the LMFT knows about the specific case being tried, and avoid speaking in generalities. *Expert witnesses should not speak on the specific case being tried. They are used to provide the court with expert knowledge on relevant subject matter.*

 b.  **CORRECT.** Speak solely from her knowledge and expertise in the field, and avoid saying anything about the specific case being tried. *This is the appropriate role of an expert witness in a court proceeding.*

 c.  **Incorrect.** Clarify for the court that no explanatory factors for abuse should be understood as making child abuse acceptable. *This is a moral, and not a scientific, stance. LMFTs in court proceedings are required to speak from their knowledge and expertise.*

 d.  **Incorrect.** Investigate the merits of the case before determining how to testify. *Expert witnesses are not called on to testify about the merits of a particular case.*

26. An LMFT turns away a prospective client after the client suggests the LMFT overbill the client's employer, who is paying for treatment through an Employee Assistance Program. The client was hoping to split the money with the therapist. Months later, the former prospective client is on trial for fraud, accused of engaging in a similar scheme with a different therapist. The LMFT is called to testify against the client. The LMFT should:

    a.   **Incorrect.** Advocate on behalf of the former prospective client
    b.   **CORRECT.** Prepare to testify
    c.   **Incorrect.** Inform the prosecutors and the court that the LMFT cannot testify
    d.   **Incorrect.** The LMFT has no obligation to respond or testify, as the person never formally became a client

There is a specific exception to privilege that applies when the therapist was sought out for the purposes of committing a crime (as was the case here) or avoiding detection after the fact. While it is ultimately up to the judge to determine whether the exception applies, the LMFT should consult an attorney and prepare to testify.

27. The client of an LMFT notices that before her session, as the LMFT is escorting her previous appointment out of the office, the LMFT and the person she is escorting out are discussing plans to have coffee together later. The client asks the LMFT about this at the beginning of her session. The client tells the LMFT that she, too, would like to have a more personal and social relationship with the therapist that involves meeting outside of the office. What should the LMFT do to manage her ethical responsibilities in this case?

    a. **CORRECT.** Consider whether the earlier appointment was confidential

    b. **Incorrect.** Inform the client that the existing relationship is not unethical as it has no negative impact on client care. Consider whether a similar relationship is possible with the current client

    c. **Incorrect.** Scold the client for inquiring about the therapist's relationships

    d. **Incorrect.** Cancel the coffee plan by phone with the client in the room, to acknowledge and take responsibility for her mistake

We have to be careful about the assumptions we make. Therapists meet with a lot of people in our offices, not all of whom are clients. The person the LMFT was escorting out of the office could have been a friend, a colleague, a business associate, or anything else. The LMFT may want to be transparent with the client about the nature of that relationship, if they can legally and ethically do so. That transparency would reduce the client's concern that another client was receiving special treatment, and reinforce the boundaries of the therapist-client relationship.

28. An online business aims to make therapy more affordable for telehealth clients by using what they call a "reverse auction" process. When a prospective client signs up with the business, the business creates a de-identified summary of client information (such as location, demographics, and presenting problem), and then allows participating therapists to "bid" on the client by posting what they would agree to charge that client per 50-minute therapy session. The therapist who has offered the lowest "bid" when the auction closes pays the business a nominal fee, and then receives the client's full information, including their name, phone number, and email address. The client is told which therapist won the auction, what fee the therapist committed to, and the therapist's contact information. How should LMFTs interact with this service?

    a. **CORRECT.** LMFTs should not participate in this service
    b. **Incorrect.** LMFTs should ensure that no actual therapy information is shared with the service
    c. **Incorrect.** LMFTs should only participate in this service if the fees they charge auction clients are in line with fees they would charge to the general public
    d. **Incorrect.** LMFTs should demand that the business do additional screening on potential clients, to address potential crisis issues

The key phrase in the question is "pays the business a nominal fee." At that point the rest of the question becomes irrelevant. LMFTs cannot charge a fee or pay a fee for referrals, and this business structure would require LMFTs to pay for each specific referral the business would generate for them. It is thus against the law for LMFTs to participate.

29. In the client's second session, the individual client of an LMFT requests a letter that would allow the client to have an emotional support dog in their apartment. The client reports that their apartment building does not typically allow dogs, but their pet dog who is currently in the care of a family member helps the client to manage their panic attacks. Considering the LMFT's legal obligations, the LMFT is required to:

    a.   **Incorrect.** Seek records from the client's prior treatment to support the need for an emotional support animal, prior to issuing such a letter

    b.   **Incorrect.** Observe the animal directly in order to be able to attest to the animal's safety

    c.   **Incorrect.** Observe the animal and the client together to directly assess the animal's impact on the client

    d.   **CORRECT.** Establish at least a 30-day clinical relationship with the client, including a full clinical assessment

Under state law, LMFTs and other therapists issuing letters for emotional support dogs must first establish a 30-day therapeutic relationship, and conduct a formal assessment, among other requirements. The therapist is not required to seek prior records, to evaluate the animal directly, or to attest to the animal's safety.

30. An LMFT is providing individual therapy to a young adult who is planning her wedding. The client and her partner are both part of a tight-knit religious community, and the LMFT believes that other members of the community could benefit from the LMFT's services, as the LMFT is familiar with this community despite not being a part of it. The client expresses that she and her partner are building the guest list for the wedding, and are struggling with the question of whether to invite guests from outside the religious community. Considering the LMFT's ethical obligations, what would be the most appropriate course of action for the LMFT to take?

    a.  **CORRECT.** Inquire further about the reasons behind the couple's struggle

    b.  **Incorrect.** Directly request an invitation to the wedding, while ensuring the couple that their confidentiality will be protected

    c.  **Incorrect.** Discuss the potential benefits to the community of inviting outsiders as guests, potentially but not necessarily including the LMFT

    d.  **Incorrect.** Express the LMFT's belief that the therapist's services could be of benefit to the community, and ask the client what the best way would be for the LMFT to support the wedding while building community connections

Note that there is nothing in the question to suggest that the client has even considered, much less that they are in favor of, specifically inviting the LMFT to the wedding. The LMFT is interested in doing so for their own sake, not out of support for the client. Seeking an invitation, influencing the client's decision by only highlighting the benefits of including outsiders, or using the wedding to build the LMFT's connections within the community are all examples of exploiting the client's trust. The LMFT should set aside their business interests and focus on supporting the client.

31. An LMFT is working with a family that chooses not to vaccinate their children or to receive most medical care because of the family's religious beliefs. Though the parents take their children to a physician for annual checkups, they otherwise avoid what they describe as the "toxic western medical establishment." The LMFT has not encountered these beliefs before, but largely dismisses them as irrelevant to the treatment being provided. The family is working in therapy on the father's anger, one child's difficulty in social relationships, and another child's regressed behavior. Considering the LMFT's ethical responsibilities, the LMFT should:

   a. **Incorrect.** Report suspected child neglect
   b. **CORRECT.** Seek out additional information on the family's religion
   c. **Incorrect.** Provide the family with information about the benefits of vaccination, while supporting their decision-making autonomy
   d. **Incorrect.** Inquire about any possible connections between the family's religion and the maladaptive behaviors of its individual members

Because the LMFT has not encountered these beliefs before, and religious beliefs can deeply impact behavioral norms and expectations, the LMFT should seek to expand their scope of competence in order to serve the client family effectively. None of the other options reflect ethical obligations.

32. An LMFT is diagnosed with a serious illness and told that they need to immediately discontinue their clinical practice. The illness is not contagious, but the LMFT's doctor believes that the LMFT cannot provide competent care due to the illness, and will need to focus all of their energy on treatment. Most clients are successfully transferred to other clinicians, but one of the LMFT's clients goes into crisis and threatens suicide if they cannot continue seeing the LMFT. The client offers to meet by telehealth instead of in-person, in hopes that this will allow for continued services. Considering their ethical responsibilities, how should the LMFT proceed?

   a. **Incorrect.** Given the risks involved, continue seeing this one client via telehealth, while discontinuing all other clinical practice
   b. **Incorrect.** Discontinue all contact with the client, as they have been notified of the transition and further contact may only further escalate them
   c. **Incorrect.** Provide two sessions on an emergency basis, but make clear that the LMFT cannot provide any further treatment
   d. **CORRECT.** Contact the client to apologize for the transition and attempt a warm handoff to another clinician

The LMFT should take reasonable steps to address the client's crisis needs, but should not continue practicing in any way while impaired to the point of incompetence. The best option is a warm handoff.

33. An LMFT in private practice is planning to raise her fees and limit her schedule in order to spend more time with her family. For most clients, she is charging $100 per session, and would like to double this to $200. She is seeing some reduced-fee clients for $50 per session, and would like to double this to $100. Considering her ethical responsibilities, what is the LMFT's best path forward in regard to raising her rates?

    a.  **CORRECT.** Provide significant advance notice of the change to ongoing clients who will be impacted

    b.  **Incorrect.** Limit the fee increase to no more than 10% per year until her fees are where she would like them to be

    c.  **Incorrect.** Apply the increase only to full-fee clients, and not to reduced-fee clients, as they are the ones most likely to experience hardship as a result of higher fees

    d.  **Incorrect.** See what fees are being charged in the local market, to ensure that her new fees are not exploitive

LMFTs are ethically obligated to provide reasonable notice of fee increases. Given the size of the increases here, it would be reasonable to provide a significant amount of advance warning. While LMFTs should provide some services at reduced rates, there is no requirement that fee increases be limited to a certain percentage, or that clients at reduced fees never experience fee increases. Whether the LMFT's new fees would be exploitive or not is dependent on the circumstances of her clients and on her own motivations, not what others in the local market charge.

34. A wealthy celebrity client continues working with an LMFT via telehealth whenever the client is traveling within California. The LMFT agrees to accommodate the client's travel schedule by arranging a telehealth session on a Saturday, when the LMFT normally does not see clients. A short time after the session concludes, the LMFT sees that the client has paid triple their usual fee, with a note that the client attached to the payment simply saying "Thank you for making time in your weekend for me." Ethically, the LMFT should:

    a. **Incorrect.** Refund the client's overpayment and explain that making it was inappropriate
    b. **CORRECT.** Discuss the meaning of the client's overpayment with them at the next session
    c. **Incorrect.** Donate the client's overpayment to a charity of the LMFT's choosing
    d. **Incorrect.** Apply the client's overpayment as a credit toward future session fees

It may be ethically sound to accept a gift from a client, depending on the clinical and cultural implications involved. In this case, the client is wealthy, so the gift does not likely represent a financial burden. Nothing in the question suggests that the client is expecting special treatment in exchange for the gift, or that they want or expect it to change the nature of the clinical relationship in any way. Such expectations are possible, and that is all the more reason for the LMFT to initiate a discussion of it at the next session. But from the information provided, the LMFT is not obligated to refuse or donate the gift, only to fully consider what it might mean.

35. An LMFT is testifying in a court case involving a 15-year-old who is accused of sexually assaulting a 14-year-old classmate. The LMFT has been seeing the 15-year-old for individual therapy, and in that process has learned that the 15-year-old was raped when they were 12. The LMFT believes this is a critical factor in the court and the victim understanding the 15-year-old's actions, but the client has been insistent that the LMFT not share this information, even though the client otherwise has given permission for the LMFT to testify. Considering state law, how should the LMFT address this situation?

   a. **CORRECT.** Seek a private meeting with the judge to explain that the minor is the victim of a crime, and that in the eyes of the LMFT, disclosure of that fact is in the client's interests
   b. **Incorrect.** Maintain confidentiality around the rape, as the client has specifically requested that information not be shared
   c. **Incorrect.** Include information about the rape in the LMFT's testimony despite the client's wishes
   d. **Incorrect.** Submit a friend-of-the-court brief, separate from the LMFT's courtroom testimony, noting that many minors who engage in inappropriate sexual behaviors have themselves been victimized

The facts here suggest that an exception to privilege applies. The minor is the victim of a crime, and in the eyes of the therapist, disclosure of that fact is in the minor's interests despite the client's expressed preferences. However, it is never up to the LMFT to determine whether an exception to privilege applies. That is a determination for a judge to make, and so the LMFT should seek to privately inform the judge of the relevant facts.

36. An LMFT is preparing to transition from working for a nonprofit organization to launching the LMFT's own private practice. The LMFT is planning to see clients under the clients' insurance, and to submit claims electronically. In preparing for the transition, the LMFT has joined the panels of three popular insurance networks. Considering the LMFT's legal obligations, the LMFT must:

    a. **CORRECT.** Conduct a formal risk analysis regarding how client data will be gathered, stored, and shared

    b. **Incorrect.** Obtain from each insurance company their list of denial and exclusion criteria, and provide this to each insured client prior to beginning therapy services

    c. **Incorrect.** Offer a sliding fee scale to clients who have other insurances or are paying out of pocket for mental health care

    d. **Incorrect.** Review the insurance contracts to ensure that the LMFT is receiving the same per-session fee from each insurance company

The fact that the LMFT is planning to submit insurance claims for payment electronically establishes that they will be a "covered entity" under HIPAA, and the risk analysis is a required component of HIPAA compliance. None of the other options here reflect a legal obligation. The LMFT is free to accept different rates from different insurers if they so choose, as long they are not violating the terms of any individual contract by doing so. Sliding fee scales for cash-pay clients also may be offered if they do not violate the terms of any specific insurance contract, but sliding scales for cash-pay clients are not legally required. The LMFT does not need to provide information about a client's insurance coverage to the client prior to beginning services.

37. A same-sex couple contacts an LMFT to arrange couple therapy. The LMFT informs the couple that, as part of the LMFT's standard couple assessment process, the LMFT will meet with the couple together first, and then with each partner individually. The couple agrees and schedules a session at the therapist's office. As the clients are walking into the office, one partner pulls the LMFT back, and quietly asks whether it is possible to tell the LMFT about "some things" that the client does not want their partner to know about. Considering the LMFT's ethical obligations, how can the LMFT best manage this situation?

    a.  **Incorrect.** Inform the client that the LMFT cannot hold individual secrets in couple therapy

    b.  **CORRECT.** Establish a policy that both partners agree to regarding how individual secrets will be handled

    c.  **Incorrect.** Ask the client to further define "some things" so that the LMFT can determine whether they would undermine the overall course of therapy

    d.  **Incorrect.** Explain that individual confidentiality is absolute, so the client can feel safe in sharing this information at the appropriate time

While there is no specific policy on secrets that is demanded by current ethical standards, those same standards indicate that the LMFT should have some policy on the issue, and it should be one that the clients have agreed to. Encouraging the client to share individual secrets without first settling on a policy could be problematic in a number of ways. Individual confidentiality is not absolute, even in individual therapy, so such an assurance would be misleading.

38. An associate marriage and family therapist is working under the supervision of an LMFT in private practice. The LMFT encourages the associate to take clients who are on the LMFT's waiting list and have an insurance plan that the LMFT participates in. For billing, the LMFT encourages the associate to use the LMFT's standard claim template, showing the LMFT as the provider. The LMFT explains that this is so that payments will be made to the LMFT and not the associate. Considering their legal obligations, the associate should:

   a. **CORRECT.** Add a note or comment onto billing documents that identifies the associate as the person who performed the therapy
   b. **Incorrect.** Adjust any billing documents to reflect the associate's name and the LMFT's license number for sessions conducted by the associate
   c. **Incorrect.** Form a separate business entity that can bill for services rendered by the associate, while still designating the LMFT as the payee
   d. **Incorrect.** Avoid billing insurance for any sessions provided by the associate

While associates can bill for services, and some insurance plans will pay for mental health services provided by associates, it would be unprofessional conduct (and potentially insurance fraud) to submit a document that suggests that the LMFT actually provided the billed services, or that the associate is actually licensed when they are not.

39. An LMFT is working with an 8-year-old girl and her mother in therapy. In their first session after the 8-year-old returned from visiting her grandparents out of state, she is shifting and squirming in her seat. Her mother tells the LMFT that the child has taken a sudden interest in learning about sex, and that the daughter has made vague statements about "learning things" on the trip but refuses to be more specific. How should the LMFT proceed?

    a.   **Incorrect.** Refer the family to the child's pediatrician to assess for possible sexual abuse

    b.   **Incorrect.** Interview the child alone to establish specific facts from the visit and investigate the likelihood that abuse took place

    c.   **CORRECT.** Report suspected child abuse to the LMFT's local child protective service agency

    d.   **Incorrect.** Because any possible abuse would have taken place outside of California, encourage the mother to report possible abuse to the appropriate agency where the grandparents are located

There is enough here for the LMFT to have reasonable suspicion of abuse. The LMFT should make a report themselves. There is no need to investigate, and in any event, investigation is not the therapist's role. When reporting abuse that occurred outside of CA, an LMFT should report to their local child protective service agency, and let that agency determine how to best coordinate with similar agencies or law enforcement where the abuse occurred.

40. The client of an LMFT has been engaged in a difficult custody battle over her two sons. The client has shown the LMFT photos, emails and text messages her husband has sent her, where he regularly talks about being drunk and often appears intoxicated. Though the children are all healthy, the client expresses fear for her children's safety around the father, and asks the LMFT to inform the court that her husband may have a substance use disorder. The LMFT should:

a. **Incorrect.** Consider whether a report of child neglect is appropriate. *While the husband's behavior is potentially troubling, simple use of a substance in and of itself – without evidence that the use has occurred in the presence of the children, and without evidence that they have been harmed or endangered – would not be enough to support a report of suspected neglect.*

b. **Incorrect.** Refuse to review these photos, emails, and text messages in the future, focusing instead on the client's reaction to them. *The information may be clinically relevant. There is no obligation to discontinue reviewing them.*

c. **Incorrect.** Provide the court with a letter stating that, based on the limited information available, the LMFT believes the husband may have a substance use disorder and should be further assessed. *The CAMFT Code of Ethics specifically prohibits LMFTs involved in court cases from offering a diagnosis of someone the LMFT has not personally assessed or treated.*

d. **CORRECT.** Refuse the client's request. *The CAMFT Code of Ethics specifically prohibits LMFTs involved in court cases from offering a diagnosis of someone the LMFT has not personally assessed or treated. The simple fact that someone regularly uses a substance is not sufficient for a diagnosis of Substance Use Disorder.*

41. A couple is seeing an LMFT as the couple considers whether to divorce. The couple is expecting their first child, and they invite the LMFT to a party where they will reveal the baby's sex to friends and family. The couple explains to the LMFT that they do not want others to know they are in therapy, but they are worried about their conflict and anger coming up during the party, and if that happens they may need the LMFT to mediate. How should the LMFT proceed, considering the LMFT's ethical obligations?

a. **Incorrect.** Have the couple sign a release authorizing the LMFT to attend the party, understanding the risks to confidentiality involved
b. **Incorrect.** Attend the party in a coach or consultant role
c. **CORRECT.** See whether a compromise solution, such as the LMFT being on-call during the party for an emergency telehealth session, is available
d. **Incorrect.** Reinforce therapeutic boundaries and urge the couple to reconsider whether the party is a good idea

The LMFT is not in a place to push the couple to not have the party. It is possible that attending in the LMFT role could be acceptable, if the couple is willing. (Changing to a coach or consultant role for such an event would likely introduce more problems than it would solve; changing roles in this way is not advisable.) However, because the couple does not want others to know they are in therapy, a compromise solution may help ensure that the party goes smoothly while protecting the couple's confidentiality.

42. An LMFT is working with a young adult client who operates a channel on a popular video sharing web site. The client tells the LMFT that the channel involves older people, some over 100 years old, "flashing" their breasts or genitals. The client insists that they have consent from all of the participants in their videos, and that most participants find the videos to be "harmless fun." Only one participant has ever objected, and that participant was edited out after the video that featured them was published. The client is paid by the web site for their videos, but the client does not share this revenue with the video participants. The LMFT finds the channel to be exploitive and potentially harmful to the video participants. Which statement best summarizes the LMFT's legal obligations?

    a.  **CORRECT.** The LMFT may report suspected elder abuse, but is not required to

    b.  **Incorrect.** The LMFT must investigate the videos further to determine whether abuse is occurring

    c.  **Incorrect.** The LMFT must report suspected elder abuse

    d.  **Incorrect.** The LMFT must maintain confidentiality

The reporting standards for elder and dependent adult abuse give LMFTs the opportunity, but not a mandate, to report suspected abuse when that abuse does not fit neatly into the categories defined for mandated reports. In this case, the LMFT's suspicion that participants are experiencing mental suffering due to the client suggests that the LMFT could make a report here if they chose to. But no specific reporting mandate is triggered.

43. A client comes to therapy expressing concern about his 94-year-old mother. The client tells the therapist that his mother, who lives a few houses down from the client, has been refusing to eat and is unwilling to leave her home to see a doctor. She is losing weight and appears to be in declining health, but wants simply to be left alone. The client is unsure of how to help. The LMFT should:

    a.   **Incorrect.** Encourage the client to openly discuss his concern with his mother. *An open discussion is unlikely to resolve the problem and does not address the LMFT's responsibilities.*

    b.   **Incorrect.** Encourage the client to transport his mother to a doctor for evaluation even if it means doing so against her will. *Transporting the mother to medical care against her will is questionable on a number of levels, and also does not address the LMFT's reporting responsibility.*

    c.   **Incorrect.** Encourage the client to report the situation to his local adult protective service agency. *Encouraging the son to report does have the advantage of the adult protective service agency being notified, but it would still represent a failure on the LMFT's part to report in a mandated reporting situation.*

    d.   **CORRECT.** Report the situation to the local adult protective service agency. *The mother's refusal to attend to basic needs (eating and medical care) and her apparent declining health suggest self-neglect. Even though the LMFT did not learn about the problem directly from the elder, the LMFT has enough information to reasonably suspect elder neglect. Reporting fulfills the LMFT's obligation and may help the mother receive the services she needs.*

44. An LMFT takes notes during sessions in order to track key moments in session and important words or phrases used by various clients. The LMFT keeps these handwritten notes separate from clients' files. The LMFT receives a court order for all available treatment records on one of the LMFT's clients. That client has an extensive file, as the LMFT had seen the client for more than 100 sessions. The LMFT should:

   a. **Incorrect.** Respond to the court order by asserting privilege. *A court order must be obeyed. The LMFT could assert privilege in response to a subpoena, but the fact that it is a court order suggests that a judge has already determined that the records must be provided.*

   b. **Incorrect.** Respond to the court order by providing a treatment summary. *The court order was for "all available treatment records," so a summary would be an insufficient response.*

   c. **Incorrect.** Respond to the court order by providing the full file for the client, without the handwritten notes that had been kept separately. *While the handwritten notes may fall under the definition of "psychotherapy notes" in HIPAA that is different from the client's medical record, both types of records are subject to subpoena or court order. When a court order demands all available treatment records, both types of records must be provided.*

   d. **CORRECT.** Respond to the court order by providing the full file for the client and all handwritten notes pertaining to the client's sessions. *This is a full and appropriate response in keeping with the court order.*

45. An LMFT is working with a religious family whose son has been diagnosed with a blood disorder. While not fatal, the disorder could impact the boy's growth and development. The family tells you that after meeting with multiple doctors, they have elected to use only spiritual healing for their son, and to put his health "in God's hands." The LMFT should:

    a.   **Incorrect.** Advise the clients to utilize Western medicine techniques known to treat the disorder. *This would be providing medical advice, which is outside the LMFT scope of practice.*

    b.   **Incorrect.** Report suspected child abuse. *There is no evidence of abuse in the question. See option C below for consideration of neglect.*

    c.   **Incorrect.** Report suspected child neglect. *State law provides an exception to the definition of neglect. That exception allows parents to choose spiritual or religious-based treatment for their children as long as they have met with a physician who has assessed the child and the parents' decisions are "informed and appropriate."*

    d.   **CORRECT.** Discuss with the family how they reached their decision and what its possible impacts could be. *State law provides an exception to the definition of neglect. That exception allows parents to choose spiritual or religious-based treatment for their children as long as they have met with a physician who has assessed the child and the parents' decisions are "informed and appropriate." While the LMFT in this case may not agree with the parents' decision, they have had the boy assessed by a physician, and their decision does not appear to put him in significant danger.*

46. A client comes to an LMFT and identifies himself as the victim of intimate partner violence. He describes instances of his wife physically assaulting him and threatening him with a gun. He tells the LMFT that his wife is a police officer who is skilled with technology and monitors their bank accounts closely. He asks the LMFT to see him on a cash-only basis with no physical receipts, and to not keep any records of her treatment, as he is worried those records could be used by his wife to discover where he is currently staying and to describe him in future divorce proceedings as mentally unfit for custody of their children. Considering the LMFT's ethical responsibilities, the LMFT should:

a. **Incorrect.** Agree to the client's requests
b. **CORRECT.** Inform the client that neither of his requests can be honored
c. **Incorrect.** Agree to the client's requests surrounding payment, and inform the client that records from treatment of intimate partner violence are not subject to subpoena
d. **Incorrect.** Agree to the client's requests surrounding payment, and inform him that clinical records must be kept, but that those records will not include any information about his mental health

There are a lot of pieces we could unpack here, as there are potentially workable options outside of what is presented in the response choices. However, of the choices here, the best one is (B). We rule out (A) because clinical record-keeping is an ethical requirement; the clinician cannot agree to an arrangement where no records will be created. We rule out (B) and (C) because both contain incorrect elements. If the client has active mental health concerns, it would not be adequate to document her treatment without documenting those concerns (D). And California law offers no exception to subpoena for records relating to intimate partner violence (C). You could make an argument for alternate arrangements here that involve clinical-recordkeeping without financial recordkeeping (recall that the CAMFT and AAMFT codes disagree in whether financial records are specifically necessary), but considering the options available here, (B) is the only one that works.

47. A young adult seeks the services of an LMFT to help him determine his life path. He specifically asks the LMFT to help him learn how to perform household tasks like laundry and help with financial management, explaining that since he had spent many years in a series of foster homes as a child, he never learned these skills. The LMFT should:

    a. **CORRECT.** Turn away the client and refer him to community resources. *The client is seeking services outside of the LMFT's scope of practice.*

    b. **Incorrect.** Turn away the client and refer him to three other therapists. *The client is presenting with goals that are not appropriate for psychotherapy.*

    c. **Incorrect.** Accept the client and focus on the skills he is asking to learn. *The client is presenting with goals that are not appropriate for psychotherapy.*

    d. **Incorrect.** Accept the client and focus on the trauma he suffered in the foster care system. *The simple fact that the client was involved in the foster care system does not necessarily mean that he was traumatized by that involvement.*

48. An LMFT has been working with a client who describes himself as a computer hacker. Sessions have focused on his difficulty in building friendships and romantic relationships. In session, the client tells the therapist that he was easily able to obtain a great deal of personal information about her, including her home address, bank account balances, and social security number. He sees that the LMFT is unsettled by this, and assures her he has no intention of misusing the information. The LMFT should:

a. **Incorrect.** Contact law enforcement and report the data theft, without revealing that the person suspected is a client. *The LMFT only developed knowledge of this in a confidential context. In order to say anything about the data theft or the person suspected, the LMFT would have to reveal information learned in that confidential context, and no exceptions to confidentiality allow such disclosure in this situation.*

b. **Incorrect.** Discontinue treatment and refer the client to at least three other therapists. *This could be considered client abandonment. While it may rightly be considered a boundary violation, given the nature of the treatment it would make more sense to address the issue clinically.*

c. **Incorrect.** Make it a condition of treatment that the client delete all of this data from any place where he has it stored. *This would be a clinical consideration, not a legal or ethical issue for the therapist to address.*

d. **CORRECT.** Consult with an attorney and monitor her accounts closely. *This is the appropriate response, though the LMFT would need to be cautious about what information is even shared with the attorney.*

49. A client who has expressed great concern about anyone knowing she is in therapy passes out in the middle of a session. The LMFT the client was seeing is able to wake her long enough to learn that she has recently been struggling with illness and has pain from a neck injury, and the LMFT knows from the client's intake paperwork that she has a blood disorder. The LMFT should:

- a. **Incorrect.** Stay with the client and continue attempting to wake her. *Passing out mid-session may be indicative of a medical emergency. Absent other information, it should be treated as an emergency.*
- b. **Incorrect.** Call 911 and transport the client outside of the office into a public area to protect her privacy. *Calling 911 is appropriate, but attempting to transport the client is not, particularly given her known neck injury.*
- c. **Incorrect.** Call 911 and summon paramedics without providing any information about the client or her illness. *Paramedics may need information on the woman's recent illness and blood disorder in order to treat her appropriately. It is acceptable to share this information with other health care providers in an emergency, and the LMFT can do so without revealing anything about the woman's therapy.*
- d. **CORRECT.** Call 911, summon paramedics, and inform them of the client's medical issues. LMFTs *are allowed to share medical information in an emergency situation, and the LMFT in this instance can do so without revealing any information about the client's therapy.*

50. A few days after a particularly difficult session, a client asks her therapist (an LMFT) to show her the information the LMFT wrote in the client's file about that session. The client had discussed childhood trauma and tells the LMFT she wants any information about that trauma removed immediately from the file. The LMFT empathizes with the client, but had included information about the trauma in progress notes and believes it is important to the client's treatment. Legally, the LMFT should:

a.   **Incorrect.** Comply with the client's request by sharing the progress note and removing any offending information from the file within 15 days.

b.   **CORRECT.** Inform the client that the client is free to review the file but that the LMFT cannot comply with the client's request to change the note. *It is the therapist, not the client, who determines the content of the file and must ensure it meets the standard of care. If the information about trauma is important to the treatment, it belongs in the file.*

c.   **Incorrect.** Inform the client that she may replace the progress note from the session with a statement of up to 250 words that she has written herself. *The client legally may add such a statement to the file, but not to replace the therapist's existing record.*

d.   **Incorrect.** Refuse the client's request and process her reasons for wanting to keep the information secret. *The LMFT cannot simply refuse to show the client the file. If the LMFT believes that seeing the file will be harmful to the client, they must document that decision and inform the client that they can bring in another LMFT of their choosing to review the file.*

51. A client calls her therapist, an LMFT, from a train headed outside of California. The two have typically been working via video with the client's consent, so the LMFT is initially surprised that the client called in by phone. The client tells the LMFT that she expects the train will cross out of California in about 20 minutes, but that there is no way for her to know when exactly that happens. The LMFT should:

    a.   **CORRECT.** End the conversation within about 20 minutes. *Assuming that the LMFT is not licensed in the other state, the LMFT cannot treat the client once the client crosses the state line.*

    b.   **Incorrect.** Continue the session for the fully scheduled time. *See option A.*

    c.   **Incorrect.** Conduct a crisis assessment and then immediately end the call. *There is no evidence that the client is in crisis; either way, the LMFT could treat the client for as long as the client is in California.*

    d.   **Incorrect.** Confirm the client's formal state of residency. *The client's state of residency is not relevant when determining whether a California licensed therapist can work with a client who travels out of state.*

52. A middle-aged man who is seeing a psychologist to work on his symptoms of anxiety inquires with an LMFT about the possibility of the man and his wife seeing the LMFT for couple counseling. The man explains that while some of his anxiety is about how others in his life perceive him, this is improving with treatment and he sees this as being markedly different from the work he and his wife would do with the LMFT. The couple have been together for eight years and have two children. The LMFT should:

    a. **Incorrect.** Defer the request and ask the man to wait for couple counseling until the individual treatment is concluded. *While professional ethics encourage caution and coordination when a client is seeing two therapists simultaneously, it is not prohibited and may be clinically appropriate.*

    b. **Incorrect.** Accept the man and his wife as a couple client, and encourage the man to discontinue individual therapy while the couple work is in progress. *While professional ethics encourage caution and coordination when a client is seeing two therapists simultaneously, it is not prohibited and may be clinically appropriate. Discontinuing the individual therapy is not necessary and may be inappropriate.*

    c. **CORRECT.** Consider the potential conflicts involved in the man seeing two therapists simultaneously for treatment of issues that may be intertwined. *While professional ethics encourage caution and coordination when a client is seeing two therapists simultaneously, it is not prohibited and may be clinically appropriate.*

    d. **Incorrect.** Refuse the request on the grounds that his anxiety is already being appropriately treated. *The anxiety does seem to be receiving appropriate treatment, but the client is asking for assistance with his relationship. Refusing the request for couple therapy on this basis does not make sense.*

53. A client asks to use her insurance to pay for therapy with an LMFT, as she would not be able to pay out of pocket. The client's husband works for a large multinational corporation, and the client's insurance is provided through that corporation. The client tells the LMFT that she believes she may have Borderline Personality Disorder and Substance Use Disorder, and does not want her husband or the corporation to learn of these diagnoses. The LMFT should:

    a.   **Incorrect.** Provide referrals to low-fee clinics. *It is possible that the client does not qualify for the diagnoses she fears, and that she could receive insurance coverage for treatment without her diagnoses being revealed. Referrals at this point would be premature.*

    b.   **CORRECT.** Discuss what information is provided to insurers, and what the client's treatment options may be. *LMFTs are ethically obligated to review what information is shared with third-party payors. Reviewing the client's treatment options in that context is appropriate.*

    c.   **Incorrect.** Contact the insurer to advocate for the client. *While professional ethics support advocating for clients with third-party payors, first it must be determined what needs advocating. If the client does not qualify for the diagnoses she fears, if diagnoses are not necessary for the insurer to pay for treatment, or if the insurer would not share the diagnoses as a matter of current policy, no advocacy would be necessary.*

    d.   **Incorrect.** Advise the client to seek a court order that will seal her treatment records. *This would be giving legal advice, which is outside of the LMFT's scope of practice.*

54. A couple has been seeing an LMFT for premarital counseling. Toward the end of the counseling, they ask the LMFT whether she would be willing to attend the wedding and speak briefly at the reception about what makes the couple such a good fit. They say they have no problem with introducing the LMFT honestly and describing her role, saying she has been very helpful to them. They believe their families would be happy to meet her and to share their thanks as well. The LMFT should:

a. **Incorrect.** Politely refuse the request.
b. **CORRECT.** Consider the cultural implications of the request and the potential impact on any future treatment.
c. **Incorrect.** Attend the wedding, but decline to speak, and ask that she not be introduced as a therapist.
d. **Incorrect.** Have the clients sign a release of information authorizing the LMFT to speak candidly, and then do so, consistent with the clients' request.

Accepting the invitation would arguably create a dual relationship. However, many such relationships are not prohibited. For a dual relationship that is not prohibited, therapists are required to consider the risk of exploitation for the client, and the impact on clinical judgment for the therapist. In this case, there is not enough information in the question to conclude that attending would be appropriate or inappropriate (options A or D). Asking to be falsely introduced (option C) may protect the clients' confidentiality but appears to go against why the clients want the therapist there. The LMFT should engage in the consideration spelled out in option B.

55. An adolescent male client tells an LMFT that he is drawn to violent movies and video games, and spends a great deal of time fantasizing about what he would do if confronted with a situation where he would need to become violent to survive. Though he has no history of violence or substance use, the client is struggling in school and the family has guns in the home. The LMFT should:

a. **Incorrect.** Assess for safety and for psychotic disorder. *For an adolescent male to be drawn to violent movies and games is not particularly unusual, and is not evidence of a psychotic disorder.*

b. **Incorrect.** Assess for substance use disorder. *No evidence of substance use disorder, or even any form of substance use, appears in the question.*

c. **Incorrect.** Develop a safety plan. *The potentially violent fantasies and the presence of guns in the home are risk factors, but nothing in the question suggests an immediate safety concern.*

d. **CORRECT.** Engage in discussion of what makes the games, movies, and fantasies so appealing. *No specific ethical or legal responsibilities are triggered by the information in the question.*

56. An Associate MFT has been working under supervision in a private practice setting for two years. The Associate achieves licensure, and informs the supervisor that the Associate will be starting their own private practice. The now-former Associate would like to bring their current clients along to the new practice. How can the Associate MFT best address their ethical responsibilities?

    a.  **CORRECT.** Understand that the clients are ultimately clients of the supervisor, and allow the clients to determine how they wish to proceed

    b.  **Incorrect.** Understand that the clients are ultimately clients of the supervisor, and allow the supervisor to determine which clients may follow the new licensee into their private practice

    c.  **Incorrect.** Retain the files for all clients who wish to follow the new licensee into their private practice, allowing the supervisor to make copies if the supervisor wishes

    d.  **Incorrect.** Allow the clients to determine whether to follow the new licensee into private practice, paying the supervisor a fee for each client who does so. This fee covers the supervisor's costs for marketing that brought the clients in to see the Associate originally

While supervisors bear ultimate responsibility for client well-being, clients retain their freedom of choice when it comes to selecting their treatment provider. The supervisor cannot make that choice for them (B). Files are the property of the employer, not the clinician seeing the client (C); clients following the new licensee to private practice would actually need to sign releases allowing the new licensee to copy current files and bring them along to the new practice. And paying a fee for referrals is explicitly prohibited by both ethical code and state law (D).

57. After consulting with an attorney and a colleague, an LMFT makes a child abuse report. The LMFT had learned from a family being seen together in treatment that the parents engage in physical punishment of their children. Three weeks after the report was made, the parents in the family ask directly in session whether the LMFT was the person who made the report. The parents have been frustrated and hope to confront the reporting party, as they do not believe their behavior is abusive and are embarrassed and angry that an investigator from the local child protective service agency visited their home and their child's school. The investigator was ultimately unable to substantiate the abuse report. Ethically, the LMFT should:

    a. **CORRECT.** Acknowledge having made the report and share the specific reasons why the LMFT did so. *This is most in keeping with the general ethical principle of Fidelity.*

    b. **Incorrect.** Acknowledge having made the report, apologize for having done so, and work to repair the relationship. *Presuming that the LMFT had justifiable grounds for reporting, it would not be appropriate to apologize for having made the report.*

    c. **Incorrect.** Deny having made the report, and empathize with their emotional response to the investigation. *Denying having made the report serves no clear ethical or legal purpose. It runs contrary to the general ethical principle of Fidelity.*

    d. **Incorrect.** Deny having made the report, and guide the conversation back to the reasons why the family is in treatment. *Denying having made the report serves no clear ethical or legal purpose. It runs contrary to the general ethical principle of Fidelity.*

58. An LMFT receives a request from a former client for their complete therapy records. The client's treatment occurred four years ago. When the LMFT locates the former client's file, the LMFT finds that the file is disorganized, and consists mostly of brief, handwritten notes. The LMFT, whose current record-keeping is much improved, is embarrassed by the state of this old file. How should the LMFT address their legal responsibilities in this case?

    a. **Incorrect.** Only agree to provide the client a written treatment summary in lieu of the full record

    b. **Incorrect.** Recreate the handwritten notes in a more structured, typed format, adding details as needed. Discard the handwritten notes and provide the updated record within 10 days of the client's request

    c. **Incorrect.** Refuse to release the file, on the grounds that it may be damaging to the LMFT's relationship with the former client

    d. **CORRECT.** Release the file in its current form, and offer to address any questions the former client may have

While treatment summaries (A) are often preferable responses to requests for client records, in this case the client specifically requested their *complete* record. With some limitations, they have a legal right to that record. Altering the record and presenting it as if it were the original record (B) could be considered fraud. While LMFTs can refuse to release records if they believe doing so would harm the client, there's nothing in the question to suggest such risk of harm. The LMFT's embarrassment is not adequate justification to refuse a record request (C). The LMFT is obligated to release the file. Offering to address any questions is not a legal obligation, but may alleviate any confusion on the part of the client.

59. In group supervision, several MFT associates and their supervisor (who is a licensed MFT) are discussing whether the client of one of the associates should make a report of suspected child abuse. The associate who has seen the client says she does not believe the situation warrants a report. The other associates believe there is enough information to form reasonable suspicion of abuse, based on what the associate who has seen the client has said in describing the case. The supervisor validates the arguments being made by both sides, and after a long discussion, their positions are unchanged. The Associate MFT who has seen the case should:

    a.  **CORRECT.** Make a report of suspected child abuse. *The legal definition of "reasonable suspicion" says, essentially, that if other similar professionals presented with the same information would reasonably suspect abuse, then so should you. In this case, several other similar professionals suspect abuse based on the information available. (The supervisor has not taken a stance on either side.) In fact, everyone in the room who has expressed an opinion believes the case should be reported except the treating MFT. A report should be made.*

    b.  **Incorrect.** Defer a decision on reporting until she can conduct further assessment. *Once reasonable suspicion has been determined, the decision to report is made and should not be deferred.*

    c.  **Incorrect.** Hold to her belief that a report is not warranted unless new information comes to light that would change her view. *Based on the opinions of others in the room, she needs to change her view and make a report.*

    d.  **Incorrect.** Consult with the local child protective service agency. *Such a consultation may be helpful but is not definitive. Based on the MFT's experience in supervision, reasonable suspicion of abuse exists and a report must be made.*

60. An individual client tells an LMFT that she is in fear of her husband. The couple has a long history of severe intimate partner violence, and there are protective orders in place requiring that they couple stay away from each other except when meeting in supervised locations to hand off their children. Now that the couple is finally divorcing, the husband has begun leaving threatening voicemails. The client plays one such voicemail for the LMFT, who agrees that the client may be in danger. The LMFT should:

a. **Incorrect.** Notify law enforcement and warn the victim. *The victim is aware of the danger. The LMFT does not need to notify law enforcement as the dangerous person is not a client.*

b. **Incorrect.** Attempt to contact the husband to reduce the danger. *Without a release, this could be a violation of confidentiality; in any event, reducing the danger in this case is not a responsibility of the LMFT.*

c. **CORRECT.** Encourage the client to notify law enforcement. *The client has the information needed to notify law enforcement.*

d. **Incorrect.** Notify the court that the husband is violating the protective order. *LMFTs are neither obligated nor authorized to make such a report in this instance. The client may notify the court if she chooses.*

61. An LMFT has been working with a family for several sessions and plans a session where the entire family will participate in a ceremony relieving the oldest daughter of the responsibility she has taken on as a co-parent. Shortly before the session, the mother informs the LMFT that she will be away on a business trip and asks whether she can participate in the session by phone or videoconferencing. The mother's frequent absences are part of the reason why the daughter felt obligated to take on parenting tasks. The LMFT should:

    a. **Incorrect.** Contact the BBS to see whether the LMFT can include the mother in session while she is on her trip. *The BBS does not provide legal advice, and even asking the question may require providing information that is confidential.*

    b. **Incorrect.** Include the mother in the session and in the ceremony via phone or videoconference, and clarify that her involvement is consultation rather than therapy. *Simply calling the mother's involvement consultation does not make it something different from therapy. This is especially true considering that the entire purpose of her presence in session is to be involved in a therapeutic intervention that the LMFT designed.*

    c. **CORRECT.** Refuse the mother's request and reschedule the ceremony for a time she can attend in person. *LMFTs are required to carefully assess whether telemedicine services are appropriate in a given case. Here, the mother's absence would likely have a major impact on the planned ceremony; having her participate by phone or videoconference rather than in person appears likely to impact the effectiveness of the intervention.*

    d. **Incorrect.** Contact the other family members to see whether they believe including the mother would be appropriate. *While the family may be able to offer useful clinical feedback on this question, it is not the role of the family to resolve the LMFT's legal and ethical concerns.*

62. An LMFT's new 34-year-old client recently moved to the US from another country. Though the LMFT not familiar with the other country's culture, the LMFT finds that they strongly like the client. The client appears intelligent and confident, and tells the LMFT that the client is also interested in becoming a therapist someday. The LMFT finds it difficult to develop concrete therapeutic goals with the client, as it seems the conversation in therapy over the first two sessions has been more social in nature. The LMFT should:

    a.  **CORRECT.** Learn more about the other country's culture and social norms, to determine whether the client's behavior is normal

    b.  **Incorrect.** Because the client is from a culture that is not familiar to the LMFT, refer the client to another therapist due to scope of competence

    c.  **Incorrect.** Attend therapy to address the pathology that underlies the LMFT's immediate fondness for the client

    d.  **Incorrect.** Assign the treatment goals the LMFT feels would be best, reminding the client that the client is free to participate or not participate in therapy as the client sees fit

This client offers the LMFT the opportunity to expand their scope of competence. Doing so will help the LMFT determine whether the social conversation in the first two sessions is a culturally accepted way of building trust and familiarity with a professional, or whether it is more troublesome. (B) is incorrect because this could be considered discrimination based on national origin. (C) is incorrect because it is not automatically pathological for an LMFT to like a client who is confident and intelligent. While the LMFT would want to remain aware of how the LMFT's biases may be impacting treatment, simply liking a client does not require an LMFT to go to therapy. (D) is incorrect because it is not up to the therapist alone to determine the goals of treatment. Goals should be established collaboratively, and to do otherwise may violate a client's right to autonomy.

63. A 37-year-old married client wishes to use their insurance to pay for substance use treatment provided by an LMFT. The LMFT is not in-network with the insurance company, but provides the client with superbills that the client then submits to the insurer. The insurance company contacts the LMFT to ask for more information on the client's treatment, including the client's diagnosis, the client's date of birth, and a copy of the treatment contract, before issuing payment. The LMFT attempts to contact the client but is unable to do so. Considering the LMFT's legal responsibilities, how may the LMFT address the insurance company's request?

    a. **Incorrect.** File a complaint with the state Department of Managed Health Care

    b. **Incorrect.** Contact the client's spouse to seek their permission to release records on the client's behalf

    c. **CORRECT.** Provide the requested documentation to the insurer

    d. **Incorrect.** Provide a copy of the client file, and a copy of the insurer's request, to an external licensed therapist to determine whether the insurer's request it reasonable under the circumstances

Legally, LMFTs may share documentation with a third party in order to facilitate payment for services without needing to get the client's permission. While ethical considerations typically lead LMFTs to obtain permission anyway, it is not a legal requirement. However, other options here involve inappropriate breaches of confidentiality. The client's spouse has no automatic right to information about the client's treatment, and the LMFT cannot share the client file with an external clinician to address this question without client permission. In the absence of any evidence of insurer wrongdoing, there is no legal reason for the LMFT to file a complaint with the Department of Managed Health Care.

64. An LMFT is planning her retirement in a few months, and has agreed to sell her private practice to a local colleague. Several weeks before she turns the practice over, the LMFT should:

    a.   **Incorrect.** Inform clients of her plans, and instruct them to continue as usual with the colleague as the colleague takes over. *Clients have autonomy in choosing their treatment provider. The therapist can make referrals, but cannot simply instruct clients to transfer to the new provider.*

    b.   **CORRECT.** Inform clients of her plans, and request that each client who wishes to continue treatment with the colleague sign a Release of Information form allowing their files to be transferred. *While the office location may be the same, the clients who continue with the colleague are changing treatment providers. It makes good sense to formally allow the transfer of records and even to sign a new informed consent document with the colleague.*

    c.   **Incorrect.** Inform clients of her plans, and offer to do a series of transitional sessions with each client while they are simultaneously starting therapy with the colleague. *Concurrent treatment can be problematic in several ways, including the possibility that the retiring therapist may (even accidentally) undermine treatment with the new therapist. Here, if the retiring LMFT wishes to engage in a "warm handoff," it would be better to sit in on a session or two with the therapist taking over the practice, or to more actively coordinate care during the transition period.*

    d.   **Incorrect.** Inform clients of her plans, and draft a transition document for the colleague. *It is not clear what such a document would or should entail.*

65. A client asks whether her 75-year-old mother can be part of her therapy. The mother speaks English, but can only read and write in her native language, which the LMFT is not familiar with. The LMFT believes that including the mother in the therapy may be helpful to the client. The LMFT should:

    a.  **Incorrect.** Have the mother sign the informed consent form and join the therapy

    b.  **CORRECT.** Verbally discuss the process, risks, and benefits of therapy with the mother to help her decide whether to join the therapy, and document the discussion and her response

    c.  **Incorrect.** Refer the mother to a therapist who speaks her native language, and ask the client to sign a Release of Information form authorizing the LMFT to speak to that therapist

    d.  **Incorrect.** Ask the mother to teach the LMFT her native language so that the LMFT can provide all appropriate paperwork in her language

Consent for therapy should be documented, but the client's consent does not need to be in writing. Such a requirement would make it impossible to work with clients who are illiterate. A verbal conversation is the best way to ensure that the mother is truly able to exercise her autonomy and provide informed consent for treatment. A is incorrect because the mother's signature would not mean much on a form she could not understand. C is incorrect because it would not fulfill the request of the client, to have the mother be part of the client's therapy, which you also believe may be helpful. D is incorrect because this would be both time-consuming and a potentially inappropriate dual relationship.

66. A mother presents her 11-year-old child for treatment from an LMFT. The mother notes that the child has been struggling in school and in social relationships, and the mother is concerned that the child may be experimenting with drugs. The mother says she is willing to provide consent for treatment, and notes that she and the child's father were never married. Legally, the LMFT must:

   a. **CORRECT.** Have the mother provide consent for the child's treatment
   b. **Incorrect.** Seek consent from both the mother and the child's father
   c. **Incorrect.** Evaluate the 11-year-old's capacity to independently consent for treatment
   d. **Incorrect.** Report suspected child neglect based on the 11-year-old's potential drug use

When parents were never married, one parent's consent is sufficient to provide services to a minor. Minors younger than 12 cannot consent independently. Even if the minor has experimented with drugs, something that is not clear from the question, this would not necessarily indicate reasonable suspicion of neglect.

67. An LMFT is working with an individual client who is contemplating moving out of the state. The client has twin 5-year-old children with her spouse, and the client says she is prepared to let her spouse have primary custody. The client explains that her marriage is failing and she cannot find work in California, but that her family in another state is prepared to give her a place to live and help connect her with possible jobs. She says she wants to be a good parent and maintain good relationships with her spouse and children. How should the LMFT proceed?

    a.  **CORRECT.** Help the client develop and consider possible outcomes of the move, and possible alternatives

    b.  **Incorrect.** Consider the family to be the client and support maintaining the family structure until instructed otherwise by the client

    c.  **Incorrect.** Offer to connect the client with a therapist in what will be their new state, including sending records if the client will allow

    d.  **Incorrect.** Inform the client that the therapist will listen and reflect as the client weighs their options, but that the LMFT will not guide the discussion in any way

The question says the client is contemplating the move, not that the decision has been made. The LMFT should not assume that the move will happen, or that it shouldn't. But the LMFT also does not need to be passive. They can best fulfill their role by helping the client see the full range of their options, and the potential outcomes of each.

68. An LMFT is working for a large nonprofit agency, which handles all aspects of client billing. The agency informs the LMFT that, as of one week from today, the agency will begin reporting unpaid balances to a collection agency when the balance is more than 30 days overdue. The LMFT objects, arguing that current and past clients with overdue balances have not been informed of this and that such reporting may have negative impacts on clients with both financial and mental health struggles. The agency insists that letters will be sent to all clients with overdue balances. How should the LMFT manage the ethical issues in this case?

   a. **Incorrect.** Since the business relationship is between the client and the agency, not between the client and the LMFT, no action is required
   b. **Incorrect.** Offer to personally take on the balances of clients who owe the agency, such that the therapist can collect balances as they see fit
   c. **Incorrect.** Discontinue their employment at the agency, and seek alternative employment instead
   d. **CORRECT.** Attempt to negotiate with agency administrators for more notice to potentially-impacted clients

Here, professional ethics and agency obligations are in conflict. The CAMFT code of ethics requires LMFTs in such situations to make known their commitment to the code of ethics and take reasonable steps to resolve the conflict. While personally taking on the clients' debt is not reasonable, seeking a compromise that provides clients with additional notice would be.

69. To show support for the local high school basketball team, an LMFT advertises that new clients can receive their first six sessions at a per-session fee equal to the number of points scored by the basketball team's opponent in their most recent game. So, if the team plays great defense, new clients receive lower fees. After six sessions, clients who wish to continue therapy would do so at the LMFT's standard rate of $120 per session. Which best reflects the LMFT's legal obligations related to this promotion?

    a.  **Incorrect.** The LMFT cannot include a temporary or promotional fee in their advertising

    b.  **Incorrect.** The LMFT must include both the promotional rate and the standard rate in all advertisements

    c.  **CORRECT.** The LMFT must inform each new client, prior to the beginning of services, what their specific rate would be and why

    d.  **Incorrect.** The LMFT must set a minimum and maximum rate to protect both clients and the therapist from potential exploitation if basketball scores are unusually high or low

LMFTs are not required to disclose fees in their advertising, but they are allowed to do so. Advertising temporary or promotional pricing is also allowed, though any limits on these fees should be disclosed. LMFTs are legally required to inform each client what their specific fee will be, and the basis for how it was computed, before beginning services. In this case, the advertisement may explain the basis for the fee, but not all new clients may have seen the advertisement.

70. A couple in their 40s brings their 15-year-old child into therapy and expresses concern for the 15-year-old's safety and wellbeing. The parents report that the 15-year-old has begun identifying as a lesbian, and the parents are worried that this will cause problems in the family's conservative community. The parents say that they support their child, but are hopeful that the LMFT will help the child to also become more attracted to men, or at least to reduce attractions to women until such time as the child is old enough to move out. The LMFT expresses sensitivity to both the child's orientation and the parents' safety concerns, and is unsure of how to proceed. Considering the LMFT's ethical obligations, what should the LMFT do in this situation?

    a. **Incorrect.** Provide services to the family under the banner of coaching or consulting, not as an LMFT

    b. **CORRECT.** Seek articles and trainings related to adolescents who have faced similar situations

    c. **Incorrect.** Work with the child toward a temporary identification as asexual, until such time as it is safe for them to identify openly as lesbian

    d. **Incorrect.** Agree to provide services to the family as an LMFT only if doing so is consistent with every family member's religious beliefs, including the minor's

While reparative or conversion therapy – any effort to change a minor's sexual orientation through therapy – is defined as unprofessional conduct in state law, this question asks about the LMFT's ethical obligations, not their legal ones. Ethically, the LMFT is obligated to practice in accordance with current science, and to remain current on developments in the field. Each of those obligations suggests that the therapist should not provide the requested services, but instead should seek articles and trainings on the topic, which will help inform the LMFT of how to best support the family and the minor while affirming the minor's sexual orientation and identity.

71. A 61-year-old individual client of an LMFT and the client's 66-year-old spouse were vacationing at a popular theme park when an argument between the spouses about what to get for lunch turned violent. They wrestled each other to the floor and had to be separated by park security. Both spouses were treated for their injuries and escorted out of the park. When the client tells this story at their next session, they tell the LMFT that the couple has been violent with one another for 10 years, since shortly after their youngest child moved out of the house. What must the LMFT do next?

a. **Incorrect.** Report the couple's extensive violence to local law enforcement

b. **CORRECT.** Report to the local adult protective service agency that the 66-year-old is a victim of suspected elder abuse

c. **Incorrect.** Require the partners to live in separate homes until they have established at least a 90-day window of nonviolence

d. **Incorrect.** Gather information from the theme park, including any notes and reports the park made about the incident, to determine whether any additional reporting is necessary

The 66-year-old is an elder under state law, for the purposes of mandated reporting. The 61-year-old is not. While both partners are victims of violence, the LMFT's mandated reporting responsibility is specific to the violence experienced by the 66-year-old. The LMFT would only report violent acts since that spouse turned 65, not the couple's full history of violence. The LMFT does not need to investigate the park's actions to reasonably believe that abuse took place. And the LMFT has no obligation to demand a window of non-violence, particularly considering that the LMFT is engaging in individual treatment with the client.

72. A 29-year-old woman brings her 19-year-old brother to an LMFT's office and explains that the brother needs therapy to address issues of grief and depression. The brother has some developmental delays and is illiterate, but is a legal adult and is not under conservatorship. The woman explains that she would be willing to provide consent for the brother's treatment and take financial responsibility for it, and could be in or out of the therapy based on the brother's preference and the LMFT's assessment. How should the LMFT fufill his ethical responsibilities?

    a. **Incorrect.** Allow the sister to provide consent signatures for herself and her brother, and assess to determine the most appropriate unit of treatment

    b. **Incorrect.** Ask the brother whether he is comfortable allowing his sister to consent to treatment on his behalf, and document his decision

    c. **Incorrect.** Inform the sister that she can participate in therapy if the brother allows, but that he must be financially responsible for his treatment

    d. **CORRECT.** Interview the brother individually to discuss risks and benefits of treatment, and assess his desire to participate

Because the brother is an adult and not under conservatorship, he can consent to therapy on his own if he chooses to do so. The sister's efforts to support him may be well-intended, but she cannot consent to treatment on his behalf. She can, if she wishes, accept financial responsibility for his treatment. But first, the LMFT should get verbal consent from the brother, understanding the potential risks and benefits of treatment. Consent does not need to be obtained in writing, but it does need to be documented in the client's records.

73. Six months after the end of their supervision relationship, an LMFT supervisor and their former supervisee encounter one another at a party. They express their attraction to each other and would like to develop a sexual relationship. The LMFT supervisor is still serving as therapist to a few clients that had previously been seen by the former supervisee. Which of the following best reflects the ethical obligations of both therapists?

    a.  **CORRECT.** The LMFT supervisor and the former supervisee may enter into a sexual relationship

    b.  **Incorrect.** The LMFT supervisor and the former supervisee may not enter into a sexual relationship until two years have elapsed since their last professional contact

    c.  **Incorrect.** The LMFT supervisor and the former supervisee may not enter into a sexual relationship until the LMFT supervisor has terminated therapy with all of the former supervisee's former clients

    d.  **Incorrect.** The LMFT supervisor and the former supervisee may not enter into a sexual relationship until the former supervisee is licensed, making the two professional equals

While LMFT supervisors may not enter into sexual relationships with active supervisees, ethical standards do not prohibit such relationships once the supervisory relationship has ended.

74. At a busy group practice, an LMFT observes that a colleague has been increasingly letting sessions go past their scheduled end time, and that the colleague's office has become disorganized. The colleague explains that they have been going through a divorce, and fighting for custody of their children. The colleague has been using cocaine to keep their energy up for client care, but feels "out of gas" to maintain client boundaries or organize their office. Considering the LMFT's ethical obligations, the LMFT should:

    a. **Incorrect.** Pause referring clients to the colleague, and take no further action
    b. **CORRECT.** Offer to connect the colleague with legal, substance use treatment, or other resources
    c. **Incorrect.** Report the colleague's behavior to the BBS
    d. **Incorrect.** To protect the interests of clients, threaten to inform the owners of the group practice about the colleague's behavior unless the colleague enters substance use treatment

The CAMFT Code of Ethics encourages LMFTs to offer support to colleagues who are experiencing impairment due to substance abuse or mental health issues.

75. During the assessment process in outpatient therapy, a 38-year-old woman describes to an LMFT the woman's long history of troubled romantic relationships. The woman carries a diagnosis of Borderline Personality Disorder. She reports that she was sexually abused as a child, had several difficult dating experiences, once had a threesome with the therapist she and her husband were seeing for couple therapy, later divorced that husband, and has had a series of brief romantic relationships with married people. She has been through a great deal of therapy, she says, but she asks the LMFT not to request prior treatment records. Considering the LMFT's legal responsibilities, the LMFT should:

    a.   **Incorrect.** Contact the client's prior clinicians to request records from prior treatment

    b.   **Incorrect.** Consider whether the client's statements are likely to be truthful, considering all relevant assessment data

    c.   **CORRECT.** Provide the client with a copy of the brochure *Therapy Never Includes Sexual Behavior*

    d.   **Incorrect.** Consider whether the client is in need of a higher level of care

The only specific legal obligation triggered by the information in the question is the obligation to provide the brochure *Therapy Never Includes Sexual Behavior*. Whether the therapist believes the client is telling the truth does not matter; a client is reporting a sexual relationship with a previous therapist, and that is enough to trigger the obligation.

# Appendix:
# Exam Plan with Index

# Board of Behavioral Sciences

## Licensed Marriage and Family Therapist
## California Law and Ethics Examination Outline

This document provides detailed information about the LMFT California Law and Ethics Examination, including a description of each content area, subarea and the associated task and knowledge statements.

**Each question in the examination is linked to this content.**

*Note: The exam outline, including all task and knowledge statements, comes from the BBS outline published online. Page numbers in the following charts refer to where the relevant information can be found within this text.*

# I. Law (40%)

This area assesses the candidate's ability to identify and apply legal mandates to clinical practice.

## IA. Confidentiality, Privilege, and Consent (14%)

| Task Statement | Knowledge Statement | Page |
|---|---|---|
| T1. Comply with legal requirements regarding the maintenance/dissemination of confidential information to protect client's privacy. | K1. Knowledge of laws regarding confidential communications within the therapeutic relationship. | 35 |
| | K2. Knowledge of laws regarding the disclosure of confidential information to other individuals, professionals, agencies, or authorities. | 35 |
| T2. Identify holder of privilege by evaluating client's age, legal status, and/or content of therapy to determine requirements for providing treatment. | K3. Knowledge of laws regarding holder of privilege. | 36-37 |
| | K4. Knowledge of laws regarding privileged communication. | 36-37 |
| T3. Comply with legal requirements regarding the disclosure of privileged information to protect client's privacy in judicial/legal matters. | K4. Knowledge of laws regarding privileged communication. | 36-37 |
| | K5. Knowledge of laws regarding the release of privileged information. | 37 |
| | K6. Knowledge of legal requirements for responding to subpoenas and court orders. | 37 |

| Task Statement | Knowledge Statement | Page |
|---|---|---|
| T4. Comply with legal requirements regarding providing treatment to minor clients. | K1. Knowledge of laws regarding confidential communications within the therapeutic relationship. | 35 |
| | K2. Knowledge of laws regarding the disclosure of confidential information to other individuals, professionals, agencies, or authorities. | 35 |
| | K3. Knowledge of laws regarding holder of privilege. | 36-37 |
| | K4. Knowledge of laws regarding privileged communication. | 36-37 |
| | K7. Knowledge of legal criteria and requirements for providing treatment to minors. | 38 |
| T5. Maintain client records by adhering to legal requirements regarding documentation, storage, and disposal to protect the client's privacy and/or the therapeutic process. | K8. Knowledge of laws regarding documentation of therapeutic services. | 39 |
| | K9. Knowledge of laws pertaining to the maintenance/disposal of client records. | 39 |
| T6. Respond to requests for records by adhering to applicable laws and regulations to protect client's rights and/or safety. | K10. Knowledge of laws pertaining to client's access to treatment records. | 39 |
| | K11. Knowledge of laws pertaining to the release of client records to other individuals, professionals, or third parties. | 40 |
| T7. Provide services via information and communication technologies by complying with "telehealth" regulations. | K12. Knowledge of laws regarding the consent to and delivery of services via information and communication technologies. | 41 |
| T8. Comply with the Health Information Portability and Accountability Act (HIPAA) regulations as mandated by law. | K13. Knowledge of legal requirements of the Health Information Portability and Accountability Act (HIPAA). | 42 |

# IB. Limits to Confidentiality / Mandated Reporting (16%)

| Task Statement | Knowledge Statement | Page |
|---|---|---|
| T9. Report known or suspected abuse, neglect, or exploitation of dependent adult client to protective authorities. | K14. Knowledge of indicators of abuse, neglect, or exploitation of dependent adults. | 55 |
| | K15. Knowledge of laws pertaining to the reporting of known or suspected incidents of abuse, neglect, or exploitation of dependent adults. | 53 |
| T10. Report known or suspected abuse, neglect, or exploitation of elderly client to protective authorities. | K16. Knowledge of indicators of abuse, neglect, or exploitation of elderly clients. | 55 |
| | K17. Knowledge of laws pertaining to the reporting of known or suspected incidents of abuse, neglect, or exploitation of elderly clients. | 53 |
| T11. Report known or suspected abuse or neglect of a child or adolescent to protective authorities. | K18. Knowledge of indicators of abuse/neglect of children and adolescents. | 52 |
| | K19. Knowledge of laws pertaining to the reporting of known or suspected incidents of abuse/neglect of children and adolescents. | 49 |
| T12. Comply with legal requirements regarding breaking confidentiality to protect the client in the presence of indictors of danger to self/others and/or grave disability. | K20. Knowledge of symptoms of mental impairment that may indicate the need for involuntary hospitalization. | 56 |
| | K21. Knowledge of legal requirements for initiating involuntary hospitalization. | 56 |
| | K22. Knowledge of laws regarding confidentiality in situations of client danger to self or others. | 57 |

| Task Statement | Knowledge Statement | Page |
|---|---|---|
| T13. Comply with legal requirements to report and protect when client expresses intent to cause harm to people or property. | K23. Knowledge of methods/criteria to identify situations in which client poses a danger to others. | 58 |
| | K24. Knowledge of laws pertaining to duty to protect when client indicates intent to cause harm. | 59 |
| | K25. Knowledge of situations/conditions that constitute reasonable indicators of client's intent to cause harm. | 59 |
| T14. Comply with legal requirements regarding privilege exceptions in client litigation or in response to breach of duty accusations. | K26. Knowledge of laws regarding privilege exceptions in litigation involving client's mental or emotional condition as raised by the client or client's representative. | 60 |
| | K27. Knowledge of laws regarding privilege exceptions in which client alleges breach of duty. | 60 |
| T15. Comply with legal requirements regarding privilege exceptions in court-appointed and/or defendant-requested evaluation/ therapy. | K28. Knowledge of laws regarding privilege exceptions in court-appointed evaluation or therapy. | 60 |
| | K29. Knowledge of laws pertaining to privilege exceptions in defendant-requested evaluation or therapy. | 60 |
| T16. Comply with legal requirements regarding reporting instances of crime perpetrated against minor clients. | K30. Knowledge of laws pertaining to the reporting of crimes perpetrated against a minor. | 60 |
| | K31. Knowledge of laws regarding privilege exceptions in crime or tort involving minors. | 60 |

# IC. Legal Standards for Professional Practice (10%)

| Task Statement | Knowledge Statement | Page |
|---|---|---|
| T17. Comply with laws regarding sexual contact, conduct, and relations between therapist and client to prevent harm to the client and/or the therapeutic relationship. | K32. Knowledge of laws regarding sexual conduct between therapist and client. | 65 |
| | K33. Knowledge of legal requirements for providing client with the brochure *Therapy Never Includes Sexual Behavior*. | 65 |
| T18. Comply with legal parameters re: scope of practice. | K34. Knowledge of laws that define the scope of clinical practice. | 66 |
| T19. Comply with legal parameters regarding professional conduct. | K35. Knowledge of laws that define professional conduct for licensed practitioners. | 66 |
| T20. Disclose fee structure prior to initiating therapy. | K36. Knowledge of laws regarding disclosures required prior to initiating treatment. | 69 |
| T21. Comply with legal regulations regarding providing treatment when interacting with third-party payers. | K37. Knowledge of laws and regulations regarding third-party reimbursement. | 70 |
| | K38. Knowledge of parity laws regarding the provision of mental health services. | 70 |
| T22. Comply with laws regarding advertisement of services and professional qualifications. | K39. Knowledge of laws regarding advertisement and dissemination of information regarding professional qualifications, education, and professional affiliations. | 71 |
| T23. Comply with laws pertaining to the payment or acceptance of money or other consideration for referrals. | K40. Knowledge of legal requirements regarding payment or acceptance of money or other considerations for referral of services. | 72 |

# II. Ethics (60%)

This area assesses the candidate's ability to identify and apply ethical standards for professional conduct.

## IIA. Professional Competence and Preventing Harm (18%)

| Task Statement | Knowledge Statement | Page |
|---|---|---|
| T24. Consult with other professionals and/or seek additional education, training, and/or supervision to address therapeutic issues that arise outside the therapist's scope of competence. | K41. Knowledge of limitations of professional experience, education, and training to determine issues outside scope of competence. | 77 |
| | K42. Knowledge of situations that indicate a need for consultation with colleagues or other professionals. | 77 |
| | K43. Knowledge of ethical standards regarding the protection of client rights when engaging in consultation/collaboration with other professionals. | 77 |
| | K44. Knowledge of ethical methods of developing additional areas of practice or expanding competence. | 78 |
| | K45. Knowledge of the ethical responsibility to remain current in developments in the profession. | 78 |
| T25. Consult with other professionals to address questions regarding ethical obligations or practice responsibilities that arise during therapy. | K42. Knowledge of situations that indicate a need for consultation with colleagues or other professionals. | 77 |
| | K43. Knowledge of ethical standards regarding the protection of client rights when engaging in consultation/collaboration with other professionals. | 77 |

| Task Statement | Knowledge Statement | Page |
|---|---|---|
| T26. Evaluate therapist's own mental, emotional, or physical problems/impairment to determine impact on ability to provide competent therapeutic services. | K42. Knowledge of situations that indicate a need for consultation with colleagues or other professionals. | 77 |
| | K46. Knowledge of problems/impairments that interfere with the process of providing therapeutic services. | 78 |
| | K47. Knowledge of referrals and resources to assist in meeting the needs of clients. | 79 |
| | K48. Knowledge of methods to facilitate transfer when referrals to other professionals are made. | 79 |
| T27. Provide referrals to qualified professionals when adjunctive/alternate treatment would benefit the client. | K41. Knowledge of limitations of professional experience, education, and training to determine issues outside scope of competence. | 77 |
| | K43. Knowledge of ethical standards regarding the protection of client rights when engaging in consultation/collaboration with other professionals. | 77 |
| | K47. Knowledge of referrals and resources to assist in meeting the needs of clients. | 79 |
| | K48. Knowledge of methods to facilitate transfer when referrals to other professionals are made. | 79 |
| T28. Manage therapist's personal values, attitudes, and/or beliefs to prevent interference with effective provision of therapeutic services and/or the therapeutic relationship. | K49. Knowledge of the potential impact of therapist's personal values, attitudes, and/or beliefs on the therapeutic relationship. | 80 |
| | K50. Knowledge of methods for managing the impact of therapist's personal values, attitudes, and/or beliefs on the client or the therapeutic relationship. | 80 |

| Task Statement | Knowledge Statement | Page |
|---|---|---|
| T29. Evaluate potential conflict of interest situations to determine the impact on the client or the therapeutic process. | K51. Knowledge of conditions/situations that may impair judgment and/or lead to client exploitation. | 81 |
| | K52. Knowledge of methods for managing boundaries and/or professional relationships with the client. | 82 |
| | K53. Knowledge of methods for protecting the client and the therapeutic relationship in potential conflict of interest situations. | 82 |
| T30. Maintain professional boundaries with client to prevent situations or relationships that may impair professional judgment and/or adversely impact the therapeutic relationship. | K51. Knowledge of conditions/situations that may impair judgment and/or lead to client exploitation. | 81 |
| | K52. Knowledge of methods for managing boundaries and/or professional relationships with the client. | 82 |
| | K54. Knowledge of relationships that can be potentially detrimental to the client and/or the therapeutic relationship. | 82 |
| | K55. Knowledge of methods to prevent impairment to professional judgment and/or client exploitation in situations where dual/multiple relationships are unavoidable. | 83 |
| T31. Adhere to ethical guidelines regarding sexual intimacy/contact with prospective, current, or former clients and/or client's spouse, significant other, or family members to avoid causing harm or exploitation of the client. | K56. Knowledge of the potential for client harm or exploitation associated with sexual intimacy/contact between a client and therapist. | 83 |
| | K57. Knowledge of ethical standards pertaining to sexual intimacy/contact with clients and/or client's spouse, significant other, or family members. | 84 |
| | K58. Knowledge of ethical standards regarding entering into a therapeutic relationship with former sexual partners. | 84 |

# IIB. Therapeutic Relationship (27%)

| Task Statement | Knowledge Statement | Page |
|---|---|---|
| T32. Obtain informed consent by providing client with information regarding the therapist and the treatment process to facilitate client's ability to make decisions. | K59. Knowledge of the ethical responsibility to provide client with information regarding the therapeutic process. | 89 |
| | K60. Knowledge of disclosures that facilitate client's ability to make decisions regarding treatment. | 89 |
| | K61. Knowledge of client's right to autonomy and to make decisions regarding treatment. | 89 |
| | K62. Knowledge of methods for communicating information pertaining to informed consent in a manner consistent with developmental and cultural factors. | 90 |
| | K63. Knowledge of the right and responsibility of legal guardian/representative to make decisions on behalf of clients unable to make informed decisions. | 90 |
| | K64. Knowledge of methods for protecting client's welfare when client is unable to provide voluntary consent. | 91 |
| T33. Evaluate for concurrent psychotherapy the client is receiving with other therapist(s) to determine implications for entering into a new therapeutic relationship. | K65. Knowledge of the effects of concurrent treatment relationships on the treatment process. | 91 |
| | K66. Knowledge of ethical guidelines for providing concurrent psychotherapy. | 92 |
| | K43. Knowledge of ethical standards regarding the protection of client rights when engaging in consultation/collaboration with other professionals. | 77 |

| Task Statement | Knowledge Statement | Page |
|---|---|---|
| T34. Address confidentiality and/or therapeutic issues associated with therapist's role, treatment modality, and/or involvement of third parties to protect the client's welfare and/or the therapeutic relationship. | K67. Knowledge of methods to identify the "client" and the nature of relationships when providing therapy to more than one person. | 92 |
| | K68. Knowledge of the impact of treatment unit, treatment modality, and/or involvement of multiple systems on confidentiality. | 92 |
| | K69. Knowledge of methods to manage factors that impact the therapeutic relationship. | 93 |
| | K70. Knowledge of methods to manage potential conflicts when providing concurrent therapy to more than one person. | 94 |
| | K71. Knowledge of methods for managing confidentiality and privacy issues when providing treatment to more than one person. | 94 |
| | K72. Knowledge of methods for managing confidentiality and privacy issues when treatment involves multiple systems or third parties. | 94 |
| T35. Manage the impact of confidentiality/limits of confidentiality on the therapeutic relationship by discussing with the client issues/ implications that arise during the therapeutic process. | K73. Knowledge of ethical standards regarding the management of confidentiality issues that arise in the therapeutic process. | 95 |
| | K74. Knowledge of methods for managing the impact of confidentiality issues on the therapeutic relationship. | 95 |
| T36. Manage the impact of safety and/or crisis situations by evaluating risk factors to protect the client/others. | K75. Knowledge of methods for assessing level of potential danger or harm to client or others. | 95 |
| | K76. Knowledge of ethical obligations regarding the management of safety needs. | 97 |
| | K77. Knowledge of procedures for managing safety needs. | 97 |

| Task Statement | Knowledge Statement | Page |
|---|---|---|
| T37. Manage the impact of legal and ethical obligations that arise during the therapeutic process to protect the client/therapist relationship. | K78. Knowledge of the impact of legal and ethical obligations on the therapeutic relationship. | 98 |
| | K79. Knowledge of methods for protecting the best interest of the client in situations where legal and ethical obligations conflict. | 99 |
| | K80. Knowledge of methods for protecting the best interest of the client in situations where agency and ethical obligations conflict. | 99 |
| T38. Manage diversity factors in the therapeutic relationship by applying and/or gaining knowledge and awareness necessary to provide treatment sensitive to client needs. | K81. Knowledge of diversity factors that potentially impact the therapeutic process. | 100 |
| | K82. Knowledge of ethical standards regarding nondiscrimination. | 99 |
| | K83. Knowledge of ethical standards for providing services congruent with client diversity. | 100 |
| | K84. Knowledge of methods to gain knowledge, awareness, sensitivity, and skills necessary for working with clients from diverse populations. | 101 |
| T39. Provide treatment that respects client's autonomy and right to make decisions. | K85. Knowledge of the collaborative role between therapist and client in the therapeutic process. | 101 |
| | K61. Knowledge of client's right to autonomy and to make decisions regarding treatment. | 89 |
| | K86. Knowledge of methods to assist client make decisions and understand consequences. | 102 |

| Task Statement | Knowledge Statement | Page |
|---|---|---|
| T40. Advocate with and/or on behalf of the client with third party payers to assist client in accessing mental health care. | K87. Knowledge of methods for evaluating client's capacity to advocate on own behalf. | 102 |
| | K88. Knowledge of ethical standards pertaining to interacting with third-party payers. | 102 |
| T41. Maintain practice procedures that provide for consistent care in the event therapy must be interrupted or discontinued. | K89. Knowledge of ethical considerations and conditions for interrupting or terminating therapy. | 103 |
| | K90. Knowledge of referrals/resources to provide consistent care in the event therapy must be interrupted or discontinued. | 104 |
| | K48. Knowledge of methods to facilitate transfer when referrals to other professionals are made. | 79 |
| T42. Terminate therapy when no longer required or no longer benefits the client. | K91. Knowledge of factors and/or conditions that indicate client is ready for termination of therapy. | 104 |
| | K92. Knowledge of factors and/or conditions that indicate client is not benefiting from treatment. | 105 |
| | K93. Knowledge of methods for managing the termination process. | 105 |
| | K94. Knowledge of methods to prevent client abandonment and/or client neglect. | 105 |

# IIC. Business Practices and Policies (15%)

| Task Statement | Knowledge Statement | Page |
|---|---|---|
| T43. Advertise services by adhering to ethical guidelines regarding the use of accurate representations and information to promote services and/or expand practice. | K95. Knowledge of ethical guidelines regarding the use of accurate representation of qualifications and credentials in advertisements and/or solicitation of clients. | 111 |
| | K96. Knowledge of ethical guidelines pertaining to the solicitation of testimonials or statements from clients or others. | 111 |
| | K97. Knowledge of ethical guidelines regarding the recruitment of clients through employment and/or professional affiliations. | 112 |
| T44. Maintain client records by adhering to ethical guidelines to document treatment and/or protect the client's confidentiality. | K98. Knowledge of ethical guidelines regarding the documentation of therapeutic services consistent with clinical practice. | 112 |
| | K99. Knowledge of methods for providing reasonable protection of the confidentiality of client records. | 113 |
| | K100. Knowledge of ethical guidelines for releasing client records upon request. | 112 |
| T45. Clarify role(s) when acting in a professional capacity other than providing treatment or supervision to avoid confusion, maintain objectivity, and/or protect the therapeutic relationship. | K101. Knowledge of the ethical responsibility to clarify roles when acting in a professional capacity other than providing treatment or supervision. | 113 |
| | K102. Knowledge of ethical guidelines regarding engaging in conflicting and/or dual roles. | 113 |
| | K103. Knowledge of methods for maintaining impartiality and/or professional integrity when engaging in legal proceedings. | 114 |

| Task Statement | Knowledge Statement | Page |
|---|---|---|
| T46. Implement policies/procedures that address ethical issues associated with the use of electronic media and technology in the course of providing therapy. | K104. Knowledge of the potential for harm to the client or therapeutic relationship with the use of electronic media in the therapeutic process. | 115 |
| | K105. Knowledge of ethical standards for interacting with clients via electronic media. | 114 |
| | K106. Knowledge of the limitations and risks associated with electronic means of service delivery. | 115 |
| T47. Maintain fee/payment policies that are commensurate with services provided and protect the therapeutic relationship. | K107. Knowledge of methods and conditions for determining fees commensurate with professional services. | 116 |
| | K108. Knowledge of prohibited business practices/forms of remuneration for making/accepting client referrals. | 117 |
| | K109. Knowledge of the potential for client exploitation or harm that may result from bartering/exchanges for services. | 117 |
| | K110. Knowledge of ethical standards pertaining to the collection of unpaid balances. | 117 |
| | K111. Knowledge of ethical obligations regarding providing for continuation of treatment to the client. | 118 |
| | K112. Knowledge of ethical guidelines regarding the provision of therapeutic services when interacting with third-party payers. | 118 |
| | K47. Knowledge of referrals and resources to assist in meeting the needs of clients. | 79 |

| Task Statement | Knowledge Statement | Page |
|---|---|---|
| T48. Adhere to ethical guidelines regarding the acceptance of gifts and/or tokens of appreciation from clients. | K113. Knowledge of conditions/situations that may impair the integrity or efficacy of the therapeutic process. | 119 |
| | K114. Knowledge of ethical standards regarding the acceptance of gifts from clients. | 119 |
| T49. Adhere to ethical guidelines for protecting the welfare and dignity of participants when conducting research related to the provision of therapeutic services. | K115. Knowledge of procedures to safeguard participants when conducting research projects. | 119 |
| | K116. Knowledge of disclosures required to inform participants of the nature and role of research projects. | 120 |
| | K117. Knowledge of client rights regarding participation in research projects. | 120 |
| | K118. Knowledge of methods for protecting client confidentiality and data when conducting research projects. | 120 |
| T50. Address unethical or incompetent conduct of colleague by taking action to promote the welfare and interests of clients. | K119. Knowledge of conditions/situations that may impair the integrity or efficacy of the therapeutic process. | 121 |
| | K120. Knowledge of guidelines for addressing unethical or incompetent conduct of colleagues. | 121 |
| T51. Adhere to ethical guidelines for engaging in the supervisor/ prelicensure practitioner relationship. | K121. Knowledge of ethical guidelines governing the supervisor/prelicensure practitioner relationship and responsibilities. | 122 |